THE DEVIL IN DISGUISE

Frontispiece This image is a detail from a print depicting a Whig, John Rothmel or Rawthmel, who kept a coffee house in Covent Garden. He is depicted as a devil with a mask. The motif of the mask disguising a sinister inner self is one that recurs repeatedly in this book. Although catalogued as *c*.1700 the image may belong to a slightly later period, when the coffee house hosted the Society of Arts.

THE DEVIL IN DISGUISE

DECEPTION, DELUSION, AND
FANATICISM IN THE EARLY
ENGLISH ENLIGHTENMENT

MARK KNIGHTS

OXFORD

UNIVERSITY PRESS

OXFORD
UNIVERSITY PRESS

Great Clarendon Street, Oxford OX2 6DP

Oxford University Press is a department of the University of Oxford.
It furthers the University's objective of excellence in research, scholarship,
and education by publishing worldwide in

Oxford New York

Auckland Cape Town Dar es Salaam Hong Kong Karachi
Kuala Lumpur Madrid Melbourne Mexico City Nairobi
New Delhi Shanghai Taipei Toronto

With offices in

Argentina Austria Brazil Chile Czech Republic France Greece
Guatemala Hungary Italy Japan Poland Portugal Singapore
South Korea Switzerland Thailand Turkey Ukraine Vietnam

Oxford is a registered trade mark of Oxford University Press
in the UK and in certain other countries

Published in the United States
by Oxford University Press Inc., New York

British Library Cataloguing in Publication Data

Data available

Library of Congress Cataloging in Publication Data

Data available

Typeset by SPI Publisher Services, Pondicherry, India
Printed in Great Britain
on acid-free paper by
MPG Books Group, Bodmin and King's Lynn

ISBN 978-0-19-957795-8

1 3 5 7 9 10 8 6 4 2

ACKNOWLEDGEMENTS

My aim in writing this book has been to provide an accessible intro-duction to the later seventeenth and early eighteenth centuries. I wanted to be able to explain why the period is important, lively and thought-provoking and hence to persuade students and the gen-eral reader that it is interesting and worthy of study. I also hoped that exploring the early Enlightenment and what I have called a 'cultural revolution' in a holistic way through an extended set of linked case studies might have something to say even to those who already know something about the period. So what follows owes much to my students, both those past (who have helped me explore the sources and ideas presented here) and those imagined as future readers.

I first came across the Cowper archive when working in the early 1990s at the History of Parliament, a project to research and write the history of Westminster, and the book has been in gestation ever since, accruing debts of thanks along the way. Anne Kugler generously shared material with me and Beverly Adams, who began work on a fine thesis about the Hertford Quakers shortly after I left the History of Parliament, kindly allowed me to have first stab at telling the story.

I am very grateful to the British Museum for permission to repro-duce many images and can only commend the Museum's website, which is an outstanding resource for both academics and the wider public. I am also grateful to the British Library; the Ashmolean Museum; the Houghton Library; the Palace of Westminster; the National Library of Scotland; the Beinecke Library, Yale; the Pepys Library, Cambridge; the V&A; the Library of the Religious Society of Friends in Britain; the Wellcome Trust; the National Trust; and the Provost and Fellows of Oriel College, Oxford for granting permission to use images.

Since I was aiming at a wider audience than in my previous work I foisted drafts on family and friends, and am extremely grateful to Ed, Jo, and Emma for their feedback. I am also grateful to Bernard Capp, David Beck, Penny Roberts, Fara Dabhoiwala, Peter Marshall, and Simon Middleton for their comments.

The book is dedicated, with love, to Emma, Sam, and Caitlin.

CONTENTS

List of characters   ix
Chronology   xi
List of Figures   xv
List of Abbreviations   xix
Note to the Reader   xxi

INTRODUCTION   1

1. THE TRIAL OF SPENCER COWPER   10
   Dead Bodies Float   14
   Scientific Reputations   18
   An Anatomy of London Doctors   22
   Dead Dogs and Public Science   25
   False Man's Cruelty   30
   Summing up   34
   Zara's story   37

2. PARTISAN FEUDS   45
   The Whigs   46
   The Tories   54
   Hertford Tories   59
   Popular Politics and Party Rivalries   63

3. QUAKERS   70
   Persecution   71
   Spiritual Warfare   77
   The Lustful Quaker   82
   The Trial Verdict and its Aftermath   89
   Consequences   95

4. MORAL PANIC AND MARITAL AFFAIRS   98
   Rethinking Religion   100
   Rethinking Marriage   109

The Quakers, Marriage, and Morality   113
Sarah Cowper and the Slavery of Marriage   116
Will Bigamy   125
Justifying Polygamy   132
Manley and the *New Atalantis*   138

5. FANATICS AND FALSE BRETHREN   142

Sacheverell and his Sermons   144
The Trial   148
Hypocrisy   160
Sacheverell and Print Fever   166
Censorship and Censuring   181
Fanaticism   186
Sacheverell's Longer-term Legacy   190

6. DESPAIR AND DEMONISM   193

Melancholic Despair and Suicide   197
The Despair of the Deist and Atheist   202
Shifting Attitudes   206
Animal Spirits   207
A Political Witch-hunt   213
Jane Wenham   220
The Debate over the Impossibility of Witchcraft   228
Vindicating Jane Wenham   237

CONCLUSION: AN EXCEPTIONAL STORY?   241

Glossary   247
Endnotes   253
Further Reading   267
Index   273

LIST OF CHARACTERS

Queen Anne	The daughter of James II; became queen on William III's death in 1702.
Ralph Battell	Hertford vicar; his son, of the same name, assisted his father's clerical duties and also taught in the town's school. Both were High Church.
Francis Bragge	Grandson of Sir Henry Chauncy; chief polemicist in the 1712 witchcraft debate.
Charles Caesar	MP for Hertford 1701–8, 1710–15, and 1722–3, and then for the county; High Church Tory.
William Camlin	Physician to the Cowper family.
Sir Henry Chauncy	Lawyer, recorder of Hertford; historian of the county; High Church Tory; grandfather of the chief prosecutor of Jane Wenham for witchcraft.
Sarah Cowper	Diarist; wife of Sir William and mother of Spencer and William Cowper.
Sarah Cowper	Daughter of William Cowper, who, like her grandmother, kept a diary.
Spencer Cowper	Whig lawyer; tried for murdering Sarah Stout; MP for Bere Alston 1705–10 and Truro 1715–27.
William Cowper	Brother of Spencer; Whig lawyer who became Lord Keeper in 1705 and Lord Chancellor in 1708; MP for Hertford 1695–1700, Bere Alston 1701–5.
William Cowper	Anatomist; gave evidence at Spencer Cowper's trial. – no relation
Sir William Cowper	Father of Spencer and William; Whig MP for Hertford 1680–1, 1689–1700.
Edmund Curll	Unscrupulous publisher who attempted to publish a life of Manley; published items in the 1712 witchcraft debate.
John Dimsdale snr	Surgeon and Tory mayor of Hertford 1682, 1688, 1697–1700; key figure in local politics and in the evidence against Spencer Cowper.
John Dimsdale jnr	Surgeon who told the coroner that Sarah Stout must have committed suicide but later changed his mind, perhaps under pressure from his father; Tory and active in Hertford politics, becoming mayor in 1706 and 1711, and a parliamentary candidate in 1708.
Robert Dimsdale	Graduate physician; son of John Dimsdale snr; part of the group of doctors who concluded Sarah Stout must have been murdered.

William Dimsdale	Convert from Quakerism to Haworth's Independent congregation; kinship with the other Dimsdales likely, perhaps through Quaker line of John Dimsdale snr's brother, but precise relationship unclear.
Samuel Garth	London doctor and poet; gave evidence at Spencer's trial; Whig.
Richard Goulston	Tory MP for Hertford 1701.
William Haworth	Dissenting minister (Independent) in Hertford who waged a campaign against the town's Quakers.
Benjamin Hoadly	Controversial Low Church cleric, hated by High Churchmen and often seen as the antithesis of Henry Sacheverell.
Sir John Holt	Judge who heard initial evidence against Spencer Cowper and imprisoned him; opponent of witchcraft trials.
King James II	Formerly James, duke of York; fled at the Revolution of 1688–9.
Sir Thomas Lane	Whig London alderman; character witness for Spencer Cowper at his trial; Dissenter; responsible, as magistrate, for hounding a witch.
Delarivier Manley	Journalist; author of scandal novels about Whig hypocrisy (including the story of the Cowpers), for which she was arrested.
Thomas Marshall	Friend of Spencer Cowper who had courted Sarah Stout.
John Marson	Arrested with Spencer Cowper and tried for murder of Sarah Stout.
Judge John Powell	Appeal judge in Spencer Cowper's case and presiding judge at Jane Wenham's trial for witchcraft, instrumental in securing her stay of execution.
Dr Henry Sacheverell	High Church cleric who was tried by Parliament in 1710 for an inflammatory sermon against 'revolution principles'.
(Sir) Hans Sloane	Doctor who gave evidence at Spencer's trial and advised on witchcraft pamphlets; founder of the British Museum.
Henry Stout	A prominent Hertford Quaker; father of the dead Sarah; a reasonably well-to-do brewer.
John Stout	Sarah Stout's half-brother.
Mary Stout	A prominent Hertford Quaker; mother of the dead Sarah.
Sarah Stout	Quaker found dead in Hertford mill pond.
Henry Sweeting	A leading Quaker in Hertford and active in town politics.
Bostock Toller	Whig undersheriff; friend of the Cowpers, who frustrated the appeal against Spencer and was imprisoned for contempt of court.
Jane Wenham	Convicted of witchcraft but reprieved.
King William III	Invaded England in 1688 and crowned joint monarch with his wife, Mary (James II's daughter), and then, after her death in 1694, as sole monarch.

CHRONOLOGY

1642–8	Civil War between royalists (supporters of Charles I) and parliamentarians.
1649	Charles I executed and a republic created.
1660	Restoration of the monarchy, with Charles II (son of Charles I).
1661–5	Religious 'penal code' placed penalties on dissent from the Church of England.
1670	Charles II signed secret Treaty of Dover with Louis XIV of France, agreeing to wage war on the Dutch and convert England to Catholicism.
1672	Declaration of indulgence granted by Charles II giving freedom of worship by royal decree.
1673	Charles II forced to abandon his declaration of indulgence.
1678	Popish Plot revealed—an alleged attempt to kill Charles II and forcibly reconvert the country to Catholicism. This heightened anti-Catholicism and led to parliamentary attempts to bar the Catholic James duke of York from succeeding to the throne. The 'succession crisis' also gave an opportunity for an attempt to revise the 'Restoration settlement' more fully.
1681–5	'Tory reaction', when the Tories purged Whigs from local office-holding and prosecuted Dissent.
1683	Rye House Plot to assassinate King Charles II.
1685–8	Reign of James II whose pro-Catholic policies alienated many. In 1687 the king issued a declaration of indulgence, granting freedom of worship by royal decree. In 1688 he required the clergy to read this in church.
1688	Glorious Revolution—the invasion of William of Orange (James II's son-in-law) and the transfer of the crown in 1689 to him and his wife Mary.
1689	The quelling of forces loyal to James II in Scotland; passage of the Toleration Act; start of war with France.
1690	The quelling of forces loyal to James II in Ireland; Tory victory at general election but the two sides were quite evenly poised and King William attempted to construct a government from elements of both parties.
1694	Triennial Act passed to ensure that new parliaments were held every three years; creation of the Bank of England. Whig support increasingly necessary to sustain the war against the French.
1695	General election—Whig victory.
1696	Law passed to allow Quakers to affirm rather than swear oaths; assassination attempt on William III's life, leading to mass signatures of an 'association' of loyalty to him
1697	Peace negotiations concluded temporary cessation of war with France.

1698	General election produced narrow victory for Court Whigs
1699	Trial of Spencer Cowper for the murder of Sarah Stout; the Whig government unravelled.
1700	Tories recruited to government.
1701	Two general elections: one in January relatively indecisive and the second in December gave the Tories a victory; Tory reluctance to re-engage in war against France, made necessary by France's support for the Pretender, created dilemmas for the king about where to place political trust.
1702	William III's death, Anne's accession; general election produced decisive Tory victory; Sacheverell preached Oxford sermon against Dissenters; Parliament introduced the first of a series (1702–5) of bills banning Occasional Conformity, aimed at curbing Dissenting power. Tory ministry created.
1704	High Church Tory ministers dismissed and a more moderate ministry emerged.
1705	General election produced Whig gains and Whigs (including William Cowper) were appointed to government; Tory anxiety that the Church of England was in danger.
1707	Union with (Presbyterian) Scotland created Great Britain but deepened Tory worries about position of the Church.
1708	Removal of Robert Harley as Secretary of State, as government became more Whiggish; general election confirmed shift to Whigs; duke of Marlborough victorious militarily abroad and influential at home via partnership with Lord Treasurer Godolphin.
1709	Sacheverell preached sermon against 'false brethren in Church and State' and Whigs voted to impeach him.
1710	Trial of Sacheverell; Anne's breach with Marlborough's wife, Sarah; Godolphin dismissed; general election produced Tory landslide and new Tory ministry.
1711	Peace negotiations with France; fourth Occasional Conformity Bill became law.
1712	Wenham trial; removal of remaining Whigs from office; Stamp Act taxes periodicals.
1713	Tory victory at general election.
1714	Death of Anne; accession of George I (Hanoverian); Whig government (including William Cowper) returned to power.
1715	Widespread rioting against the Hanoverian succession, necessitating introduction of the Riot Act.

THE NORTH PROSPECT OF THE TOWN OF HERTFORD FROM PORTHILL.

Drawn on Stone from the Original Engraving of G. I. Tyler

To the Right Worshipfull y.ͤ Mayor, Recorder & Aldermen of the Town of
Hertford; This Plate containing y.ͤ North Prospect of the Town of Hertford, as it was taken from
Porthill;

Is humbly dedicated by your Worshipps' Humble Servants,

J. Drapentier.

Pub.ᵈ by; J.M. Mullinger, typo. Stanford.

This view of Hertford is taken from Sir Henry Chauncy's *Historical Antiquities of Hertfordshire* (1700), showing the town as it looked at the turn of the century from Porthill, where the Quakers had their burial ground. The large building in the middle is the Castle, where the Cowper family lived.

FIGURES

Frontispiece: Detail from 'Rotaveltragopann', BM Sat. 1414.   ii
View of Hertford, from Sir Henry Chauncy, *The Historical
Antiquities of Hertfordshire* (1700). Courtesy of the Bodleian
Library, University of Oxford.   xiii

1.1.   William Cowper, plate facing the 'Thirty Second Table' of *The
Anatomy of Human Bodies* (1698), Wing C6698. Courtesy
of the Wellcome Library, London.   13

1.2.   From *False Mans Cruelty*, broadside ballad (1681–4), Wing
F344B. Courtesy of the Pepys Library, Magdalen College,
Cambridge.   39

1.3.   Portrait of Spencer Cowper. Courtesy of the Provost
and Fellows of Oriel College, Oxford.   42

2.1.   The governance of Hertford.   51

2.2.   *A Genealogie of Anti-Christ*, BM Sat. 820.   55

2.3.   Portrait of Sir Henry Chauncy, from William Blyth Gerish,
Sir Henry Chauncy (1907). Personal collection.   58

3.1.   The Hertford Meeting House, flickr.com/photos/98826199
@No0/444981026.   75

3.2.   From Francis Bugg, *A Seasonable Caveat Against the
Prevalency of Quakerism* (1701), 7, ESTC T47255. Courtesy
of the Library of the Religious Society of Friends in Britain.   79

3.3.   From William Jones, *Work for a Cooper* (1679), Wing J1002.   83

3.4.   *A Quaker*, BM Sat. 158, attributed to Richard Gaywood.   84

3.5.   *Yea-and-Nea the Hypocrite*, broadside ballad *c.*1690,
Wing Y19B. Courtesy of the Pepys Library, Magdalen College,
Cambridge.   85

3.6.   *The Cryes of the City of London Drawne after the Life:
The London Quaker*, after Marcellus Laroon, *c.*1688,
BM 1871, 1209.3361.   86

3.7.   *The Quakers Meeting*, by Isaac Beckett after Egbert van
Heemskerck, BM 1974, 1207.20.   87

3.8.   BM Sat. 154, *The Quakers Meeting*, after Egbert van
Heemskerck, BM 1854, 0812.49.   88

3.9.   Satire on the pursuit of money, by Thomas Cross, after Hendrik
        Goltzius, BM Sat. 802.   94

4.1.   *The Happy Marriage and the Unhappy Marriage*, *c.*1690,
        by John King, BM 1906, 0823.4.   118

4.2.   The Lord High Chancellor of Great Britain (1705–8),
        William, 1st Earl Cowper (1664–1723). Oil on canvas by
        Thomas Murray, *c.*1695. WOA © Palace of Westminster
        Collection.   129

5.1.   Youth seated, BM Sat. 1514, *c.*1709–10, anonymous.   150

5.2.   *The Modern Champions* (1710), ESTC T41303. Courtesy
        of the Houghton Library (Bute Collection) C70.   153

5.3.   From Ned Ward, *The Whigs Unmask'd* (1713),
        ESTC T147726.   154

5.4.   A playing card showing William Cowper surrendering his
        office of Lord Chancellor in the wake of the Sacheverell affair,
        from the Beinecke Rare Book and Manuscript Library, Yale
        University, Cary Collection of playing cards, Eng. 87.   159

5.5.   Frontispiece of *An Auction of State Pictures* (1710), ESTC
        T89787. Reproduced by permission of the British Library.   168

5.6.   *Needs Must when the Devil Drives* (1709–10), BM Sat. 1496.   170

5.7.   *Like Coachman like Cause* (1709–10), BM Sat. 1497.   171

5.8.   Portrait of Henry Sacheverell, print made by John Smith
        after a portrait by Antony Russell, BM 1902, 1011.4791.   174

5.9.   *The Picture of a High Church Man* (1709), ESTC T26807.   175

5.10.   Illustration by Jeremiah Cliff in a copy of *The Fables of
        Aesop* by Roger L'Estrange (1708), National Art Library
        Pressmark: Safe 6.A.10. Photo © Victoria and Albert
        Museum, London.   176

5.11.   *A British Janus* (1709–10), BM Sat. 1505.   177

5.12A. *The High Church Champion* (1709–10), BM Sat. 1498.   178

5.12B. *The High Church Champion pleading his own Cause*
        (1709–10), BM Sat. 1499.   178

5.13.   A detail from *To the unknown Author of the High Church
        Champion and his two seconds* (1709–10), BM Sat. 1501.   179

5.14.   From the mural by John Thornhill at Hanbury Hall,
        Warwickshire. Photo courtesy of the National Trust.   180

5.15.   *Jack Ketch's New and Fashionable Auction* (1710), broadside,
        Miscellaneous broadsides 981. Courtesy of the National
        Library of Scotland.   181

5.16. A detail from *Mobb's IDOL or ye pad Lockt Trompetter*, The Ashmolean Museum, B.II part XI, p. 67. Reproduced by permission of the Ashmolean Museum. 182

5.17. *Guess att my Meaning* (1709–10), BM Sat. 1503. 184

5.18. Frontispiece of Ned Ward, *The Whigs Unmask'd* (1713), ESTC T147726. 189

6.1. Laurence Braddon, *Innocency and Truth Vindicated* (1689), Wing V10. Reproduced by permission of the Huntington Library, San Marino, California. 201

6.2. From Thomas Willis, *Dr. Willis's Practice of Physick* (1684), opposite p. 44. Courtesy of the Wellcome Library, London. 208

6.3. Frontispiece of Nathanial Crouch (pseud. Richard Burton), *The Kingdom of Darkness* (1688), Wing C7342. Courtesy of the Bodleian Library, University of Oxford. 234

ABBREVIATIONS

BL	British Library
HALS	Hertfordshire Archives and Local Studies
HCR	*Hertfordshire County Records*, ed. William le Hardy (10 volumes, 1905–57)
HMC	Historical Manuscripts Commission
MS	Manuscript
ODNB	Oxford Dictionary of National Biography, online version

NOTE TO THE READER

Quotations are taken from the primary sources listed at the end of the book, where the reader will also find suggestions for further reading and details of a website that contains further images and online resources. The original spelling has generally been retained, though I have on occasion silently modified both spelling and punctuation to make the sense more accessible.

All titles were published in London unless otherwise stated.

INTRODUCTION

This book is intended as an introduction to the late seventeenth and early eighteenth centuries, a period that has been rather neglected but which can be described as the English Enlightenment. The following chapters examine the cumulative impact of Britain's two seventeenth-century revolutions and their lasting legacy. The turmoil of the civil wars and their aftermath was still felt—and often remarked on—well into the eighteenth century and provided the essential backdrop against which much later discussion took place. But the focus of the book is the second of the seventeenth-century revolutions, the so-called 'Glorious Revolution'. Whilst the successful invasion of England by a Dutch force took place in November 1688 and the subsequent coronation of William of Orange and his wife Mary followed in the spring of 1689, the impact of these events lasted very much longer. The debates they provoked were still being argued out at least a generation later and turned on divisive changes to the religious, political, moral, and cultural life of the nation. This book therefore seeks to explain how the revolutions of the seventeenth century helped to shape the eighteenth century.

That larger story can nevertheless appear a rather abstract and impersonal one about constitutions, institutions, new ideas, and State structures. This book therefore tells it through the perspective of one extraordinarily well documented and interesting family, the Cowpers of Hertford. Their dramatic history contains a murder mystery, bigamy, a scandal novel, and a tyrannized wife; and their town saw violently competitive factions, rampant religious prejudice and the last conviction of a witch in England. Each member of the Cowper family sheds light on their times. Spencer Cowper was accused of murdering a Hertford Quaker, Sarah Stout, and his brother William had two illegitimate children by his mistress or bigamous second 'wife'. Both incidents help to uncover ideas about sexuality, religious enthusiasm, forensic science, and the power of the press. Their scandalous lives became the source of public gossip, much to the horror of their mother, Sarah, who poured out her heart in a diary that also chronicles her feeling of being enslaved to her husband, Sir William Cowper. Her two sons remained in the limelight. Both were instrumental in the prosecution of Dr Henry Sacheverell, a cleric who had preached a landmark firebrand sermon about the illegitimacy of resistance and religious toleration. Sacheverell's parliamentary trial in 1710 provoked serious riots in London and a mob even threatened the house of William Cowper, who had risen to become Lord Chancellor. Just as William opposed Sacheverell's fanaticism, which offended his sensibilities, so he opposed the fanaticism of those who sought the blood of witches. Thus in 1712 he intervened to secure the life of Jane Wenham, who was convicted of witchcraft in the same courtroom in which his brother had been convicted just over a decade earlier, and subsequently gave her refuge on his estate. Partly as a result of the family's activities, but also because of much deeper rifts, Hertford was a bitterly divided community, wracked by partisan political and religious feuds. Indeed the Cowpers and their town are a microcosm of a changing world. Nearly every aspect of the macro debates affecting the nation as a whole can be explored through their micro history—debates about religious and political fanaticism, women and marriage, sex and sexuality, science and reason, truth and deluded error. Their story suggests that an early 'Enlightenment', far from being simply a movement of ideas sparked by 'great thinkers', was shaped and advanced by local and personal struggles. It was the conflict and tensions within families and small communities, as much as at Westminster or Whitehall, which changed the national culture.

Three linked episodes, each turning on a dramatic trial, provide the narrative for the book's story of revolutionary change. The first is the trial in 1699 of Spencer Cowper for the murder of Sarah Stout, whose body was found floating in a mill pond in Hertford. The manner of her death and identity of her killer (if there was one) remain uncertain; but the subsequent trial exposed key features of a society in transition. The courtroom exposed tensions about the dangers posed by religious sectarianism and highlighted the fragility of religious toleration even after the passage of an act in 1689 had granted religious freedom of worship. Sarah's parents were stalwart Quakers who had allied themselves with the tolerant Cowper family; but her death led to a dramatic breach with them, and even to a strange partnership between the Quakers and their former enemies, the local Church of England men. Another dimension of the case reflects the emergence of party politics and the fissures and passions it created. The terms Whig and Tory were first used in 1681 and the parties locked horns at the local as well as at the national level. The Stouts had been the Cowper's electoral agents in Hertford in a period of very bitter partisan strife in the town, and the Tory mayor who assisted the prosecution of Spencer stood to gain politically from his rival's humiliation. The case also reveals new scientific attitudes. Cowper's acquittal turned on the new art of forensic evidence gleaned, in part, from autopsies and experiments on drowned dogs, to rebuff a prosecution led by physicians in the town; and evidence was given to the court by some of the most famous medics of the day, including the future founder of the British Museum, Sir Hans Sloane. But Sarah's story is also a moving one of forbidden love: the married Spencer claimed that she wrote him passionate love letters and, when her feelings were not reciprocated, committed suicide, an act that the Quaker community refused to countenance as a possibility, since it flew in the face of their beliefs.

The middle section of the book advances the story a decade, exploring the 'rage of party' in the reign of Queen Anne and placing this in the context of a moral crisis perceived to be undermining family, Church, and State. These chapters examine the diary of Spencer's mother, Sarah, which reveals much about the tensions within and outside the family, and how the personal and political worlds interacted. That theme also emerges in the scurrilous but fictional and politicized account of the Cowper family's misfortunes which led to the arrest of its author, Delarivier Manley, one of the first female journalists and early novelists. Just as the trial of Spencer Cowper focused on the issue of what was true about the murder allegation, so Manley's salacious polemic explored the boundaries between fact and fiction. Manley's own bigamy, together with William Cowper's, also demand an exploration of changing relations between the sexes, a theme that Sarah's unrequited love and Sarah Cowper's love-less marriage also help to explore. The context in which Manley was writing is studied through the heated passions aroused by the almost simultaneous arrest and trial of the High Church cleric Dr Henry Sacheverell, whose defenders opposed the 'revolution principles' established in 1688. Those were principles for which both Spencer and William Cowper had taken up arms in 1688 and were now prepared to defend in court. Spencer was a key prosecutor at Sacheverell's trial and his brother William, who by then had become Lord Chancellor, was the judge in charge of proceedings. The controversy that the case provoked shows how enduring older ideas and mindsets were but also the determination of the Whigs to eradicate them.

The last chapter of the book focuses on changing ideas about the supernatural and the devil. It explores a declining attribution of suicide to the devil and investigates the last woman to be convicted in England of witchcraft, Jane Wenham, who was afterwards taken under the wing of the Cowper family. The trial in 1712 was presided over by one of the judges involved in Spencer's case, and was initiated by the same 'Church' faction involved in the prosecution against Spencer, which had become dominant in the wake of the controversy generated by the Sacheverell trial. The Wenham case split the local community and reverberated throughout the country in a violent press debate about whether or not witches existed. The arguments reveal the shift of attitudes that ended witch-hunting in England. The role of the devil is explored in the context of witchcraft but demonism and delusion more widely are considered in terms of the political, religious, intellectual, and scientific ferment explored in earlier chapters and particularly in terms of the possible suicide of Sarah Stout. Indeed, throughout, the book seeks to show that politics, religious and ideological belief, sexual morality, print, and science were all interwoven factors explaining why and how society was changing. Those interconnections can best be highlighted through a case study of one family and their locality.

The Cowpers and their town can thus be seen as emblematic of a new, post-revolutionary political culture on the cusp between old and new mindsets. A number of issues (which have a strong twenty-first-century resonance) run through the chapters that follow: religious 'fanaticism' and how to understand or deal with it; how and why cultures and mindsets change or endure; the role of women; the thin line between fact and fiction; the nature of the early Enlightenment scientific debate; the power of stereotypes; and the intertwined history of hypocrisy and the self. These can be grouped into two key themes: truth and change.

The first of these overarching themes, the quest for truth and certainty, took several forms. It can be approached by examining religion, the press, literary works, and science, as well as anxieties about hypocrisy. The nature of religious truth, for example, lay at the heart of debates over the Quakers, a sect that will feature prominently in the first chapters of the book. Both the Quakers and their opponents claimed to possess religious truth; but both sides accused the other of dangerous error. These religious fissures were the result of the first seventeenth-century revolution: the established Church was dismantled in the late 1640s, leading to the sectarianism in the 1650s that produced the Quakers This religious diversity and conflict raised the issue of how far different religious beliefs could be tolerated, a problem that bedevilled the Church after its restoration in 1660 and even after the passage in 1689 of a parliamentary Act of toleration. Religious diversity, and anxiety about tolerating it, remained unsettling factors well into, and arguably throughout, the eighteenth century. And this long struggle raised questions about how man could discover religious truth. How was God's will revealed? Was it (as the Quakers believed) through an inner light, or (as strict adherents of the Church of England believed) through clerical tradition and authority, or (as the Cowpers believed) via reason? Was it possible to distinguish what one group called delusion from what another called revelation? What contemporaries called 'fanaticism' was a highly charged subject, and remains so today.

The later Stuart period marked the emergence of a religiously pluralistic society in which truth was relativistic but hence also uncertain and disconcerting. But it was not just religion that was destabilizing truth. The problem of discerning fact from fiction in the political arena had creative and literary potential. Delarivier Manley fictionalized the lives of the Cowper family in a novel that combined sexual scandal and politics, and her fellow satirical journalists, including her colleague Jonathan Swift, took advantage of a newly free press to 'spin' politics. Uncertain truths were thus part of the political culture. Writers constantly accused each other of inventing or distorting the truth. This was partly the result of a major shift in publishing history. Temporarily in 1641, and then permanently in 1695, the government lost the power to censor material before publication. The result was an explosion in the amount of print available. The first provincial and daily newspapers began in the twenty years after the Revolution of 1688–9. The birth of a free press gave the public much more information about politics; but it also created opportunities for misinformation—scurrilous, misleading, and sometimes simply lying reports. John Arbuthnot, the inventor of that enduring national stereotype John Bull, went so far as to compile a mock prospectus for a book outlining 'the art of political lying'. Fiction was part of the culture and it is no coincidence that this period witnessed the rise of the novel. And fiction was also at stake in the testimony against witches: the prosecution of Jane Wenham involved a fabulous tale of a girl with a dislocated knee who, when possessed, could hurdle gates; of cats that talked; and of a woman who could fly.

One response to the quest for certainty was recourse to science. Science was undergoing its own revolution. This was the age of the founding of the Royal Society and when Isaac Newton was offering new explanations about gravity and the laws of the universe. The 'new' science had a real impact at the local level on the mentalities of provincial England. There was thus a public dissemination of scientific debate outside the rarefied realm of the Royal Society and learned treatises. The trial of Spencer Cowper for murder was a magnificent display of the power of the rising medical profession with its new set of ways to prove and explain truth. Tribes of medical witnesses offered 'expert' testimony; and there was much dissecting and drowning of dogs (including one experiment by Spencer Cowper himself the night before his trial), to determine precisely how much water would be found in the lungs of a murder victim. Similarly, natural causes rather than supernatural ones were offered as an explanation for the experiences of those who believed themselves inspired by God or were bewitched. And yet scientific truth was also contested—the medical evidence offered for Spencer's defence was disputed by half a dozen physicians on the other side and then in the press. Truth remained uncertain despite of, and sometimes because of, science.

Such uncertainty was all too obvious in a concern that echoes throughout the book with dissimulation and hypocrisy, with deception and delusion, with the fictions peddled by people to cover their true designs or selves. We see this first with Spencer Cowper and Sarah Stout. Spencer Cowper was satirized for hiding the relentless pursuit of his self-interest and lust under a veneer of respectability. Sarah Stout, as a Quaker, was the epitome of a deluded and hypocritical religious enthusiast who, under the cover of a pretended inner light, hid diabolical darkness. We can also see dissimulation and hypocrisy as central to the charges made by the inflammatory cleric Henry Sacheverell against what he saw as 'false brethren'. They were those who, whilst pretending to protect the Church, really undermined it. Duplicity was also central to Dalarivier Manley's novelistic satire against William Cowper, for his pretence of marrying two women simultaneously; and Sarah Cowper railed against her husband's tyranny in the household when politically he championed liberty in the State. Allegations of hypocrisy and deception were also prominent in the witchcraft trial, since the clerics who promoted the prosecution of Jane Wenham were said to be using the prosecution to advance their own power, and duplicity lay at the heart of witch-craft beliefs, since they rested on the notion of a witch, secretly in league with the devil, who needed unveiling. All these instances played with a notion that there was an inner (often sinister) self that was being disguised, one that could be revealed, unmasked, and exposed. Uncertain truth, then, was particularly troubling when it was also a matter of how you assessed the trustworthiness of any person and when the political, religious, and print culture of the day was deliberately enabling the creation of false, misleading, or double identities.

The title of the book, together with the frontispiece illustrating it in which a devil is disguised by a mask, serve to highlight this anxiety about public and private personas, about inner and outer selves. To be sure, the notion of insincerity was not new. It had been forged (or re-forged) during the Renaissance. But the duality of the partisanship that pervaded the later Stuart period heightened an awareness of the duality and duplicity of the individual. Partisanship, which became embodied in the rival camps of Whig and Tory in the later Stuart period, systematized a double vision of any event or person, which could always be seen in two fundamentally different ways. Both sides accused the other of lying to the public and misrepresenting truth.

Religious and political diversity thus meant a state of relativism, in which good and truth were subjective, and defining the motives of an individual or party became a fraught affair as the sincerity of anyone became a matter of partisan conjecture. The press encouraged both the partisanship and the anxiety about sincerity, fuelling a perception that people were pursuing selfish ends. Each age can be said to be important in the history of the emergence of the modern 'self'; but this conjunction of developments give the later Stuart period a particular-ly strong claim. Many 'self' words entered the language during the mid-seventeenth century revolution: selfish and self-conscious (by 1632, and selfishness by 1645), self-reflection (by 1644), self-advancement (by 1649), self-enjoyment (by 1652), self-consciousness (by 1655), self-inspection (by 1660), self-gratification (by 1663), self-indulging (by 1671), self-restrained (by 1700), and self-scrutiny (by 1675).[1] These words were used frequently in the later Stuart period, when it also became usual to talk of private interests undermining the public good.

A second thread running throughout the book is the duality, funda-mental to all historical study, of change and continuity. Britain in the seventeenth century experienced two revolutions, one in the 1640s and 1650s, another spanning the decades either side of the turn of the century. Together the two revolutions sowed the seeds of far-reaching change. But at the same time there were those who were deeply wedded to older ways of thinking. As a result the nation was deeply divided between those who adhered to traditional ideas about the power of the Church and monarchy on the one hand and those who envisaged a very different world of religious freedom and a right to resist tyranny. If there was no exchange of blows, this was nevertheless cultural civil war.

The different strands of this conflict interacted with and shaped each other. For example, tension in the political and religious spheres spilled over into the domestic. Governance and authority were at stake in both the State and the family. Monarchs were called fathers of the country but, in theory at least, the male head of the household ruled his family and servants like a little king. The challenge to patriarchal political ideals resulting from the execution of Charles I in 1649 and again in the unseating of the king in 1688 therefore forced a rethinking of political paternalism that threatened to spill much further into the social sphere. Mary Astell, writing at the turn of the century, has been called a 'proto-feminist' for her idealization of spaces dedicated to independent female rationality and Sarah Cowper, the mother of Spencer and William, saw herself as enslaved to her husband, railing in her diary about the disparity between her husband's commitment to political and religious liberty on the one hand and his tyranny towards her on the other. Delarivier Manley, who satirized the Cowper men by exposing their apparent desire to dominate and deceive women, herself challenged many assumptions about the subordinate role of women, since she abandoned her husband and earned her own living with her pen. Perceptions of women were also challenged in the religious sphere. The expanded role for women in Quakerism is clearly shown in the remarkable Mary Stout, the mother of the dead Sarah, who published her cause, preached her religion and fought legal battles with extraordinary determination and visibility.

Perceptions of women owed a great deal to the power of stereotypes. Stereotypes are normally associated with the mass culture of modernity—the term was invented to apply to a printing plate in the late eighteenth century but only employed in 1922 to mean a preconceived and oversimplified idea of the characteristics which typify a person. Nevertheless, they were employed everywhere in early modernity. Spencer Cowper used the stereotype of the Quaker (mad, melancholy, lustful, demonic) to nurture his acquittal; partisan Whigs and Tories used stereotypes to hack away at each other and at rival ideologies; Sarah Cowper meditated on the stereotype of a wife and mother; and the stereotype of the old, single woman as a witch was used against Jane Wenham. But stereotypes were also changing (the devil was becoming, for some at least, less frightening, as much a metaphor as a supernatural force) and transmuting (Quakers or Whigs or Tories were the new devils). In exploring such stereotypes the book will make extensive use of the printed visual culture of the time, exploiting a rich source for stereotype-deploying 'speaking pictures'. Such material has nevertheless often been neglected, used simply to illustrate accounts of the period rather than as part of them. Very few accounts of this period make much use of printed imagery, even though it was (and became even more strongly) part of the way in which polemical debate took place. This visual culture has to be reintegrated with the textual one and made part of the story.

So this book is partly about seeing things in the round, juxtaposing things that are too often kept separate and hence seeking to make connections that might not otherwise be possible. A political, social, religious, economic, intellectual, or gendered history of this period could only highlight one aspect of what was a tightly bundled knot of interrelated problems. 'Fanaticism' was thus used to describe religious enthusiasts but it was also applied to overly zealous political partisans and became the subject of medical study. Deception and delusion, too, were multifaceted, glimpsed in discussions about religion, politics, and science but also economics, social relations, and the press. The focus on one family and town also helps to show this essential interconnectedness. As the following chapters show, the Cowpers and Hertford bring together a host of issues that are all too easily treated separately but which should be seen together. Of course, the Cowpers were in many ways idiosyncratic. A dysfunctional family of egoists whose colourful and salacious story could be sold even in their own lifetimes, they are not in a strict sense representative of others. But their story does capture something of the ferment of ideas and experiences common to many who lived in the later Stuart period, and represent in extreme form some of the key characteristics that worried contemporaries.

I

THE TRIAL OF SPENCER COWPER

Early in the morning of 14 March 1699, Hertford's miller, James Berry, saw something floating in his pond. At first he could see only clothes ruffling the surface; but on taking a closer look he found the body of a woman, lying on its side. The head and right arm were 'driven between the stakes' near the weir that regulated the flow of water to the mill. A crowd soon gathered and lifted the body out of the water, carrying it into the nearby meadow, where it lay for an hour before being carried into the miller's house. One of the helpers, town crier Leonard Dell, later testified that he saw only 'some small matter of froth come from her mouth and nostrils', little enough to 'hold it all in the palm of my hand', as he put it. The body was that of Sarah Stout.

Barely three hours after the discovery of the body it was already being said in Hertford that Sarah Stout had drowned herself because she was 'with child'. Perhaps the fact that her stockings had been 'rowl'd down', her garters removed, and she had been without her gown (found much later 'torn to Raggs, without one of its sleeves'), had led to speculation about her virginity. But when local women and a midwife named Sarah Peppercorn stripped the body in order to verify this, their attention was immediately diverted by a mysterious 'great settlement of blood' behind Sarah's left ear and under her collar-bone. Moreover, they thought that the body was not at all like that of a child who ten weeks earlier had fallen into the same pond and drowned. That child's body had not floated and it had been bloated, full of water; whereas Sarah's body had appeared to float and been empty of water. Indeed, her body was 'very lank and thin'. And there was no sign that Sarah was with child. Here, then, was a macabre mystery. Might Sarah have been murdered before she entered the water?

Sarah's mother, Mary, wanted the marks on her daughter's body investigated. She called for one of the town's doctors, John Dimsdale, who later recalled that he had been very reluctant to go. His hesitation was understandable, since, as we shall see, he was part of a faction within the town who were bitter rivals of the Stouts and their local patrons, the Cowpers. Indeed, Dimsdale's father, John senior, was the town's mayor and instrumental in orchestrating an attack on the political interests of both Stouts and Cowpers. So doctor John Dimsdale junior probably resented Mary Stout's plea for help. But at the third entreaty he went, taking with him Mr Camlin, the Cowpers' doctor. The two men examined Sarah's body. Dimsdale 'found a little swelling on the side of her neck, and she was black on both sides, and more particularly on the left side, and between her Breasts up towards the Collar-bone' but that was all he saw 'at that time'. Accordingly, at the subsequent coroner's inquest, (a 'full examination' lasting six hours), he is alleged to have said it was 'no more than a common stagnation usual in dead bodies'. Certainly the post-mortem declared that Sarah Stout had drowned and that she had committed suicide, 'not being of sound mind'. She was buried in the Quaker burial ground at Hertford on 18 March. And there the story might have ended.

But Mary Stout refused to accept this verdict. She was 'was very much enraged' by the scandalous allegation that her daughter had committed suicide and by the persistent whispers that she had been pregnant. She insisted on a second post-mortem, six weeks after her daughter's death, 'to clear her reputation', even though she was warned that the body would already have started to decompose and that the results might be inconclusive. Organizing an exhumation and second examination so long after death, and with a team of new doctors to supplement the original two, was a very unusual move. As one of the new medics put it, he thought they 'should find the parts contained in the *Abdomen* so rotten, that it would be impossible to discover the *Uterus* from the other parts'. In any case, the process would probably be inconclusive, since it would be impossible to determine 'whether she was with Child unless the Infant was become boney'. Nevertheless, the dissection was performed. As Dr Coatsworth, one of the doctors involved, later graphically recalled:

> [Sarah's] face and neck to her shoulders appeared black and so much corrupted, that we were unwilling to proceed any further; but however her mother would have it done, and so we did open her, and as soone as she was opened we perceived the Stomach and Guts were as full of wind, as if they had been blown with a pair of Bellows; we put her Guts aside, and came to the *Uterus*, and Dr *Philips* shewed it us in his hand, and afterwards cut it out and laid it on the Table, and opened it, and we

saw into the cavity of it, and if there had been any thing there as minute as a hair, we might have seen it, but it was perfectly free and empty.

They then opened the stomach, breast and lungs but found 'all dry'. Coatsworth, now astonished at how well preserved the internal organs were, concluded 'this woman could not be drowned, for if she had taken in water, the water must have rotted all the Guts'.

Another of the doctors who helped to overturn the original inquest's verdict was mayor John Dimsdale senior, father of both John junior who had performed the earlier post-mortem and of another doctor, Robert, who was now also present. John Dimsdale senior noted that Sarah's body was 'as sound as any Flesh could be, no manner of putrifaction in her Lungs or any other part, but she was very full of Wind. We searched the Stomach and the Thorax, and found not one drop of water about it.' This, he thought, was very strange, for 'for if there had been water in her, that would have caused a fermentation, and that would have rotted the Lungs and Guts'; instead, they were 'firm and sound'. The coffin too was as 'close and dry as any board whatsoever'. The team of doctors conferred and were now 'all of Opinion that she was not drowned'. All, that is, except Doctor Camlin, who had originally certified drowning and was not prepared to change his opinion. According to later evidence in court, Robert Dimsdale grew 'angry' with Camlin for his obstinacy, asserting his own status as 'a graduate Physician', in contrast to Camlin, who had no formal training and, by implication, did not know what he was talking about. They 'had some words about it'.

The doctors had ruled out death by accident or suicide; the only alternative was murder. The last person who had seen Sarah Stout alive was Spencer Cowper, the son of the most eminent family in the town. Cowper had, as a result of Mary Stout's tenacity, already been examined twice about the possible murder by Lord Chief Justice Holt, but it was the exhumation that gave the evidence necessary to imprison him. A second man, John Marson, a friend of Cowper's, was bailed. Cowper himself remained in gaol for two months until, on 18 July 1699, he and Marson were tried for Sarah Stout's murder. Accused of 'not having God before their eyes and seduced by the instigation of the Devil', Cowper and Marson were alleged to have assaulted her with 'malice aforethought'.[1] They were alleged to have bound 'the neck and throat of the said Sarah' with a rope in order to choke and strangle her, before casting her into the river to conceal their crime.

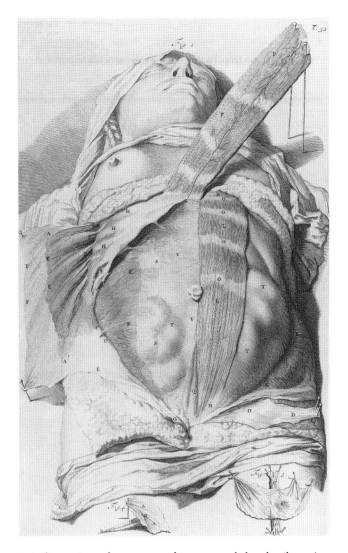

Figure 1.1 A dissection of a woman, from a work by the 'best Anatomist in Europe' who gave evidence at the Hertford trial.

The case was to have far-reaching implications, not just for Hertford, for through it and its aftermath it is possible to reconstruct the extraordinary ferment of ideas that constitute England's early Enlightenment—the process by which long-accepted beliefs, institutions, prejudices, and customs were fundamentally challenged and sometimes overturned. This book explores this contest, not through the major intellectual figures who usually figure in such accounts, nor the life of a major city, but through the rich and controversial lives of one family and their pitifully divided market town.

On the face of it we have a gruesome though not particularly unusual case, interesting perhaps only for the tenacity with which a woman pursued justice for her daughter and for the double autopsy. But it is necessary to peel away the layers of prejudice, bitterness, division, and illicit love that lay just beneath the surface of the story. This will reveal Britain at the turn of the seventeenth and eighteenth centuries as a society undergoing disturbing changes. Mapping the twists and turns of the case will illuminate a neglected but transformative part of Britain's history. This trail will lead, eventually, to two more trials, one involving both Spencer and his brother William Cowper, and the other involving the last conviction of a witch in England.

DEAD BODIES FLOAT

One question at the heart of Enlightenment debates was 'what is a fact and how can we verify a fact?' The answer to this was central to a number of subsidiary questions: how do we know that God exists (or not) or that the Scriptures are his revealed will? How do we know that a politician tells the truth and deserves a vote? How do we know what we read is true? How do we establish how the natural world works? Thus at the core of the Enlightenment lay problems about how man acquires knowledge, how to distinguish truth from error, and what authorities (if any) could be trusted—issues with which post-Enlightenment generations continue to struggle.

The problems of knowledge and fact were, of course, the concern of the courtroom as much as the pulpit, poll booth or laboratory. Indeed, it is likely that the legal notion of a fact—something verifiable by more than one public testimony, based on experience and observation and from someone of good repute and credit—was useful to these other spheres. By exploring the evidence presented by the prosecution and defence, glimpses of the different aspects of identifying truth are visible in the trial of Spencer Cowper. In particular, the role of science—already apparent in the two post-mortems conducted on Sarah Stout—will become a significant theme both of the trial and of future chapters. But we first need to flesh out the case against him.

The prosecution opened by declaring that the prisoners stood accused of 'one of the foulest and most wicked Crimes almost that any Age can remember.' The prosecuting counsel explained to the jury that, since the deed was done in the night, 'the Evidence cannot be so plain as otherwise might be'; but he put forward a scenario in which 'after she was strangled and murdered', Sarah had been 'carried and thrown into a River to stifle the Fact, and to make it supposed that she had murder'd herself'. So this was, he said, 'a double murder' and hence 'in a manner two Tryals, one to acquit the party that is dead, and to satisfie the world, and vindicate her reputation that she did not murder herself but was murder'd by other hands'.

The prosecutor explained that Spencer Cowper had come to Hertford on the day of Sarah's death, 13 March. Spencer was a barrister and the assizes were in town—the occasion when a judge from a central court went four times each year into the provinces on a tour, dispensing justice in cases that were deemed too serious for the local courts. Spencer had been conducting legal business in the town's court, for following the judge on tour meant access to the best and most lucrative cases. In an era before defendants were assigned legal assistance, he was now representing himself to defend his life.

The prosecution began to build its case. A week before the March assizes, it was revealed, Spencer's wife had written to Sarah Stout saying that she should expect him to stay with her—the families were on close terms and although the Cowpers leased Hertford Castle as a home, his parents were in London and the house was shut up and unoccupied. On arriving in Hertford, on a very 'dirty' wet day, Spencer had gone first 'to dry himself' at an inn but sent his horse to the Stout's house and:

> Some time after he came thither himself, and din'd there, and staid till 4 in the afternoon; at 4 when he went away, he told them he would come and lodge there that night, and Sup. According to his word he came there, and had the Supper he desired. After Supper Mrs *Stout*, the young Gentlewoman, and he sat together till near 11 a clock.

At 11 o'clock the maid, in Spencer's hearing, was asked to warm his bed (with a pan containing coals) and expected him to follow her upstairs:

> but it seems while she was warming of the Bed she heard the door clap together, and the nature of that door is such, that it makes a great noise at the clapping of it to, that any body in the House may be sensible of any ones going out. The Maid upon this was concern'd, and wonder'd

at the meaning of it, he promising to lye there that night; she came down, but there was neither *Cowper* nor Mrs [Sarah] *Stout*.

The maid and Sarah's mother, who concluded that Spencer and Sarah must have gone out together, 'sat up all night in the house', vainly expecting her to return.

Sarah had no obvious reason to kill herself. On the contrary, she had 'so great prosperity, had so good an estate' that she seemed to have everything to live for. Her father, Henry Stout, had been a prosperous brewer (who might possibly have given his name to 'stout ale', a term coined about this time) and had left his daughter a wealthy woman when he died in 1695. This made Sarah a great catch, for when she married her possessions would transfer to her husband. Not only was there no apparent motive for suicide and no medical evidence to back it, the bruising around her ear and neck suggested that she had been strangled. The original coroner's inquest, it was now claimed, had been a hurried and rather superficial affair; it was the second post-mortem that mattered. Moreover, the Quakers rejected suicide as incompatible with their religious beliefs; that the daughter of a leading Quaker family should have committed suicide sounded highly implausible.

It followed, the prosecution argued, that Sarah had been murdered. Spencer Cowper was 'the last man unfortunately in her Company'. And he was assisted by Marson, and by two other men, Rogers and Stevens, who had all arrived in Hertford the day of the murder. They had taken lodgings at Gurrey's (a large bed for all three accomplices, as was quite usual at this time) and then gone to dine at the Glove and Dolphin, returning at or after 11. Since it was a wet night they called for a bottle of wine and a fire to be lit and were overheard talking about Sarah Stout:

> one said to the other, '*Marson*, she was an old Sweet-heart of yours'. 'Ay', saith he, 'but she cast me off, but I reckon by this time a Friend of mine has done her business'. Another piece of discourse was, 'I believe a Friend of mine is even with her by this time . . . her business is done, Mrs *Sarah Stout*'s courting days are over'.

At the time the inn-keeper's wife was rather shocked, thinking that they meant 'some body had stole her away and got to bed [with] her'; so this incriminating talk was remembered when Sarah was dredged next morning from the water, particularly because the men had pulled out 'a great deal of Money', which looked suspiciously like a payment.[2] What is more, Spencer met with them the next day and then they left town. Had Spencer 'done her business', with the help of the three men, at least one of whom could have borne a grudge as a spurned admirer of Sarah's?

In order to reinforce the murder charge, and to rule out both accidental death and suicide, the prosecution put forward medical evidence. This rested on the notion that 'if Persons come alive into the Water then they sink'. Yet, as several prosecution witnesses testified, Sarah's body was floating on or near the surface, and little water was seen to come from it when pulled from the river. Dr Coatsworth added drama by relating how he had himself nearly been drowned. His experience of falling overboard one time, when he had swallowed 'a great deal of water', convinced him that the belly of any body that had been in the water several hours would be full of water: 'every body that is drowned is suffocated by water passing down the Wind pipe into the Lungs'. At this point, perhaps to show that he was alert to the medical evidence, Judge Hatsell remarked that he knew 'Dr Brown' had a chapter on 'the floating of dead bodies', an allusion to a book published by Dr Thomas Browne, one of the most famous physicians of the seventeenth century; but, Hatsell added disarmingly, 'I don't understand it myself.'

Several more doctors confirmed the notion that a body without water in it 'was dead before it was put into the water'. But the most vivid evidence came from Edward Clement who was a mere sailor. In 1689, almost immediately after William III had been crowned king, England had declared war against France, a war that helped propel the nation to Great Power status. The early battles had been naval ones, with many casualties (over 1 million men were to die in the conflict before its resolution in 1713). Spencer's trial took place in a lull between the fighting, for a temporary halt was called to the war in 1697, before it began again in 1702; but the memories of death were all too sharp for Clement. He had been at the battle of Beachy Head in 1690, during which he saw several dead men thrown overboard, including a friend killed by his side:

> I saw several dead Bodies floating at the same time; likewise in another Engagement, where a Man had both his Legs shot off, and died instant-ly; they threw over his Legs, though they sunk, I saw his Body float. Likewise I have seen several Men who have died natural Deaths at Sea; they have when they have been dead had a considerable weight of Ballast and Shot made fast to them, and so throw them over board;

because we hold it for a general Rule that all Men Swim if they be dead before they come into the Water, and on the contrary I have seen Men when they have been drowned, that they have sunk as soon as the Breath was out of their Bodies, and I could see no more of them. For Instance, a Man fell out of the *Cornwall*, and sunk down to rights, and seven Days afterwards we weighed Anchor, and he was brought up grasping his Arms about the Cable, and we have observed in several Cases, that where Men fall over-board, as soon as their Breath is out of their Bodies they sink downright, and on the contrary where a dead Body is thrown over-board without weight it will swim.

He took it to be 'a certain Rule that those that are drowned sink, but those that are thrown overboard do not', otherwise why would the government be at the 'vast charge' of providing three or four score hundred weight to sink the bodies of dead men? His conclusion was corroborated by Richard Gin, another sailor who had been press-ganged and 'went against [his] will in two Fights'.

The evidence against Spencer Cowper and his accomplices thus turned on the testimony of medics and seamen that the bodies of those who drown take in water and sink, whilst those who were killed before entering the water floated; that Sarah could not therefore have drowned either accidentally or by suicide (especially since she had so much to live for); and that there had to be another cause of death. This, it was suggested, was murder. The interest that the co-defendant Marson and his cronies took in Sarah was not harmless banter but deeply suspicious. Marson must have strangled Sarah at Spencer's behest or have helped Spencer strangle her with a cord, and returned to the inn in a sweat. He and his friends had received payment from Cowper; and they had ghoulishly gone to view the body of their victim, returning if not to the scene of the crime then at least to where she lay.

But if the evidence for the prosecution was sensational, the defence case proved even more so, pitting the medical experts against each other in what was one of the first trials in which forensic evidence played a major part.

SCIENTIFIC REPUTATIONS

What trust do we place in experts, such as doctors or politicians? Should we believe their evidence more than that of non-experts or, rather, how should we evaluate it? And does science offer a clear solution to the problem of establishing truth? These questions reverberated around the Hertford courtroom at the turn of the eighteenth century, just as they do in the twenty-first for issues such as global warming and the safety of GM crops. In Hertford in 1699 the doctors prepared to do battle with one another, offering rival versions of the scientific truth.

Asked to stand witness for the defence, the 'best Anatomist in Europe', William Cowper (who, despite the name, was no relation of Spencer), prepared in a rather unusual way. The night before the trial he had drowned a dog. In fact he drowned two, having already killed three in London prior to setting out for Hertford. As he told the court:

> In order to satisfie my self what quantity of water was necessary to enter the Body of an Animal and cause a suffocation in Water, I caused 3 Dogs when alive to be suddenly plunged under Water, till they were stifled.

He concluded that very little water—no more than three ounces—had penetrated the lungs and that there was none at all in the stomach. In other words, the medical evidence offered by the prosecution—that Sarah must have been killed because those who drown have a lot of water in their bodies—was wrong. William Cowper offered the court 'the testimony of the Experiments' he had performed to test the observations of the doctors, in what was a textbook example of the empirical method advocated by the 'new science' of the seventeenth century.

He began with first principles:

> This is a truth that no man can deny, who is acquainted with anything of this nature, that when the head of an Animal is under water, the first time it is obliged to inspire (or draw in air) the water will necessarily flow into its lungs, as the air would do if it were out of the water; which quantity of water (if the dimensions of the Windpipe and its branches in the lungs be considered) will not amount to 3 inches square, which is about 3 ounces of water. Nor is a greater quantity of water in the Windpipe necessary to choke any person.

When this small amount of water met with the air in the lungs it was converted to froth. It was the froth, William Cowper claimed, that blocked the windpipe and caused suffocation. And he had performed experiments to prove his case, so that his evidence was based on fact rather than supposition:

My Lord, I don't speak this by way of conjecture or Hypothesis, but I have made experiments, which have suggested what I here offer.

As one of his colleagues, Dr Morley, recounted:

We last night drown'd a Dog and afterwards dissected him, and found not a Spoonful of water in his Stomach, and I believe about two Ounces in his Lungs, while we were doing this, we drowned another, and he lay at the bottom and did not float; no more would he have done, if he had been hang'd before thrown into the water: we took him up, and upon opening him we found much about the same quantity of water in his Lungs, and little or none in his Stomach, they both froth'd at Nose and Mouth, because the water coming into the little bladders of the Lungs, and there meeting with air, a commotion arose between the water and air, which caused th' froth.

Countering the other scientific reasoning offered by the prosecution, that dead bodies float, Cowper then asserted that 'Dead Bodies necessarily sink in Water'; they became bloated with air once 'a rarefaction of humors within the cavities' set in, which caused the body to rise to the surface. 'Your Lordship may infer this', Cowper told the judge, 'from what the Seamen told you, and the great weight they use to fasten to their bodies that died of Diseases, was not of such use to sink them, as it was to prevent their floating afterwards, so that the weight was necessary for those that were killed as well as those that died of diseases.'

Cowper's testimony signalled the growing importance both of scientific experimentation—the method of establishing truth advocated by the Royal Society and its followers—and in forensic evidence in criminal cases. At stake in the trial was the question of how the truth could be determined and proven. By the end of the seventeenth century there was a growing demand for knowledge based on observation and experimentation—a reflection of the century's self-conscious shift in attitudes to understanding the natural world, towards systematic, rational, and practical exploration of it. And this was increasingly being played out before a wider public. Anyone who heard or read the trial (and, as we shall see, this audience was extensive) was exposed to quite detailed scientific knowledge. And the body of the victim was increasingly being seen as a source of evidence—by the 1720s about 40 per cent of homicides had an autopsy. Yet for all its desire to establish the truth, the 'new science' did not bring with it absolute certainty. In the trial, the prosecution had offered medical evidence, based on observation and professional knowledge, as the key plank of their case; yet Spencer countered with rival evidence, drawn from *experimental* observation, that cast the prosecution case into doubt and offered different explanations for what had happened.

William Cowper's experiments alone were not enough. Spencer Cowper also sought to invalidate the scientific conclusions of the prosecution and buttress those of his expert witness by bringing as many renowned doctors as possible to confirm William Cowper's findings. One of these London doctors, Samuel Garth, ridiculed the whole idea that Sarah had been murdered. He denied that Sarah's body had been floating; it had, he said, merely been entangled on the stakes:

> The Witnesses all agree she was found upon her side, which to suppose her to float in this posture, is as hard to be conceiv'd, as to imagine a Shilling shou'd fall down and rest upon its edge rather than its broad side.

And on the key question of how much water it was necessary to swallow in order to commit suicide, Garth was full-square behind Cowper.

> As to the quantity of water, I do not think it necessary it shou'd be very great...I believe when she threw herself in she might not struggle to save herself, and by consequence not sup up much water.

He had, he said with mathematical precision, thought of the windpipe as a cylinder and calculated that it would not hold a pint of water, 'which might imperceptibly work and fall out'. So sure was he of his opinion that he had 'offer'd a wager' about it at Garaway's Coffee House in London. Garaways was where Robert Hooke, the perfecter of the microscope, and other members of the Royal Society could be found discussing and even experimenting—on one occasion dissecting a porpoise there. Indeed the coffee houses were becoming an increasingly important venue for disseminating and demonstrating the new scientific ideas and experiments of Isaac Newton and others, a process inviting the public to judge their veracity rather as Garth was appealing to the Hertford jury to uphold his version of the scientific truth. Garth had also pointed out that no evidence had been offered about the cord which had allegedly been used to strangle Sarah and which would have left a mark, and dismissed the evidence of the prosecution's seafaring witnesses—seamen, he said, were 'superstitious people, they fancy that whistling at Sea will occasion a tempest'. To counteract them further, evidence was heard from Mr Harriot, a surgeon in the navy, and therefore a more credible, because socially superior, witness. Harriot said that when the navy weighted a body 'it was not to make them sink, but for decency sake, that they might not be driven to Shore when they began to float'. Another sailor (presumably not 'superstitious' like his colleagues) confirmed this; a Mr Bartlett told the court:

> I have been in several of the King's Ships of War that have been disabled and forc'd to lye by, in several Ingagements between the *French* and *English*, and I never saw any Bodies float either of the Men that were killed in our Ship, or in the Ships that have been near us, I have not seen a Body upon the Surface of the Water.

AN ANATOMY OF LONDON DOCTORS

Samuel Garth and William Cowper had been parachuted in from London to cast doubt on the scientific evidence that underpinned the prosecution case. The ten doctors who spoke for Spencer invoked their high status and professional competence in order to give their testimony greater weight—a good example of how scientific 'truth' was reinforced, or even determined, by social factors. Spencer's doctors were nationally and even internationally renowned men. Cowper, the anatomist, had practised in London since 1691 and been elected to the Royal Society only a few months before the trial, in January 1699. A skilled draftsman he had illustrated four volumes of anatomical works: one on muscles (which included an appendix describing the mechanism of an erection); one on the brain; a third (published in the year of the Hertford trial) on the differences between monkeys and man, with fold-out illustrations of a dissected orang-utan; and a fourth, published the previous year, *The Anatomy of Human Bodies*, from which Figure 1.1 is taken. But even medical images were not all that they seemed. The *Anatomy* involved Cowper in a dispute with the Dutch physician Govard Bidloo, who had earlier published the illustrative plates and now claimed that Cowper had plagiarized him. Cowper protested that he had acknowledged Bidloo in the introduction and that in any case, the text was his own (and better, he said, than the original); but the dispute shows that 'truth' was uncertain and malleable even in the world of medical publication. Cowper's reputation did not suffer and, perhaps a forerunner of more modern body art, in 1702 he presented to the Royal Society part of the small intestine of a dog that he had injected with wax, followed three years later with the diseased arteries of a leg which he had injected with red wax to simulate blood.

Samuel Garth had been admitted to the Royal College of Physicians in 1692 and in 1694 lectured on respiration. But he achieved more fame as a philanthropist and writer. In December 1696 he had been amongst a group of members of the Royal College who had proposed a subscription to fund a dispensary for free medical advice and cheap medicines for the sick poor. The idea had split the Royal College, for the apothecary physicians—those who traded in medicines—objected to the threat to their profits. Apothecaries were regarded as subordinate to physicians but had increasingly prescribed the drugs they prepared and sold. The dispute was a sign of the rifts within the medical profession that the Hertford trial had also begun to expose. Indeed in the spring of the same year as the trial, Garth published *The Dispensary, A Poem*, which celebrated the opening of the first public dispensary for the poor in England—and ridiculed the 'vigorous opposition' of the apothecaries. Garth's wit and political support for the Whig party—which, as we shall see, sought to establish 'revolution principles' in the wake of William of Orange's successful invasion of England in 1688—also made him a natural member of the Kit-Kat club, a Whig dining society which took its name from Christopher Catling, who made pies to feed its members. Garth's pronounced political views did not blinker him to literary talent of a different persuasion. When the arch-Tory poet John Dryden died in penury in 1700 it was Garth who arranged his burial in Westminster Abbey. There was an irony here, since Garth had acquired a reputation for lacking a Christian faith. In the funeral oration he failed to mention Jesus Christ but did eulogize 'the great god Apollo'; and he is also said to have comforted the dying Nell Gwyn, Charles II's mistress, 'by telling her on his honour there was neither God nor future state'. He was part of a trend towards irreligion that will be explored later in the book. His own death in 1719 nearly mirrored that of Sarah Stout—one report alleges that he attempted suicide.[3]

Cowper and Garth were friends of another London doctor who gave evidence on behalf of the defence, Hans Sloane. Two accounts of Cowper's dissections were published posthumously as letters to Sloane, who was also one of Garth's allies in the creation of the charitable dispensary. Sloane, like Garth, later became physician to George I and bequeathed his huge collection of natural history and other objects (including 135 of Cowper's specimens and all his notes and letters) to the public, leading to the foundation of the British Museum in 1753. Today the museum contains a superb Enlightenment gallery, displaying some of his objects, freely accessible to the public in accordance with the terms of Sloane's will. Perhaps he is as famous today as a promoter of drinking chocolate, the fruit of his travels early in his life and of his experimenting with milk to take away some of the bitterness of the cocoa bean.

Sloane will reappear at the end of this story, since he also offered advice about belief in witchcraft; but the wider point of these cameos is to stress how influential these men were in their profession and how their appearance in a Hertford court was testimony to the powerful connections of Spencer Cowper's family. By contrast the members of the Dimsdale medical clan were much more parochial, and hence the value of their expertise on behalf of the prosecution was made to seem more questionable. There was a battle of reputations and prestige going on, as credibility did not rely on scientific knowledge alone.

Nevertheless the Dimsdales are themselves an interesting case study of the growing professionalism of provincial doctors. John Dimsdale senior, the mayor at the time of the trial and leader of the medics who had challenged the findings of the first autopsy, was the son of a barber-grocer-alehouse keeper. In other words, he had little formal education in medicine, learning primarily by experience; and most surgeons were still linked to a trade guild, the Barber-Surgeons. But we have seen how his son, Robert, was a university educated physician, a sure sign that the family were on the rise. Nevertheless that was nothing compared to the fortunes of another branch of the family that lived in Essex. John Dimsdale senior's brother was, ironically, a Quaker who set up a medical practice without obtaining a licence from the bishop—as an Act of 1511 required him to. Taking refuge from persecution for his religious beliefs he bought land in the Quaker-founded colony of Pennsylvania and in New Jersey. Both his sons were Quaker surgeons and a grandson, Thomas, back in England, set up practice in 1734 in Hertford. In the 1760s Thomas began to specialize in the treatment of smallpox, inoculating patients by infecting them with a mild dose to induce resistance. In 1767 he published *The Present Method of Inoculating for the Smallpox*, which secured him international fame and the following year he was invited to inoculate Catherine the Great of Russia and her son. Dimsdale was rewarded with £10,000 and the title of baron.

The public arena of the law court witnessed a good deal of conflicting scientific evidence. Both sides used Enlightenment experiment and observation to produce rational explanations and verifiable facts; but their conclusions differed. Far from resolving the dispute, the appeal to science had muddied the waters. Thus it is not surprising that public debate about the science of the case continued after the trial, in the form both of public experiments and a printed debate. These sought to invoke the public as observers and vicarious experimenters whose verdict would help validate the scientific findings; public testimony was thus part of the new science. But science did not simply divide the debate into empiricists and non-empiricists; rather the results of the scientific experiments remained contestable. Both sides were using 'Enlightenment' observation and experiment to produce rational conclusions; but their conclusions differed. The spat is worth examining in more detail, before returning to analysis of the trial itself, to show how widely the controversy had penetrated local society, how extensively print was involved in disseminating it, and how differently the same event could be interpreted.

There had been 'two publick Experiments', one conducted at Hertford and 'the other in the River of Thames' in the weeks after the trial. The results of the first of these had been published in a national newspaper, *The Post Man*, supporting the evidence given by the London doctors for the defence. The paper reported that, at the recent assizes, a criminal:

> one William Ricles was hanged for Burglary, and afterwards stripped and flung into the River, wherein the late Mrs Stout was drowned; this was done in the presence of several hundreds, and the Body immediately Sunk to the bottom.

The experiment 'proved' that those who had been killed did not float, as the prosecution had claimed. After eight hours the criminal's body was fished out but:

> no water purged from the Nose, Mouth, Eyes, Ears or any other part, as it did in the case of Mrs Stout. This experiment was made by the people, it having been insisted upon at the late Tryal against Mr Cowper, that all dead bodies float, but so many hundreds having seen that experiment with their own eyes, the opinions of the Surgeons produced

on the part of the King [i.e. against Cowper] is thereby destroyed and exploded, and all persons convinced of the contrary.[4]

But a tract published in London, *The Hertford Letter*, whose author seems to have had very good medical and local knowledge, refuted the findings and argued for the prosecution.[5] *The Hertford Letter*'s critical response is worth quoting at length, since it ridiculed the public experiment reported by the newspaper:

> The last Assizes, here was a Man hanged, after he was Dead, was cut down, and buried without a Coffin, the Grave filled up, and the Earth well trod down; in the Evening he was digg'd up again, being pressed almost flat by the weight of the Earth, was privately cast into the River, and when it was observed that the Corps would Sink, it was exposed to publick view, and an Advertisement of it was printed in the Post-Man 25th of July last, with a great shew of Exaltation . . . What influence this Experiment may have on you, I know not; but when all the Circumstances attending it are duly considered, I am of Opinion, it will make more against them, than their Opposites: If they had been certain of Success, what need of so much Art? Why did they not insert in their Advertisement, how the Body had been managed before 'twas thrown into the Water, how they opened it afterwards, and how they made a strict Scrutiny after Water, yet could not find a drop in it? Not one word of this. Methinks this partial Relation is calculated on purpose to magnifie their own Evidences, and put a slur on the [prosecution's]. I doubt not but the ingenious Contrivers of this Experiment did not only expect it would Sink, but that it would have some Water in it also.

The Hertford Letter also claimed that the anatomist William Cowper had tried to repeat the results of his experiment with a dog in the Thames; this he was apparently unable to do, indicating that 'some Artifice' must have been used during his first 'clandestine' experiments. Moreover:

> Some Weeks since, a Surgeon [Garth], that had been an Evidence at the Trial at Hertford, going into a Bookseller's Shop, meeting some acquaintance there, he fell into Discourse about Mrs. Stout, and asserted there, what he had affirmed at the Trial, viz. That Two or Three Ounces of Water will Drown a Dog: One of the Company told him he could not conceive that so small a quantity would do the business: He replyed, Sir, I will lay a Guinea, that I will Drown a Dog in the River of Thames, and he shall not have above Three Ounces of Water in him: The proffer was no sooner made, than accepted, Time appointed, Dog brought, and with a weight tyed to his hinder Feet, flung into the River, sometime after was taken out, and dissected; where instead of Three Ounces,

there was about Thirty Three; whereby he not only lost his Wager, but in a great measure his Reputation, as to what he had so confidently asserted to the contrary on the Trial.

The author of the anti-Cowper tract supported the argument that dead bodies naturally float, suggesting that anyone who doubted this should consult with those who had been on slave ships to Africa, a trade that had grown rapidly in the last quarter of the seventeenth century in order to supply labour to the burgeoning West Indian colonies. In a rather chilling remark the author observed that:

> when they throw the Dead *Negroes* over-Board, they never lay any weight to their Feet to sink them, as they do to white Men [for decency sake, so that they sank quickly]; it is certain that all those *Negroes* do immediately Float.

The author offered the plausible suggestion that whether bodies from a battle sunk or floated depended on the injury—if their chest and belly were uninjured they floated, but 'those whose Breast and Belly are perforated, so that Water gets into their *Cavities*, through the Wound, I doubt not but they will Sink'. He then disparaged Hans Sloane's evidence as untrustworthy or plain wrong—he had particular fun with Sloane's suggestion that some of the water in the body could have disappeared 'in Vapours or Steams', since anatomically there was no exit. Moreover, he claimed that the anatomist Cowper's observations were contrary 'to the Universal Experience of the Learned and Unlearned part of Mankind'.

The author of the pamphlet then reconstructed his own version of the crime:

> I am induced to believe, she was knocked down with a Blow on her left Ear, from the large Settlement of Blood there, . . . after she was fell'd to the Ground by the Blow, it is probable, with the Gripe of a strong Hand, she was Throtled; from the Stagnation of Blood on both sides of her Neck, under her Ears, which Mr. *John Dimsdall*, Jun. swears there was; and from the Settlement of Blood on her Breast, I am inclined to believe, That the Person that Throtled her, to support his Hand, that he might Gripe the stronger, rested his Arm on her Breast.

A printed riposte, *A Reply to the Hertford Letter*, nevertheless alleged that these were 'groundless surmises'. Its author (apparently a physician and a friend of Spencer's, though the tract is anonymous) instead suggested that Sarah had committed suicide and had therefore held her breath. In such cases of 'Voluntary Drowning', little water would be swallowed. And to prove it, yet more dogs were sacrificed in another public experiment, performed (for verification) in front of the 'Gentleman porter to the Tower of London', a surgeon called John Lichfield. The anonymous physician's account was not for the squeamish:

> I took a Dog and by a Weight directly sunk him under Three Feet of Water, which was so clear, that I could perceive what happen'd to him; and to be plain with you, I observed that for almost a Minute, he threw his Head disorderly about, before he gap't; upon which, the Water getting into his Windpipe in half a Minute more, he fell down with his Neck to the Bottom, void of Sense and Motion. After this I plung'd another, somewhat less; when in like manner as the former, I found when he had turned his Neck two or three times about, he was to appearance dead in a Minute's time. Now in all this, there were none of those Violent Efforts to throw the Water out of the Lungs discernible.

Death by drowning, then, was quick and did not involve ingesting large quantities of water. He then sent for another dog and threw it into a distiller's trough, over 30 feet long, having first tied its front and back feet together, to try to emulate a 'voluntary drowning'. After half an hour of (graphically described) struggling, the dog gave up, but the body was only removed five hours later. There proved to be 'not a drop' of water in the peritonaeum and thorax, and 'very little' in the small intestine, with only four or five ounces in the stomach. Yet there was 'spumous matter' from the windpipe—the same 'froth' that had appeared coming from Sarah's mouth. The author concluded that it was the lung, not the stomach, that was critical. Successfully replicating Cowper's experiment twice—conducting it both in front of the Sergeant of the Tower, a man of 'unquestionable Probity', and 'sundry other persons, as Honest as Judicious', who could confirm the findings—the drowned dog had just 'four large spoonfulls' of water in its larynx 'mixed with a Spume or Froth'; and 'not a Drop' in its stomach'. The only people in danger of dying because of liquid in their stomachs, he quipped, were the drunks 'reeling about our streets'. As for whether dead bodies floated or sunk, the author had not 'as yet' experimented on humans; but of the other animals tested, 'both alive and dead when thrown into the Water', there was 'but one which floated'.

The relatively complex debate about floating/sinking, ingesting/not ingesting, and the large numbers of dogs sacrificed in the pursuit of both sides' arguments, are testament to a public thirst for scientific proof. Forensic evidence was in its infancy and the autopsy of Sarah Stout was still something of a novelty, organized not by the State but by the immediate family; but her case reflects a growing desire for medical evidence. Science was beginning to intrude into decisions that had previously been decided without it. Even so, until the mid seventeenth century most physicians had only limited knowledge of the inner body; and the conflicting evidence in the Stout case was a testament to the uncertain knowledge that was being acquired even at the end of that century. Whilst there was a shift towards the use of empirical knowledge, this did not at a stroke remove doubt, and could even contribute towards it by creating contested versions of what was fact. What is certain is that science was pervasive at the trial; and it was in all sense a public science. Neighbours had given accounts of how the body was found; those who attended the court heard lectures on anatomy; those who read the subsequent debate deepened their knowledge; the 'people' took it upon themselves to fling the body of a dead convict into the river; and many dogs had been drowned as part of public experiments.

The medical evidence was important; but there was even more revelation to come. Having proven, or at least raised considerable doubt, that Sarah need not have been murdered, Spencer might have rested his case. It was unlikely given the conflict of evidence that the jury would have convicted; and he did not need to show whether Sarah had committed suicide or simply accidentally fallen into the water. He nevertheless decided to shift the direction of the case by showing that suicide was the most likely explanation for Sarah's death. Perhaps he was simply trying to do everything to mount a comprehensive defence; but the speech he gave opening his defence also suggests that pride was at stake:

> I must beg your Lordship's, and the Jury's Patience, while I not only defend my Life, but justifie my self also from these things that have unjustly aspers'd me, by the Conspiracy and Artifice of my Accusers....
> I shall prove fully and clearly, in the first place, that there was no Ground at all in this Case to suppose she was murther'd by any one but her self.

Spencer was thus determined to clear his 'credit'—which at this time meant his political, financial, sexual, and personal reputation and standing. He argued that to charge an innocent man of murder was 'as Base and Barbarous as the Murther it self could be' and he would rather 'my self was Murther'd then my Reputation', which had 'suffer'd greatly'. And in refuting the 'malice and artifice' of his accusers, and exposing their 'conspiracy', he perhaps also sought revenge, deliberately exposing the depths of the divisions in the town that he believed had brought him to the dock in the first place. But it also meant revealing a fated love story.

FALSE MAN'S CRUELTY

There is something unsettling about reading a dead person's love letters, particularly someone who might have died because of the passions they evoked or reflected. The sense of unwarranted intrusion can be very strong. The historian snooping through family archives is perhaps used to that. But the trial of Spencer Cowper ensured that the type of evidence that normally remained utterly private became luridly public in 1699. Sarah's love life was paraded through the court in a way that was guaranteed to make sensational hearing—or, for those (including us) only able to follow the story in print afterwards, prurient reading.

More importantly, the exposure of Sarah's doomed relationship with Spencer Cowper raises larger questions about the relations between the sexes that will form a continuous thread throughout this book. Indeed, the evidence presented here and elsewhere suggests that something interesting was happening to sexual attitudes, under-standings of gender roles, and the institution of marriage in this period. This could be dismissed as a mere reaction against the Puritan sobriety and piety apparent in the mid-century revolution, a loosening of the moral constraints that in any case had only ever been rather patchily embraced. But this would be to ignore a wave of moral reform in the 1690s that sought to counteract the libertinism and sexual licence that many feared were being unleashed. Sarah's case also suggests a liberation of romantic love and even the existence of a romanticism—a rush of feeling that could not be contained without violence to the sincerity of the self—a century before its literary flowering. Of course, Sarah Stout was not the first young woman to fall hopelessly in love with the wrong man, nor the first whose story ended disastrously; even so, there is something about the strength of her desire that seems curiously modern and self-absorbed. If love and courtship are generally shaped by the wider cultures in which they occur, Sarah's attitudes nevertheless seem a headstrong rejection of many of those governing her own time and, as we shall see in later chapters, of the strict Quaker upbringing that had tried to instil in her a renunciation of the self and the pleasures of the flesh. Indeed it is possible that this woman, for whom we nevertheless have no directly autobiographical material, might be telling us something about changing perceptions of what constituted a 'self', with all its manifold desires.

In 1698 Mr Bowd, a Hertford shopkeeper, called on Sarah Stout to tell her about an errand he had run for her in London, where she had recently been staying. As he later told the court, he noticed that something seemed to be wrong:

> Sitting together in the Hall, I ask'd her 'what's the matter with you?'
> Saith I, 'there is something more than ordinary, you seem'd to be Melancholy'.
> Saith she, 'you are come from *London*, and you have heard something or other':
> Said I, 'I believe you are in Love',
> 'In Love!' said she.
> 'Yes' saith I, '*Cupid*, that little Boy, hath struck you home'.
> She took me by the Hand. 'Truly', saith she, 'I must confess it, but I did think I should never be Guilty of such a Folly'.

Mrs Jane Low, a friend, also recalled conversations with the love-struck Sarah:

> She often complain'd to me that she was very Melancholy and uneasy, one time particularly, as we were walking together in the Fields, I ask'd her the occasion of it, and she told me that was a secret; but, she said, she led a very Melancholy Life; saith I, 'I am apt to believe you are in Love'. She did not disown it, and with a little more speaking she own'd she was. I ask'd her who the Person was. She said, that should be a Secret, but it would end her Days.

It did end her days, but it did not remain a secret.

One possible candidate was John Marson, the man accused alongside Spencer, but a much stronger contender was Thomas Marshall, another of Spencer's friends and a fellow lawyer. Marshall been introduced to Sarah when he had visited Spencer in Hertford in 1697. Marshall himself gave evidence at the trial (in order, as we shall see, to help his friend) and told the judge that Sarah:

> afterwards gave me frequent Opportunities of approving that Acquaintance...when I came to Town, my Lord, I was generally told of my Courting Mrs. *Stout*, which I confess was not then in my Head but it

being represented to me as a thing easily to be got over; and believing the Report of the World as to her Fortune, I did afterwards make my Application to her...[though] I was not over importunate in this Affair, for I never was a very violent Lover.

Spencer agreed that:

when she was first acquainted with [Marshall] she receiv'd him with a great deal of Civility and Kindness, which induc'd him to make his Addresses to her, as he did by way of Courtship.

Indeed, she signed one of her letters to him 'your loving Duck'. Tongues wagged. A letter from Sarah about this time talks of the 'notorious Inventions and Lyes' that were circulating in Hertford. Gossip about the liaison evidently reached Spencer's sister-in-law Judith, since she teased the apparently restless Sarah:

I remember I have said to her, I believe you have Mr. *Marshall* in your Head, either have him or do not trouble your self about him, make your self either easy one way or another, and she hath said 'no' in an indifferent way, 'I cannot make my self easy'.

Sarah decided to turn Marshall down with 'a very fair Denial' when he wrote her a proposal of marriage. And she chided Spencer for his stupidity in trying to act the matchmaker. Spencer himself related the incident in court, in order to reveal Sarah's feelings for himself:

It happen'd one Evening, that she and one Mrs. *Crook*, Mr. *Marshall*, and my self, were walking together, and Mr. *Marshall* and Mrs. *Crook*, going some little way before us, she took this Opportunity to speak to me, in such Terms I must confess surpriz'd me: Says she 'Mr. *Cowper*, I did not think you had been so dull'. I was inquisitive to know in what my dullness did consist: 'Why', says she 'do you imagine I intend to Marry Mr. *Marshall*?' I said I thought she did, and that if she did not, she was much to blame in what she had done. 'No' says she, 'I thought it might serve to divert the Censure of the World, and favour our Acquaintance'.[6]

Courting Marshall had only been a cover for meeting with Spencer. Sarah was in love with him. Her secret was out. And Marshall suspected it. He had accepted her refusal 'having partly by my own Observation, but more by Mr. *Cowper*'s Friendship, been pretty well able to guess at her meaning'. Did the 'jocular' and 'jesting' nudges and winks between Marshall's friends—the three lawyers accused alongside Cowper—over a bottle the night of her death, and their morbid curiosity to see her body, now make sense? Here was the woman who had jilted their friend. Marshall had been present in London at a gathering of lawyers that 'in a jesting way' had encouraged Rogers, Marson, and Stevens to 'enquire after the Lady and give as good an account of her as they could'; and, according to Marson's account, Marshall himself had asked them to see Sarah 'his Sweetheart'.

But Spencer was a married man, having on 4 February 1688 wed Pennington Goodere, though as yet they had no children.[7] And, he claimed, he was being pursued by the infatuated Sarah, despite his attempts to distance himself. She lived for moments when she could see him. On one occasion, when she had planned to visit him in London, her disappointment when she learnt that he would be out caused her to lose colour and 'fall into a woman's Fit of Swooning'. On 5 March, a fortnight before her death, she had written to Spencer in London. Dramatically, he read the letter out in court:

March the 5th.
SIR,
   I am glad you have not quite forgot that there is such a person as I in being, but I am willing to shut my Eyes, and not see any thing that looks like Unkindness in you, and rather content my self with what Excuses you are pleased to make, than be inquisitive into what I must not know; I should very readily comply with your proposition of changing the Season, if it were in my power to do it, but you know that lies altogether in your own Breast: I am sure the Winter has been too unpleasant for me to desire the continuance of it. And I wish you were to endure the sharpness of it, but for one hour, as I have done for many long Nights and Days, and then I believe it would move that rocky heart of yours, that can be so thoughtless of me as you are; but if it were designed for that end, to make the Summer the more delightfull, I wish it may have the effect so far as to continue it to be so too, that the Weather may never be over-cast again; the which if I could be assured of, it would recompence me for all that I have ever suffered, and make me as easie a creature as I was the first moment I received breath; when you come to H[ertford] pray let your Steed guide you, and don't do as you did the last time; and be sure order your affairs to be here as soon as you can, which cannot be sooner, than you will be heartily welcome to your very sincere Friend.

Spencer claims to have immediately shown the letter to Marshall, 'as he had done several others from the same hand', and then the two of them went to find Spencer's brother William, at the Covent Garden tavern, where they also showed it to him.

Spencer produced a second, even more incriminating, letter that he also claimed was from Sarah and which he had also shown his brother:

> March 9.
> SIR,
> I Writ to you by Sunday's Post, which I hope you have received; however as a Confirmation, I will assure you I know of no inconveniency that can attend your cohabiting with me, unless the Grand Jury should thereupon find a Bill against us,[8] but I won't fly for't, for come Life, come Death, I am resolved never to desert you, therefore according to your appointment, I will expect you, and till then I shall only tell you, that I am,
> Yours.

Sarah had offered to cohabit with him and Spencer claimed to have been shocked by this. He had, he said, not gone 'voluntarily', to dine with Sarah that fateful night, but had been 'prest by her'. Sarah had been unable to press her case with her mother present at the supper table and so they had left the house for a conversation late at night; but, Spencer implied, he had refused to agree to Sarah's proposal and in despair she had committed suicide.

SUMMING UP

It is possible that the letters were forgeries. They were the only real proof of Sarah's unrequited love and the only two people who claimed to have read them at the time were Spencer's friend (who also happened to be a 'kinsman' of his wife) and his brother. Certainly Sarah's mother and half-brother refused in court to accept them as genuine, if only because the content was so out of character. Even if genuine, Sarah and Spencer clearly had some private understanding that was never properly explained in court. The letters were addressed not to Spencer directly but to a Mrs Jane Ellen at Hargrave's coffee house. Spencer claimed that this was in order to avoid raising the suspicions of the servants and postman; yet unless Sarah was used to writing to him in this disguised fashion, how had he (and indeed the coffee house owner) known that they were intended for him? And if there was an arrangement for her to write to him in this unusually secretive way, what did they have to hide, how long had the communication been going on and what was the content of the other letters? Was this, indeed, evidence of a much deeper, and possibly requited, relationship than Spencer had admitted?

There are further puzzles. At what point did Spencer tell his wife about Sarah's infatuation? If he did so before Sarah Stout's death, it seems odd that she should write to Sarah asking if her husband could stay during the assizes—would she not have wanted him safely distant at an inn rather than throwing them together?[9] So perhaps the secrecy of the letters had been to protect his wife in some way and she had remained ignorant of Sarah's infatuation with her husband until Spencer had been forced to tell her once he had been arrested? Yet does this 'noble' version of Spencer's conduct fit with a man who agreed to spend a night at the house of a woman whom he knew to be in love with him, thereby inevitably raising her hopes, merely, as he said in court, to save the cost of a night at the inn?

There is also something strange about Spencer's relationship with Marshall. Why would Spencer show Marshall the letters from Sarah if he thought he still had feelings for her, as Marshall must have, if he encouraged his friends to see her when in town? Indeed, Marshall was so bitter at being rejected by Sarah that he apparently told Spencer that if he was really his friend he should shoot her. Even if this was exaggerated, was there not the risk that Marshall might reveal the secret, the very thing that in court Spencer claimed he would only tell if the lives of others were at stake? Moreover, Spencer's account of the river walk, during which Sarah had allegedly revealed her feelings for Cowper, was also later disputed by her mother and one of Sarah's friends who denied such a conversation had taken place.

It also seems extraordinary that John Marson, the former 'sweetheart' of Sarah's and Spencer's co-defendant, was never thoroughly examined in court. Marson admitted that Sarah had 'turn'd [him] off', when he had pressed his suit, just as she had done Marshall. If Marson had also courted Sarah, and been rebuffed, should the court not have known more about this, particularly as it was Marson who, witnesses reported, had arrived at the inn in a sweat at around the time Sarah was last seen? The prosecution did get as far as establishing that Marson lied to explain his sweat, claiming he had only just ridden from London, whereas he had arrived in Hertford at least three hours earlier (though he did have an alibi for that time and also produced character witnesses in court).[10] Certainly there was speculation after the trial about Marson's motive for murder: 'what if he had stomach'd that refusal of hers to that degree, that he was resolv'd to be reveng'd of her for it?'[11] We do know that Marson had, suspiciously, impersonated Marshall when asking for directions about how to find the dead Sarah—why might he have wanted to have keep his identity secret?

And once her character had been impugned why did the court not hear character witnesses for her when there were many witnesses in court, 'some of the most reputable in that Town', ready to do so? We do know that the judge wanted to end the trial and refused Sarah's brother the chance to call witnesses on her behalf; it was left to subsequent printed vindications to assert that she lived a 'sober and blameless' life and had 'acquir'd the reputation of a virtuous and modest young woman from our whole Town'.[12] But why did the court hear so little to vindicate Sarah?

It is impossible to answer these questions because the prosecution failed to probe very effectively. The trial lasted just nine hours, which despite its brevity in modern terms was something of a marathon for the time, being described as 'very long'. There was no expectation that a murder trial would stretch over more than one day. The prosecution did, however, have time to point out one major flaw in Spencer's account. Even if his story was correct, he had lied to the coroner immediately after her death, for at that time 'he said he never knew any Distraction, or Love-fit, or other occasion she had to put her upon this extravagant Action. Now here he comes and would have the whole Scheme turn'd upon a Love fit.' Indeed when Spencer had been examined by the coroner he had been asked 'if he knew any reason why she should do such a thing, and he said, she was a very modest Woman, and he knew no cause why she should do such a thing as this'. And when asked 'if he knew any person that she was in Love with?' he had 'said he knew but of one, and his name was Marshall, and Mr. Marshall told him, that he was always repulsed [i.e. turned down] by her'. Had he said anything about the letters from her? Witnesses of the coroner's inquest denied he did; Spencer claimed he had.

What we know for certain is that Spencer's two key witnesses were hardly impartial. One, Marshall, was a friend who perhaps wanted revenge on the wealthy woman who had publicly spurned him and made him the subject of gossip. The other was Spencer's brother William, who had a secret of his own, that might, if known to the court, have invalidated his testimony. Perhaps Sarah did know and it had encouraged her thoughts about cohabitation. For William Cowper was a bigamist who allegedly persuaded his second 'wife' that she was committing no sin in cohabiting with him—a secret that will be explored shortly. This and Sarah's desire to live with Spencer raise a number of interconnected themes that will be explored throughout future chapters. Her illicit passion and his lust suggest that they were part of the 'age of immorality' that many contemporaries lamented. Such challenges to conventional morality were a feature of an interesting strand of Enlightenment thought. In particular, the nature of marriage and sexual relationships was being reassessed as the Puritan veil was lifted.

ZARA'S STORY

The trial was sensational and, perhaps because of the number of unanswered questions, prompted the publication of a number of imagined scenarios. Indeed, it was repackaged in fictional terms from the outset. A printed *Dialogue between a Quaker and his Neighbour* (1699) imagined a conversation between Hertford's citizens about the possible motives for murder and invented speeches that Spencer Cowper might have made to Sarah Stout just before her death. But in 1709 the story was given much more extensive fictional treatment. The startling courtroom revelation of her letters encouraged, ten years later, an imagined and sensationalized reconstruction of how the love affair might have been conducted. That it uses fiction is not accidental. The blurring of fact and fiction, and the possibility of malleable versions of the truth, was key to the emergence of the novel. Thus the gestation of the novel at this time was not a purely literary phenomenon. Rather it drew on wider cultural shifts, which the Cowper trial had already begun to expose. The rise of the novel has in part to be related to the debates about morality of the type that Sarah's love and suicide raised. Such subject matter had for a long time been the preserve of ballads and romances; now, the problems and dilemmas that such a moral ferment threw up became the grist of longer and more complex forms of fiction.

But it is also worth highlighting two more factors shaping the transmission of the scandal into print. One of these was the freedom of the press. After 1695 the government's legal right to censor print prior to publication was finally removed. Censorship had been a rather inconsistent and even blunt instrument before then; but the lapse of the Licensing Act in 1695 opened the press still further, both in terms of the number of titles being sold—it was the market not the government that was now in charge—and in terms of the range of its content. Since material was now only subject to prosecution *after* publication, a crop of unorthodox material began appearing. The unshackling of the press in 1695 was also important in giving a more permanent footing for periodicals. Newspapers and other journals were not new—they were an earlier seventeenth-century innova-tion—but the lapse of the Licensing Act encouraged their proliferation. The appearance of reports about the experiments involved in the Hertford case in newspapers has already been noted, but it is worth pausing to think how such periodicals also shaped the way in which people thought about what they read. Newspapers created an ongo-ing narrative of imagined characters and events, helping to shape an appetite for what the novel offered. Periodicals and newspapers were also, in this new climate, being pitched at women and the novel, too, was often associated with female readers. The press therefore drew on public thirst for dramatic news but also created a new type of imag-ined public audience.

The second factor shaping fictional writing was the political culture of the time, which will be explored more fully in the next chapter. The connection between politics and fiction will, I hope, become clearer as the Cowper case is unravelled further; but it is worth flagging here that there were a number of features of the political conflicts of the time that fostered a novelistic impulse. One was the anxiety that the new form of politics that was emerging in the later seventeenth century, one revolving around emerging political parties and frequent general elections, was both involving a wider audience and selling them a series of partial truths, fictions, or lies. Once politics became a competition at the polls to attract as many votes as possible, politi-cians had not only to present their ideas as attractively and dramati-cally as possible—honing genre and style—but were also tempted to spin their policies in as effective a way as possible or to detract from their rivals, either by creating rumours or spreading lies and innuen-do. It also became hugely tempting to use personal foibles as part of political campaigning. Of course, this was not entirely new—but, in an age of perceived growing immorality, the occasions on which this became possible and advantageous seemed to multiply. Politics and the press, politics and fiction, and politics and personal morality became closely linked realms.

Falfe Man's cruelty

While faithlefs men do Females flights   And though they do in men delight,
The more they feel loves pain,   They pay them with difdain.
                    Tune of, Jenny Gin, Bufie Fame, or, *The fair one let me in.*

Figure 1.2 A ballad from the 1680s, depicting faithless love driving a woman to suicidal thoughts.

The 1709 account of the Sarah Stout–Spencer Cowper love tryst was by Delarivier Manley. Manley is herself extremely interesting and worth returning to later, not least because her own life combined politics, print, and sexual scandal. Her version of Sarah Stout's love and death is dramatic (Manley had also written for the stage in the 1690s) and sympathetic to Sarah, whose suicide is made to seem as culpable as if Spencer Cowper had actually murdered her. It is thus politically charged, reviving accusations against the Cowpers and the Whigs more generally at what will be shown to be a critical moment in the contest between the parties. But Manley's account is also interesting because it blurs fact and fiction. Indeed, it is a good example of the factual fictions—fictions that use fact or the similitude of fact to create an illusion of reality—that characterized early novelistic writing and which lie at the heart of the genre even today. The reader is presented with a world as though it is real and enjoys the fiction as if it was a fact. It is thus an excellent example of how political culture infused and helped to shape literary style and how the emergence of the novel has to be seen in a wide historical context.

The New Atalantis, the novel which contains the account of the love affair, is worth quoting to show how fact and fiction were interwoven. In it Sarah is thinly disguised as 'Zara', with Spencer as 'Mosco'. Zara is described as 'a very pretty girl' with 'something jaunty' about her. She soon catches Mosco's eye:

> Mosco, who never saw a woman he could not have bestowed some of his favours upon, let her be handsome or indifferent, was mightily taken with pretty Zara. He had not the command of money as his elder brother had; all things moved in a much narrower sphere than at Hernando's. His lady [i.e. his wife] had been his father's mistress and his mother never forgave him his marriage with her. It would be no disadvantage to him to have the command of Zara's. The young creature took a fatal passion for him, which was not in her power to conceal, not even from his wife. If she were at the table at dinner with her, and he returned unexpectedly, her surprise and joy were usually so great, that all the world might read in her face the disorders of her soul . . . The lady did not love her the less for it; she believed her sick of a distemper she could not help and did not imagine it would arise to any guilty commerce between her and her husband. Mean time [Zara] put all her little matters in Mosco's hand; he it was that disposed of her fortune, and made what wastes and improvements he saw good. When she had affairs at [London], if he were there, she took up her constant residence at his house, perpetually put her self in the road where she might meet him. He saw this impressment and was not at all displeased with it. His soul was almost as amorous and his person almost as handsome as his brother's. He had a great deal of wit and attempt, understood very well his business, but had not the good fortune to be born an elder Brother.
>
> By pretence of business, he could often see Zara at her mother's house. Those opportunities were not lost. She was of an opinion that cohabitation makes a marriage; she would have given ten times her fortune, if she had had it, that Mosco, as he sometimes gave her hopes, would leave his wife and cohabit with her. Not that he ever intended it, but men used not to say disagreeable things to those that they come to be happy with.

But, according to Manley, Mosco soon tired of Zara's love. In this version of events the lovesick Zara brings matters to a head, urging him either to tell her he did not love her or to cohabit with her, in the Quaker style:

> Things are come to that height. I can't bear to live and not possess you all. Will you do as you promised? Will you live with me? Shall I have that sanction for my passion? My fortune may be wholly at your disposal. I will even do all that's necessary to please my mother, in whose power it is to double it. She will no longer oppose my

inclinations, when she finds you give me that proof of yours. You have but to cohabit with me to make you master of hers as well as mine. I am asking no new thing. 'Twas but what your self first proposed, the artifice by which you drew me to give you the last proof of my love, and without which I should have believed that concession highly criminal. Persons of our persuasion [Quakers] promise nothing but what they are sure to perform; you well know their very word to them is a law.

Mosco replied with 'an answer stuffed with false assurance of love and performance of his promise. He would but put his affairs in a posture not to fear his wife's anger and then he'd devote himself wholly to her.' But, of course, he did not stick to his word and merely grew colder. The afflicted Zara therefore began to deluge him with letters; 'she fatigued, she persecuted him'. He wanted rid of her. Neither 'her height of passion, youth, nor beauty, could restore lost appetite, or prevent a loathing'. And though she 'perpetually talked of dying... he knew that very few died of that distemper'. Even so, her beauty faded; she neglected herself; and became withdrawn, full of despair and sorrow. She resolved to see Mosco one last time and wrote him an imploring but also threatening letter:

> Tired out with love and disdain, too cruel friend and husband, I have resolved to suffer no more in private, but will proclaim my woes, and your delusions, even to the woman the world believes your wife, though I am only such, and will not fail to make my claim within two days at [London]. If before that time be expired, thou dost not come and relieve thy affectionate and most despairing
>
> Zara

Alarmed at the thought of exposure, Mosco was determined to 'be at rest from so troublesome an amour'. He rode to Hertford to see Zara and 'she was all joy and new transport to see him; 'twas as if she had never been in pain. She told him he must lie there that night. He said nothing to contradict her. They supped with her mother, who afterwards withdrew to order the linen for his bed.' After this awkward meal, and 'having summoned all his resolution' for what would undoubtedly be a difficult conversation:

> he asked her if they should take a walk by the riverside? The servant was above ordering his bed, but he was afraid that what he had to say would make her so outrageous, that the family would hear her and he, in the first gust of her passion, should be exposed, as well as her self. Zara consented to every thing that was agreeable to him. They began

Figure 1.3 Detail of a portrait of the 'amorous' Spencer Cowper. A lock of his hair, perhaps a love token, is preserved among the family papers.

their walk by the pale glimmerings of the moon and the agreeable noise that arose from the gentle dashes of the water.

Mistaking Mosco's presence for a sign that he had finally consented to her entreaties, Zara pushed matters on:

'Thou shalt never, my dear', says she, 'forsake me again. I have told my mother of my design to take you for my husband. We will begin this very night to cohabit together. My despair and melancholy has drawn her at length to consent. Do but utterly forgo that woman you call your wife and we require no more for making mine (in our opinion) a lawful marriage. We are above the little censure of others; the law nor magistrates do not frighten us. I make you absolute master of my fortune, only upon those conditions - my dear! why do you not speak? Thou art not come here to disappoint me. I beseech you to answer me.'

But Mosco shattered her illusions about leaving his wife in words that hypocritically stressed his adherence to the laws of marriage:

'Alas! beautiful Zara! What can I answer? Nothing, I fear, but will be disagreeable to your expectations. You don't know the world. You are ignorant of mankind. 'Tis in our power to marry our selves but once; this is a fundamental established law, as long as that wife shall live. I did not doubt but you knew this and, when I first gained the pleasures of your love, said the contrary only to allow your virtue that pretence for yielding, but we must be both utterly void of common sense to go to pass such a marriage upon the world—me to abandon a lady by whom I have so many children and other benefits, to ruin my own and for an airy notion, by which we make our selves obnoxious to the laws and hated by mankind.

Mosco at first still offered her his continued love but only if it was clandestine: 'Be contented with my love; there's nothing I shall omit to please you. I will lose no opportunity to entertain you with it, provided you are discreet and do not expose us both.' But then, despite seeing her distraught state, he callously decided to bring the breach between them to a head:

'You would do well, Madam,' says he, aiming to unlock her hands, 'to leave me in peace, and go home to compose your brain by sleep. You happen to be amorous and fantastically mad and I must be the sufferer. True, you have obliged me; I promised to make a marriage after your fashion by cohabitation. I do not think fit to perform it. What of that? Are you the first woman that has gone upon a wrong principle? My family and reputation are not to be staked for trifles. Be more moderate, or assure your self I'll never, from this instant, see you more.'

Here he threw abroad her hands, and broke from her. She fell her length upon the ground, then, getting up as fast as she could, strove to follow him for he was at too great a distance. Revenge and despair worked her up to the height of lunacy. She tore off her hood, her coif, her gown that hung loosely about her, trampling it under foot and calling after him, 'Turn, turn, but a moment, turn and see what love and rage can do, return and behold what Zara can perform! Frantic, lost to hope and love, lost to life. Ruin, despair, destruction, death, eternal misery, overtake me! Heaven, earth and hell revenge me! Heaven, earth and hell are conscious of my wrongs! I devote my self to misery eternal . . . Receive me, oh hospitable flood! into thy cold bosom, receive a devoted wretch whose flame thy water can only quench.'

Here she flounced, with all her strength, into the river, to the last moment persisting in a desire of speedy death. She held her breath and was immediately stifled, without swallowing any of the water. 'Tis very much a question if he did not hear the fall of the body, possibly not believing a woman's love could work her to such a prodigious height of frenzy and resentment.

Reading this account shortly after its publication, Spencer's mother, Sarah, confided to her diary that she thought that Spencer had indeed been culpable even if Sarah Stout was the aggressor: 'Upon some talk about that Rampant Shaker who Drown'd herself, I had this Reflection. That immodesty of behaviour makes way to lust, and gives life to wicked hopes. Schechem Sinn'd, but Dinah tempted him. She that was so light as to wander abroad alone I fear was not over difficult to yield. Lust given way to is a pleasant madness but is a desperate Madness when it is opposed.'[13] Her Biblical allusion was to the story in Genesis about Schechem, the son of the ruler Hamor, who 'violated' Jacob's daughter Dinah but then fell in love with her; Dinah's brothers nevertheless revenged her death and destroyed Hamor and Schechem for treating their sister like a prostitute. It seems possible that Sarah Cowper was admitting that her son had seduced Sarah Stout and that, as we shall see shortly, the Stouts had in revenge turned on William and his father, to destroy their political standing in the town.

And it was that political dimension that Spencer also chose to reveal in court. He argued that his prosecution had not been 'stirred till two parties, differing on all other occasions, had laid their heads together'. These two parties were his political opponents, the Tories, and his former allies, the Quakers. The aim of their unholy alliance, he said, was 'to destroy, or break at least' his family's influence in Hertford. He saw himself as the victim of a conspiracy hatched by two powerful, and hitherto antagonistic, groups. Behind his prosecution, Spencer claimed, lay the murky and bitter world of partisan politics.

2

PARTISAN FEUDS

Hertford's divisions give a concrete example of what can otherwise easily become a rather abstract discussion about the emergence of party politics and religious sectarianism. The dead Sarah Stout and Spencer Cowper, facing prosecution for murder, were individuals caught in a personal nightmare shaped by local circumstance; but they also inhabited a wider, national political culture that influenced their lives. In particular the political and religious divisions of Hertford, whilst inevitably unique in detail, reflected wider developments that have to be explored if the context of Spencer's trial is to be fully understood.[1] Fortunately, the town's records are superb and allow us to reconstruct the local feuds in which the Cowpers played a significant part; and this partisanship can be related to the national context. The contours of the divisions are a little complex, since they have a number of fault lines, but the cultural landscape is worth mapping since it helps to place the Cowpers and their town in a vibrant world of contest that shaped and sharpened the allegations against Spencer. Indeed, the Cowpers believed that he was the target of a particularly unpleasant party-political smear.

Besides explaining the motives of those ranged against Spencer Cowper, a study of partisan feuds also highlights their long genesis and how deeply ideological they were. Hertford's and the nation's divisions had long roots—at least as far back as the civil war of the 1640s and the diversity of political and religious opinion that it unleashed in the 1650s. The consequences of this crisis of authority shaped the rest of the century. And the resulting political culture—the way in which politics worked outside the narrow confines of Westminster—was to have far-reaching significance for England's Enlightenment by raising a series of interlocking ideological questions. The first related to political allegiance and structures. Was it possible to restore the authority of the Crown to its pre-civil war degree; or did the notion of popular sovereignty that had gained currency between 1649 (when Charles I had lost his head) and 1660 (when his son Charles II regained the throne) require constitutional readjustment?

This was essentially a question about representation. Who or what was the State representing? The will of God, the will of the king, or the will of the people? And how was such a will to be represented? These questions about authority in the political sphere were echoed in the religious one. Was the authority of the Church of England, which had been abolished in 1646–7 as a result of the civil war and parliamentary victory over the king, capable of being restored in order to achieve uniformity of belief or did the destruction of religious consensus require that plurality of belief be recognized in some way? These questions continue to have a modern resonance. The relationships between the State and the individual, or the State and religious belief, continue to preoccupy us as our concern with religious fundamentalism, the nature of the good citizen, and a crisis of political institutions suggest. Issues of representation and toleration endure.

It would, of course, be possible to construct a narrative of the past that stressed only the triumph of representational politics and religious tolerance; but such an account would lack a proper sense of the historical process, and distort its outcome by looking only for the genesis of what we now call liberal values. A more interesting approach is to examine the very different ideological positions that were taken in the past and take seriously the contest between them. The English Enlightenment was not simply about the triumph of a 'modern' set of ideals over a set of backward-looking ones; rather, it was a struggle, a process, an engagement during which both sides shaped each other. Those who championed one set of fundamental principles or institutions had necessarily to react to those who disagreed with them and in the process they and their principles were reshaped by that exchange. Opposing views were stated; but there was also interplay between them. Moreover disputes in one sphere—religious, political, scientific—drew on disputes in another, producing a swirl of argument rather than a linear move forward. The Enlightenment was thus the outcome of a series of dialogues, not an ever-louder monologue of modern ideas. That debate was all too clearly audible in the vituperative and contested politics of Hertford.

THE WHIGS

The emergence of what by 1681 was called the Whig Party can be seen in the career of Spencer's father, Sir William Cowper. The first Whigs were an amalgam of different factions united by a hostility to 'popery and arbitrary government'. That pejorative phrase is worth unpacking. 'Popery' meant a politicized form of Catholicism presided over by the pope or, to the Church of England's critics, an unreformed national 'High' Church that placed an ungodly stress on formalized, unscriptural ritual and obedience to clerical hierarchy. 'Arbitrary government' meant governance where rule by law, right, and the constitution had been set aside in favour of rule by royal will and priests. Sir William claimed kinship with one of the leaders of the emerging Whig Party, Anthony Ashley Cowper, first earl of Shaftesbury, who in the 1670s accused the government of popery and arbitrary government. Besides sharing a surname the precise relationship between the two men is unknown; but when Shaftesbury found himself in the Tower in 1677 for challenging King Charles II over the legitimacy of the Parliament (there had been no general election for sixteen years and Shaftesbury claimed that it was no longer legal), Sir William visited him regularly in prison, until prevented by royal order. In 1680 he joined Shaftesbury in trying to prosecute the king's brother, James duke of York, for his Catholicism, with a view to excluding him from the succession to the throne (James stood next in line because Charles had no legitimate son to inherit the crown). James's conversion to Catholicism and his belief in strong monarchy made him personify the threat of 'popery and arbitrary government'. In three successive parliaments held in 1679, 1680, and 1681, in each of which Sir William Cowper represented Hertford, there were attempts to bar the duke of York from the throne; and, so far as we can tell, Cowper supported all of them. The succession crisis was nevertheless symptomatic of a wider crisis—about the source of political authority, about religion, about the autonomy of local governance, and about England's relationship with France, where the powerful, Catholic, Louis XIV seemed to represent another link in the chain of popery and arbitrary government. The crisis of 1679–81 had been brewing since the restoration of the monarchy in 1660, for the 'settlement' had left key problems largely unresolved—or rather, settled in the interest of only one, namely the Tory part of the nation.

It was the succession crisis that gave rise to the labels Whig and Tory, which were used to describe major political divisions until the rise of the Liberal Party in the nineteenth century. The name Whig originally meant a Scottish rebel. The Scottish Presbyterian 'covenanters' were deeply hostile to the religious forms imposed on them from London and wanted to push the Reformation much further, north of the border, than King Charles I or II had been prepared to allow, even to the extent of aiming to overthrow the established Church. The name Tory originally meant Irish Catholic thieves and plunderers. These terms, Whig and Tory, were applied to English politics in 1681 as terms of abuse. Those who challenged royal power and the Church were nicknamed Whigs; those who supported the rights of the Catholic heir to the throne were castigated as Tories.

The development of party politics took time but Spencer's brother, William, later wrote an account of the party system in which he identified the late 1670s and early 1680s as a pivotal moment in their evolution. In an ostensibly 'Impartial History of Parties', prepared for King George I in 1714, William Cowper noted that the two parties, Whig and Tory, 'began to form themselves and give names to each other about the time the Exclusion Bill was set on foot, in the reign of Charles II' (in other words in 1679–81) to bar James from succeeding to the throne and that only the Whigs 'would venture all to support the Protestant succession'.[2] The failure to prevent a Catholic succession (with all tyranny that went with it) had led to the disastrous reign of James II and required the Revolution of 1688–9 to put it right. And Cowper argued that Georgian Britain rested on the same foundations as that revolution.

What, then, did Sir William Cowper and his Whig allies stand for? A Protestant succession was one core demand. In 1679–81 this meant backing the exclusion of the Catholic James, but it could also mean support for Charles II's illegitimate but Protestant son, the duke of Monmouth. On 16 August 1682 a bonfire had been lit in Hertford market place and Sir William Cowper's men Henry Radford and Thomas Draper threatened one man, Nelson Stratton, that if he did not drink the duke of Monmouth's health they would 'kick him into the fire'. When Stratton refused, adding that he would not 'drinke any phanatick's health whatsoever', Radford replied 'that he would fight against any man that ... would take ye Duke of Yorke's part'.[3] James duke of York did nevertheless become king in 1685, as James II, but his Catholicizing policies provoked another crisis both at home and abroad. In November 1688 the Dutch William, Prince of Orange and James's own son-in-law, invaded England. So strongly did the family support the prince that William and Spencer Cowper raised troops and joined his revolutionary army. William wrote an excited letter to his wife describing the unfolding drama: 'You cannot conceive ye Pleasure there is in seeing ye fountain of this Happy revolution & ye new face of things at Court', he wrote.[4] They were delighted to see William crowned king; and both William and Spencer were again strong advocates of a Protestant succession, by the Hanoverians in 1714, when the issue of the succession was once more in dispute.

A Protestant succession alone, however, was insufficient security. There were other 'revolution principles' safeguarding political and religious liberties that the Cowpers and Whigs prized. Thus in February 1681 Sir William Cowper had been presented at his election with a document setting out the Hertford electors' desire for Protestant unity against 'popery and arbitrary government'.[5] This, it set out, meant the repeal of the Corporation Act, which had been passed in 1661 to prevent anyone who was not a member of the Church of England from holding office in a 'corporation'—a town council but also any body of men that was legally incorporated into an association. Although rather haphazardly enforced in the 1660s and 1670s, the Corporation Act excluded those who were unable to conform to all the doctrines and forms of worship prescribed by the Church of England. The passage of an Act in 1662 requiring religious uniformity created a group of Protestants, called Dissenters, who were unable to conform to the forms and doctrines of the national Church. Whereas the Church of England saw itself as the one and true Protestant Church, in the eyes of the Dissenters it was still riddled with remnants of popery that had not been purged at the Reformation. The Protestant world was thus divided. On the one hand was the restored institution of the national Church of England; on the other were groups of Protestants who objected to the Church's theology or forms of worship and refused to attend its services.

The Dissenters, or 'non-conformists' as they were also called, harboured a desire to widen or even overturn the terms of the Church settlement imposed in the early 1660s. In fact settlement was a misnomer because the Dissenters remained dissatisfied, especially as the legislative penalties against them became even more punitive. Sir William Cowper not only sympathized with the plight of the Dissenters; as we shall see, he himself held distinctly unorthodox religious views. Both his sons were deeply attached to the idea of religious toleration; which is in part why the breach with the Quakers during the trial was so shocking, since it pulled apart two natural bedfellows. Hertford's desire in 1681 for the repeal of a law which prevented Cowper's Dissenting friends from holding political office showed how deeply religious and political issues were intertwined.

The Hertford address of 1681 had also asked for other civil liberties. One was a means to safeguard 'frequent Parliaments'. The right to call and dismiss Parliament had been deeply contested since the early seventeenth century. One of the concessions forced on Charles I before the Civil War had been to renounce royal control of Parliament's meetings. But the restoration of Charles II had seen the restoration of this royal power; and the new king had used it not only to keep a subservient Parliament in existence between 1661 and 1679, but also to dismiss MPs at crucial moments. Thus the bills to exclude James duke of York had been frustrated by the Crown's power to dismiss MPs at will. The Hertford address had also called for the defence of the right to petition. Signing a petition was conceived of as a right inherent in all 'free born Englishmen' as a way of allowing the voice of the people to be heard when other forms of representation had been silenced. The king's deliberate refusal to let Parliament sit or, as in 1681, his dismissal of MPs when they still had business to finish, had led to petitioning campaigns. The one in the winter of 1679–80 had been particularly impressive, with huge rolls being presented to the nonplussed king. Charles II had responded with a proclamation in December 1679 forbidding 'tumultuous' petitioning, that is to say petitioning by a crowd or 'mob', a word coined during this period.

Sir William responded to the 1681 address by urging his Hertford supporters to 'Agree as English men and Protestants in asserting our Civil and Religious Liberties' against those who sought to undermine 'our Old English Government' by parliament and the law. And he called those who held positions at Court 'State Vermin' who sold 'English Liberties' to buy their own advancement.[6] Part of the Whig identity thus derived from a visceral hostility to a High Church Tory 'other', which was imagined to be sinisterly conspiring against them and the public good.

Sir William also maintained a populist position, asserting that the law upheld the rights of the people against magistrates intent on increasing their own powers and that of their party. The focus of this dispute was the town's charter, the official document codifying the powers of Hertford's local rulers and of its citizens. In November 1680 the Crown had given the town a new charter that was to cause controversy for many years to come. It allowed the mayor to be chosen by the corporation, thereby ensuring a self-perpetuating oligarchy. The mayor and his officers had sweeping powers—of justice, arrest, fining, regulating trade, and making by-laws. In 1682 the mayor was John Dimsdale senior, whose medical evidence was to be so crucial in leading to Spencer's arrest; he was chosen again in 1688 and in 1697. Indeed at the time of Spencer's trial he had, controversially, monopolized the post for several years, ignoring a convention that it should rotate annually. The new charter of 1680 had also unleashed a wave of religious intolerance. Since it was granted specifically to men 'conformable to the Church of England' the Dissenters were made to feel the power of the churchmen. In December 1681 one Dissenting trader was granted his freedom only after he had 'promised to go to church & receive the sacrament & go to conventicles no more'—in other words, to stop attending the Nonconformist services that often took place in houses, barns, and warehouses.[7] In April 1682 it was decided that no one could be made free or licensed to trade or keep an alehouse in the town unless he fully conformed to the Church of England.[8] And money raised by fining Dissenters was only to go to the conforming poor, with the clergy in charge of its distribution.[9] In the early 1680s the borough courts heaved with prosecutions of non-conformists, including Henry Stout (Sarah's father) and his Friends (as Quakers called each other).[10]

Sir William Cowper had taken none of this lying down. In 1681 he was accused of reflecting on some of the Hertford magistrates and was alleged to have said that 'the King would bring in arbitrary government and popery'.[11] In 1683 he was also charged with 'making

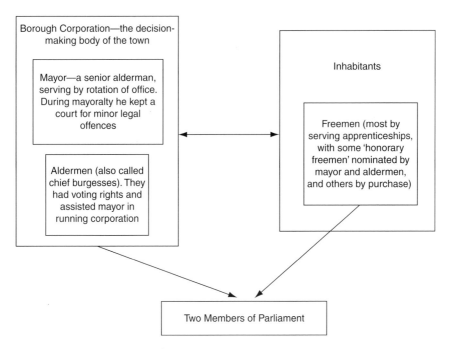

Figure 2.1 The governance of Hertford.

mouthes and distorted faces at ye minister in All Saints Church when he prayd ... for ye King and Duke of York and also for saying that there is never a Bishop in England but what are popishly affected'.[12] Although his party's fortunes were at a low ebb in the 1680s, and he himself had been required to find £3,000 in 1683 as 'security' in the wake of the Rye House Plot (an alleged assassination attempt on the king's life), Cowper saw the Revolution of 1688–9 as an opportunity to reassert Whig principles and his leadership of the locality. And that meant pursuing a feud with mayor and doctor John Dimsdale senior.

The controversial 1680 charter had bolstered Dimsdale's power by securing his own and his clique's control over the 'freemen'. Being a freeman meant possessing both an economic and a political liberty. Freemen were free to trade as masters of their crafts; and their freedom also empowered them to vote in national elections. In Hertford, the corporation also claimed a right to be able to create 'honorary freemen'. These were freemen who were not tradesmen in the town but often neighbouring gentry and clergy, who thereby gained a vote. The corporation also claimed a right to sell freedoms ('by redemption') to the sons of men who were already free but who had not served an apprenticeship. The right of the corporation to create or sell freedoms was not spelt out in any of the documents relating to the town's constitution; but neither was it ruled out. Mayors and aldermen—the higher magistracy of the town—who were dominated by Dimsdale and his friends, had thus gerryman-dered the freemen to give them electoral supremacy. In 1681—the year after the new charter—they passed an order legitimizing this process. The Tory design threatened the political power and influence of Sir William Cowper, who had first been elected to represent Hert-ford in 1679. He claimed that 'these arbitrary magistrates and multi-pliers of electors' had created honorary freemen 'on purpose to exclude' him from further representation of the town at Westminster.

At the time of the Revolution, in late 1688 or early 1689, Sir William Cowper published *The Case of the Ancient Borough of Hertford* in which he asserted the rights of all inhabitants, 'whether free or not free', to vote in parliamentary elections.[13] This was clearly designed to break the Tory corporation's hold on the town. He further asserted that 'some arbitrary magistrates' had engaged in 'a very enormous and plainly illegal practice, by making great numbers of clergy-men, gentry and others free of their corporation', with a 'design, and sometimes upon condition, that they should give their votes in Election of Burgesses to sit in Parliament, according to the

interests and direction of the corporation; thereby in effect transfer-
ring the Election from the Borough (where the law of the land hath
placed it) into the corporation and its adherents' This, he believed,
was 'very near Treason', for it took power out of the hands of the
people and placed it in the narrow, oligarchical circle of the corporation elite. Moreover, he said, in 1688 a new charter had been given to
the town that deliberately restrained the right of election 'to a select
Number, on purpose to keep me out of Parliament: But I always
esteemed it more honourable to suffer than to be a tool to any
power or interest whatsoever.' He now sought to vindicate the rights
of the Commons in England. His enemies, who had invaded his 'civil
rights and liberties', were, he said with characteristic bluster, worse
than common robbers. And he extolled the virtue of the Prince of
Orange: 'By the Eminent Goodness and Providence of God there is
placed at the Helm of our Government so great an example of wisdom,
justice, humanity and candor, that the reliever of the oppressed is
almost become his very name.' The prince 'with the Assistance of the
English Protestant Nobility and Gentry joined in Association under
him' had started to rescue religion and liberty. Sir William, or perhaps
his son, was so moved that he wrote a poem enthusing that Prince
William stood not for the:

> wild Lust and Pleasure of the Prince
> But pure Religion and the People's good.[14]

It was thus outrageous, Sir William argued in his 1688/9 tract, that 'a
few Under-Agents, Members of a poor and (at present) ill-grounded
Corporation, should yet be so hardy as to persist in those partial
Tricks and unreasonable Actings, which in the late corruption of
affairs they were so early taught and employed in'.

Sir William Cowper and his sons thus stood for a number of
revolution principles. Hostile to 'popery and arbitrary government'
they supported a Protestant monarchy, even if this meant altering the
line of succession. They sympathized with the plight of Dissenters
who found themselves persecuted and excluded from civil office.
They sought constitutional safeguards to protect representative institutions and championed the rights of citizens over the oligarchical
interests of magistrates. These principles brought the Cowpers into
direct confrontation with John Dimsdale and his friends, who headed
a Tory faction. It was a story of local division that could be repeated
across the rest of the nation.

John Dimsdale senior had been instrumental in reversing the original decision that Sarah had not been murdered, for he had taken a leading part in the autopsy that formed the chief piece of evidence against Spencer; and he had appeared in court to drive home his allegation. But his testimony, for all its ostensible scientific impartiality, had been deeply partisan. Dimdsale's enmity with the Cowpers was long-standing, and had its roots in a power struggle to control the town. Dimsdale was the leader of a Tory group in Hertford who opposed the Cowpers and their allies at every turn.

The Tories could be divided into two sorts. One, represented by Dimsdale, was hostile to Whig principles and any opposing party, but was pragmatic and essentially loyal to a vision of a Protestant Church and king working in close alliance, upholding a constitution which defended the Church, enshrined monarchical power and safeguarded the liberties of the subject. The second sort of Tory (to which Dimsdale was nevertheless also allied) was far more ideological. These 'High Church Tories' believed that the restored Church of England was God's true Church and that any weakening of the Church was a danger to both salvation in Heaven and order on earth. They believed that the Civil War had been caused in part by religious fanatics who had deluded the people into rebellion and promoted dangerous anti-monarchical doctrines that, given half a chance, would plunge the country back into civil war. And they were convinced that such enemies of the nation should not only be excluded from political office but, where they challenged the power of the Church, should also be persecuted, fined, imprisoned, and even transported to the colonies.

One of the casualties of the Civil War had been the (already fragile) state-sponsored national Church of England. The Civil War in the 1640s and the experiment in republican rule in the 1650s had unleashed a torrent of what Tories saw as religious heresy that had fractured Protestant unity. In the place of a single national Church governed by bishops to which all subjects were expected to belong, there had emerged first a Presbyterian form of Church (which removed the bishops and the Church's hierarchy) and then a variety of Protestant sects who disputed the need for any national Church at all. These 'Independents' believed that each congregation was its own sovereign power and could find its own way to God. But to many churchmen this state of affairs seemed the road to damnation.

Figure 2.2 A High Church Tory print produced in the early eighteenth century showing the vices associated with religious fanaticism. The title, *A Genealogie of Anti-Christ*, may be a reference to Hertford's very radical minister of the 1640s, Chrisopher Feake, who in 1650 had published *The Genealogie of Christianity and of Christians*.

Figure 2.2 depicts what many High Church Tories saw as the genealogy of such anti-Christian belief. It shows Oliver Cromwell as the figurehead of the Puritan revolution of the 1650s, symbolizing the root of all evil. The print identifies the types of 'fanatics' that emerged: Presbyterians (who wanted to be rid of bishops), Independents (who believed in gathered communities rather than a national Church), 'Anabaptists' (who believed in adult baptism), Quakers (a group that will be analysed shortly in some detail, since Sarah Stout belonged to it), and Socinians (who denied the orthodoxy of a trinity of God, Holy Spirit, and Christ). The print also blames the Puritans for unleashing the forces of atheism and irreligion—the table lists 'Libertines', 'Profaneness', and 'Blasphemers' as offspring of the anti-Christ. Perhaps the most interesting feature of the image, however, is the association of a set of vices with religious heterodoxy or unbelief, in order to demonize a rival ideology. Thus the religious 'fanatic' and 'enthusiast' is embued with pride, ignorance, hypocrisy, self-conceit, wrath and hatred, strife and sedition, envy and rebellion, discord, civil war, and anarchy. These in turn lead to oppression, contention, tumults, murder, regicide, confusion, and beggary. The table, even down to its devils, contains many of the themes that will recur throughout the book. The image is an extraordinarily effective lesson in the interaction of religion, politics, and their wider cultural impact. It also shows the power of a lexicon of highly charged words that could be fired pejoratively at opponents.

Without the guidance of the Church of England, the High Church-men feared, souls would be lost when people began to adopt all sorts of erroneous beliefs. When men claimed—as the Dissenters did—that their conscience was superior to everything else, all secular authority was effectively subject to the power of that conscience; and people would easily mistake their wills and whims for what their conscience was telling them. Making conscience—the internally audible voice of God—the seat of authority was thus to place the imagination, fancy, and will above everything else, creating a bizarre upside-down world in which men and women merely appealed to their conscience in order to sanction the most outrageous errors. Unless the conscience was properly guided by the established Church, the High Church Tories argued, it would lead to irreligion, blasphemy, and atheism. Indeed, it had been the pursuit of individual freedom of conscience and the attempt to remove the bishops that had led to civil war in the first place. Britain had, in the eyes of the Tories, experienced a religious civil war which had spawned an ideology hostile to authority and to monarchy. At the restoration of the monarchy in 1660, therefore, the Church of England had also been restored, and an attempt had been made to force the sectarians—the Nonconformists or Dissenters—back into the fold, by persecution if necessary. Force was necessary for the Dissenters' own good. The Corporation Act, which the Hertford address of 1681 had resented, was seen instead by the High Church Tories as entirely beneficial. It had removed Dissenters from office—in 1662 Hertford had been purged of those who did not conform and only two of the town's officers who had served during the Interregnum escaped the purge.[15] One simple maxim held by the Tories was that every Dissenter was a rebel, either to Church or king, and probably to both; the proscription of Dissenters from civil office was thus a good thing.

To the Tories, the republic of the 1650s had inverted the natural order and unleashed a flood of chaos that only the restoration of the monarchy had stopped. The attempts to exclude James in 1679–81 seemed therefore a dangerous attempt to dredge up seditious ideas that had driven the country onto the rocks once before. The Tories feared that if Parliament claimed to have power to alter the succession, as Cowper asserted it did, it followed that the 'people' were superior to their king and were the sovereign power. In the seventeenth century, 'democracy' was still a term of abuse and the notion of popular sovereignty was deeply controversial, since it implied that the people had a right to resist, and hence to overthrow, their rulers when they felt they were being tyrannized. It was that doctrine, the Tories believed, that had resulted in civil war and the execution of Charles I in 1649. Popular sovereignty was also a doctrine that, they said, had ushered in a highly intolerant and illiberal republic that had purged royalists from office, imprisoned them, and uprooted true religion.

The Tories were thus very clear about what they disliked. They hated religious Dissent and they feared the undermining of monarchical authority. They deeply distrusted the notion that the people were the source of power and that monarchs were merely created by the people, who could judge and overthrow them whenever they liked. The Tories therefore formulated an alternative ideology. This championed both the Church of England and the monarchy, advocating a doctrine of obedience to both. Some of them went so far as to argue that the monarch owed his power only to God, that he was the heir of the biblical Adam to whom God had literally given the world.

The Revolution of 1688–9 had therefore posed a problem for many Tories. Habituated to seeing Church and king as natural allies, they

Sir Henry Chauncy, Kn^{t}

after. J.Savage.

Figure 2.3 Sir Henry Chauncy, one of the leaders of the Hertford Tories.

had been forced to choose between their two beloved institutions because of James II's Catholicizing policies. Used also to magnifying the monarch's powers over the subject and to asserting that non-resistance was a core doctrine of their Church, the Tories in 1688 faced an uncomfortable dilemma about whether or not to join the revolutionary forces. Even after the Revolution, they also had anxieties about William's coronation as king—whilst the 'legitimate' King James was still alive—and how far the Church could or should be altered to accommodate the Dissenters. They successfully saw off attempts to alter the forms of worship and the doctrines of the Church; but they could not resist a measure of toleration for Dissenters, which became law in 1689. Despite, and sometimes because of, that concession the Tories retained a strong devotion to the Church and a hostility to Whig principles that took only a short time to resurface after 1688, not least because many Whigs—Sir William Cowper among them—were intent on revenge for their treatment when the Tories had been dominant in the 1680s. The Tories were helped by the fact that the new king, William, had no desire to become a prisoner of the Whig Party and sought to balance the parties, if only because he needed support for his costly all-out military assault on the power of Catholic France.

HERTFORD TORIES

The Hertford Tories exemplify many of these points about the national party. Foremost among them was one of Dimsdale's allies, Sir Henry Chauncy, a High Churchman who played an important part not just in the feud with the Whigs and Dissenters, but also in the witchcraft trial examined later in the book. Chauncy, a lawyer, had been appointed in 1675 as chief steward of Hertford borough court and, in the controversial new charter of 1680, the town's first recorder or legal officer. Indeed, according to one report, he had 'by ill practices' surrendered the charter in 1685 'in order to get a new one & himself elected' as a Member of Parliament for the town.[16] But in 1688 Sir William Cowper, along with seventeen inhabitants (again including Sarah's brother, John Stout), petitioned the king to intervene in the 'disorders' of the town and accused Sir Henry Chauncy of neglect and abuse of office.[17] Indeed, it is possible that this attack was the culmination of what Chauncy was obliquely referring to in the preface of his *Historical Antiquities of Hertfordshire*, which he finally published in 1700. Explaining how his work had been frustrated and delayed, Chauncy blamed an unnamed enemy who 'almost every Body knows'—very probably Cowper:

> When I found my self fatally disappointed in the once-dear Object of my most flatt'ring Hopes [presumably a reference to his ambition to become the town's MP]; when I found Him by mean, disingenuous and clandestine Methods, contriving and pursuing the Ruin (as far as in him lay) not of Me alone, but of those other Persons whose Interests were embarqu'd on the same Bottom with mine, and were to me much dearer than my own . . . I was under a necessity of applying no Small Sums, by Me intended to defray the Charge of Collecting and Transcribing whatever would be needful for this Work, to other Uses, for the Just Vindication of my Self and Family, against the Sinister attempts of this Degenerate Branch and his Malicious Accomplices.[18]

In an unpublished version of this preface, Chauncy went so far as to suggest that his enemies wanted to 'stifle' his work.[19] From a Whig perspective it is easy to see why Cowper and others might have wanted to do so. For although a work of history and genealogy, Chauncy's *Historical Antiquities* betrayed its author's vehement monarchical and Church bias. Thus Chauncy admitted that he had spent many pages describing the churches and chapels of the county so that posterity would know how generously they had been 'built, richly adorn'd and prudently set apart for Divine Service, thinking no Cost too great, no Charge too extravagant, for beautifying and embellishing the Temples of the Almighty'.[20] Here, then, was a reverential history of the Church, based on the testimony of pre-Reformation monks, so 'that our successors may be sensible of the great Honour and reverence which their Ancestors and Predecessors formerly paid to these Holy Places'. He even defended nunneries. It was thus not surprising that Chauncy was accused of having turned Catholic. He also went out of his way to condemn the sad fate of the bishops in the 1640s 'whose rights were invaded by an unlawful Convention, in the late Rebellion, consisting only of some Factious Members of the then House of Commons in conjunction with other seditious Partizans in the Army'. If his High Church sympathies were all too obvious, so was his Tory ideology. He claimed that 'all the Rights and Priviledges, the Liberties and Freedomes which the People now enjoy, have been since derived [from] the Crowne, by the gracious concessions of the kings of this Realme'. Talking of the Norman Conquest, but no doubt with one eye on 1688, Chauncy said that his history showed 'the dangerous consequences that attends the Invasion of a Forreigne Prince; let the Pretence be never so specious; for tis the usuall method of Conquerors to destroy the Natives and Proprietors, who are, or may be capable to oppose them; and to advance all those who shall favour their broken Titles'.

His work also laid out the Tory view of the local constitution, and by implication, the proper role of the people in government. He argued, against Cowper, that the inhabitants did not have the sole right of election and that those who thought they did had a poor understanding of the customs of the town. The 'commonalty' referred to in the charter from James I's reign, he said disdainfully, did not mean *all* the inhabitants 'for then they would extend to all Sorts of People, Men, Women, Children, Servants, Labourers, who would have equal Right in the Choice of Officers and in the Government of the Borough, which was in no Age known'. Rather, he said, the 'Word Commonalty extended no farther than the Governing Council of the Place'; in other words, the oligarchical corporation. The 'commonalty' were not *the people* but only 'a select company chosen for their wisdom and long experience'. Hostile to the populace, Chauncy complained that 'Divers persons of small estates' had illegally voted in recent elections; and because of their poverty they 'valued Loaves and Drink spent at elections' to bribe them, more than they did the common good.[21] Here then was also an element of social friction. Chauncy, Dimsdale, and their faction represented the better off in the town—Chauncy was a successful lawyer, Dimsdale was already worth £5,000 in 1680 and his friend Benjamin Jones, a dyer, was worth £4,000.[22] Of course, the Cowpers were wealthy too, but, as we have seen, they courted the popular vote.

Tory principles were clearly enunciated from the town's pulpits as well as from the pages of Chauncy's history—a combination of politics and religion that was to prove highly divisive. Ralph Battell, son of the minister of All Saints in Hertford and assistant both to his father and to the town's school, offers a good case study of a High Churchman. We know about him from his published writings since he was nationally known for his attempts to promote Church music and his forthright views on the constitution, and we can therefore reconstruct his outlook and those in the town who shared his views.[23] Like Chauncy, he had a desire to revive the authority of Church and monarch. His High Church principles are clear from a sermon preached at the Hertford assizes in March 1684, at the height of the so-called 'Tory reaction' against the Whigs. Battell's sermon was provocatively titled *The Civil Magistrates Coercive Powers in Religious Matters Asserted*.[24] Battell denied that 'the Common People' could 'censure the laws of the state'; otherwise 'farewell all Government'. He suggested that the 'Factious and Schismatical Malcontent (for usually they go together)' cried out against persecution but really wanted to lay 'his Prophane and Sacrilegious Hands upon the Crown and the Church'. The Civil War had been begun, he said, 'under the Banner of Hypocrisie entitled Religion' which had been used as a cloak for villainy. Battell also developed a justification of intolerance. It was not true that compulsion in religion, he argued, was 'either unprofitable or unlawful', since it could rescue the persecuted from error. Since 'thousands' had separated from the Church only through 'the Neglect of hearing what they might hear and learning what they might be taught' in church, persecution was thus really 'a great piece of Charity'. He urged magistrates into activity, for this would silence those who turned 'Religion into Rebellion and Faith into Faction'. And he ended the sermon with a warning against 'the counsels of any State Achitophel', a veiled reference to Sir William Cowper's kinsman, the first earl of Shaftesbury, who had been satirized under that name in John Dryden's anti-Whig poem *Absolom and Achitophel*. Achitophel had, in the Bible, counselled rebellion against King David.[25]

In the previous year Battell had outlined a Tory philosophy of governance in a work with another give-away title: *Vulgar Errors*. He had spoken of the 'great love' he had for 'Kingly Government' because he thought it was the least oppressive form of authority. He was convinced that the king was above the law and criticized the views of Thomas Hobbes, who in 1651 had suggested that society was formed by a contract. Instead Battell suggested, using a biblical metaphor, 'some mighty Nimrod' had, in the early stages of society, induced the heads of families 'to give up their Right to one whom they called a King'. Force, not consent, was the basis of authority. This reflected Battell's (and the Tories') horror of disorder and civil war, which had to be avoided at all costs, through force if necessary: 'even Tyranny it self is not so bad as Anarchy', Battell insisted, and 'to rebel seems to me a remedy worse than the disease at all times'. Resistance was thus never justified. Kingly government was ancient and natural; whereas a commonwealth or republic was the result of ambition, envy, and discontent. The common people, who ruled in republics, were 'incompetent judges' in State affairs.[26] Subjects must obey the laws and even an ungodly king.

In the 1680s, then, Hertford Tories such as Battell had set out principles of devotion to Church and king. Did the Revolution of 1688–9, which replaced James II with William III and hence did violence to the principle of hereditary succession and the Church's exhortation not to resist a lawful monarch, therefore mean that their tenure on power was at an end? How, if at all, did these ideological disputes affect the people? And how did the Whig–Tory contest contribute to the allegations of murder against Spencer Cowper?

POPULAR POLITICS AND PARTY RIVALRIES

One key process, characteristic of the Enlightenment, was the undermining of the sacred authority of monarchy and Church, and a consequent rethinking of the foundations of obligation and belief. The mid-seventeenth-century Civil War had, of course, done much to advance this process; the Revolution of 1688–9 reinvigorated it. Both revolutions reflected and enabled popular participation in affairs of State and the emergence of an ideology that grounded legitimacy in consent. These developments were nevertheless controversial and disputed, as Hertford illustrates very well. There, as elsewhere, popular participation and consent were both the subject of controversy and the means by which that controversy was engaged in. For several generations after 1688 it seemed conceivable that popular sovereignty might be espoused not just in theory but also given some practical expression. The passage of the Triennial Act in 1694 guaranteed parliamentary elections at least every three years; in practice, they were held even more frequently: on average once every two and a half years between 1679 and 1716, when the Triennial Act was repealed. During that period England witnessed one of the most vibrant periods of popular politics, with a higher rate of adult male participation in elections than at any time before the second Reform Act of 1867.

The animosity between the parties in Hertford was not immediately apparent in the early 1690s. The Revolution of 1688–9 had wrongfooted many Tories. The transfer of the crown from James to William; the passage of the Toleration Act in 1689; ongoing rebellion in Scotland and Ireland by forces loyal to James; and the pursuit of a large-scale war against France all posed searching and disorienting questions about the Tories' attitude to the new regime and its policies. Yet in the mid 1690s a number of factors came together to galvanize Tory concerns. One was a resurgent Whig Party that had captured most of the important governmental posts and achieved electoral success in 1695. Thus in Hertford Sir William Cowper and his son William were returned as the town's two MPs (most constituencies returned two MPs and each elector accordingly had two votes to cast), excluding the Tories from representation at Westminster. A second factor was a growing anxiety that the Whig regime was dangerous, both to the Church and to the national interest. The lapse of the Licensing Act, which removed pre-publication restrictions on the press, was seen as part of this threat, since Tories feared it would unleash a flood of anti-monarchical and heretical works. The war effort against France had also resulted in considerable social and economic strains. Taxes had increased; the currency was in crisis; and the beneficiaries appeared to be the Whigs and Dissenters who invested in the Bank of England, created in 1694 by a Whig Chancellor of the Exchequer. Moreover, an assassination attempt on King William's life in February 1696 was used by the Whigs for political advantage. The Whigs invited all men over eighteen to sign an 'oath of association', recognizing the king as 'rightful and lawful' monarch and promising to revenge any further attack. Anyone who refused to sign was accused of favouring the exiled James. This represented a massive exercise in translating political theory into practice, unseen since the parliamentarian regime's oaths of the 1640s. It was also an attempt to exploit the Tories' reservations about the legality of the transfer of the crown to King William and thus an attempt to trump the Tory card that it was the party of loyalty. Indeed by exposing those Tories who refused to sign as Jacobites—adherents of the exiled James II—the Whigs gained considerable political capital.

At first the growing tensions between the rival parties in Herford manifested itself only in a few scuffles and intemperate words. In September 1695 'in the publique market place' Sarah Stout's half-brother John told Alderman Jones (a former mayor and Dimsdale crony, who had been responsible in 1678 for the decision to renew the charter) that the Tory mayor and aldermen were 'a pack of as great rogues as any that ever robb upon the highways' and promised to pull their 'Charter apeices'.[27] He was prosecuted for it in December and fined. The war of words escalated, for exactly a year later Jones and Robert Dimsdale, the physician son of the mayor John Dimsdale, assaulted Leonard Dell, one of the witnesses at Spencer's trial. Dimsdale and Jones had given Dell a beating in an alehouse—serious enough to endanger his life—and thrown cold water over his head; but the humiliation of a prosecution, 'for speaking desperate and profane oaths, and uttering threatening, malicious and scandalous speeches against Sir William Cowper, Bt and William Cowper', may have temporarily cooled their overheated passions.[28]

Determined to break the Cowpers' influence, the Tory faction in the corporation nevertheless went on the counter-offensive. Over the next two years forty-two new freemen were created in an obvious manoeuvre to increase their vote, and in November 1697 John Dimsdale senior entered the first of four consecutive years in mayoral office, 'contrary to the charter and usage of the town' and 'the better to perfect the destruction' of his rivals.[29] The Tories, headed by Dimsdale, were intent on control of the town. On becoming mayor Dimsdale extended the practice of creating non-resident freemen—those who lived outside the town—and even enfranchised some local Tory MPs. This enraged Hertford's inhabitants, who feared a design by the town's magistrates to render their votes meaningless. In January 1698, 138 of them (including John Stout) signed a petition against the mayor and aldermen's creation of honorary freemen. Another petition, perhaps intended for Parliament, traced the townsmen's grievances back to the end of Charles II's reign when 'three or four aldermen, either to draw the power of the . . . elections into their own hands or by direction from the Court (as is most probably and was then pretended) did make great numbers of honorary freemen . . . merely in order to overbalance such as were the rightful electors'. Dimsdale, it alleged, had been 'a principal agent in the said breach of the petitioners' rights' and, knowing that an election was imminent, had 'again begun the said practice in order to outvote the rightful electors at the next election and draw to themselves such as they shall think fit to qualify, the power of imposing what representatives they please'. Dimsdale and his allies granted 'the said freedoms in a clandestine manner with the doors of their council chamber shut and obliging their officers to secrecy' and threatened 'to make so many as shall carry the election in the manner they please'.[30]

In this heightened atmosphere two printed satires, evidently produced by the Chauncy/Dimsdale faction, sought to undermine the Cowpers' electoral hold on Hertford. One reported a fictional conversation between Sir William, Henry Stout, and other Dissenters. The imagined exchange took place in the Cowper home, Hertford Castle, satirized as 'an Obsolete and Neglected Castle, haunted with frightful Apparitions, sometimes in the ugly shape of Empty-Pint-Bottles'.[31] The invented dialogue highlighted tensions that must have already been apparent between Sir William and the Quakers, and between the Quakers and the other Dissenters, over religion, politics, and the Cowpers' immorality. Prefiguring what was no doubt the Dimsdale faction's aim, the tract ends with the Dissenters abandoning their support for the Cowpers. A second pamphlet was aimed more at the Church of England vote.[32] In it, a thinly disguised Hertford—renamed as Scydromedia—is depicted as a wretched, divided, and irreligious town that was nevertheless beginning to turn against the Cowpers. Sir William was described as 'a Man greedy of Honour', who was 'destroying the Unity and Friendship of the Town, dividing it into Parties and begetting Hatred and Malice against one another'. He is said to have called the 'Aldermen and all the Church party... Arbitrary, Insolent Magistrates, Multipliers of Electors, Thieves, Treasonable, Impudent Fools, Injurious, Time-Servers, Carriers on of Tricks, Men of black Designs, men of no Reason, Frantick Under-takers'. The tract ends with a powerful attack on Dissenters and their doctrines, the humiliation of Sir William and cries of 'Church and King! Church and King!' The two tracts represent one of the earliest attempts to use the newly liberated press to influence the outcome of a single constituency, but its authors were also using a fictionalized Hertford to stand for the battle between Whigs and Tories that was being waged throughout the nation.

The July 1698 election was thus a very bitter one. Sir William and William Cowper stood again, with a rallying cry of 'Double Cowper',[33] opposed by two Tories, Sir William Leman and Charles Caesar, whose father had helped to pay for the 1680 charter which had done so much to entrench his faction's power. Voting records for the election still exist. They show that the Dimsdale faction supported Leman and Caesar, but the Cowpers' allies, including John Stout (Sarah's half-brother) carried the day, even if not by the 'greatest majority' that one newspaper claimed.[34] Indeed, the narrowness of the defeat (just seven votes between William Cowper and Leman) only increased Dimsdale's determination to break the Cowpers' hold. On 3 August 1698, eighty-three new freemen were created, all known Tories; and when Alderman Keynton, one of Cowper's only supporters within the corporation, objected, they 'struck his name out' of the list of office-holders.[35] Moreover, Dimsdale, Chauncy, Battell, and their allies drew up a counter-petition to the earlier inhabitants' one, complaining that Cowper's supporters were 'men of small estates or none' and 'for the greatest part are disaffected and enemies to the Church of England, as Quakers, Anabaptists and of other sects and persuasions'. Referring to Cowper's loose tongue they also complained that their enemies 'frequently if not daily greet your magistrates in the said borough with opprobrious language and print and publish scandalous libels against them and do all they can to create disturbances in the said borough'. They called for the arrest of Cowper and his cronies.[36] It was certainly true that 'as the mayor, aldermen and recorder were coming from a monthly meeting' Sir William Cowper called them 'a pack of rogues' and threatened to 'bring them before Parliament to answer for their roguery'; and on another occasion he called Dimsdale 'a blockhead'.

It fell to the Attorney General, Sir Thomas Trevor, to adjudicate between the inhabitants' petition and the corporation's counter-petition. He decided that Chauncy had not been delinquent in his duty and that other Tory office-holders were not disloyal to the king, as the inhabitants had claimed. On the other hand, he found no evidence that the Quakers and other Dissenters were disloyal, or that they had published libels against the corporation (though he admitted someone had); he also noted that Dimsdale had only managed to obtain the signatures of 72 of the borough's 300 freemen.[37] Such a careful, balanced judgment failed to satisfy either party. In December 1698 the Whigs sought legal advice about the legality of the Tory creations of freemen and were no doubt encouraged to hear that they could take action.[38] Proceedings were duly begun in January 1699 and the corporation prepared to fight their corner. In February 1699 it elected a new legal officer, Thomas Filmer, to replace Chauncy, and recruited what were described by their enemies as 'topping' lawyers from London, including Sir Bartholomew Shower, an eloquent Tory MP who knew all about how to handle Dissenters, since his brother was one of the leading London Nonconformist ministers. In response, the Whigs employed three London lawyers, including William Cowper. On 31 January 1699 the dispute was heard in one of the highest courts of the land, King's Bench, a good example of how the central courts became umpires between disputing local parties and hence how the law offered a means to try to resolve partisan tensions. Dimsdale and the Tories lost this particular battle and were told to enfranchise only those who lived in Hertford rather than give votes to Tories who lived outside the town.[39]

The point, of course, in all this is that Dimsdale's role in Spencer's prosecution for murder was highly political and that it represented the culmination of several years of campaigning against the Cowpers in Hertford. Dimsdale perhaps saw in the death of Sarah Stout an opportunity to turn the tables on the Whigs, at a critical time when his own actions were being scrutinized and criticized by the central court. The Hertford feud may have been unusual in its intensity and the degree to which personal hostilities were involved, but bitter divisions were common throughout a nation that was gripped by partisan rivalries. These permeated England's political culture, and ensured that national and local divisions were intertwined. To be sure, factors on the ground shaped such struggles—much depended on personalities, the nature of the towns' governmental structure, the balance of local gentry influence, the extensiveness of religious Dissent, and how far populations and trade were affected by the war—but the bitterness of division was widespread. What is perhaps particularly striking, to a modern age in which voter turn-out is so low and a sense of alienation widespread, is how important national elections were in the later Stuart period and how inclusive politics had become. Here was a vigorous, if not particularly attractive, form of politics that extended quite far down the social scale, to inhabitants whose vote was contested.

Hertford's troubles were also symptomatic of a shift towards a new type of politics, one in which the assumptions of consensus were replaced by ones of division and where such division was fought out not on the battlefield but in town halls up and down the land, a culture in which physical violence had largely (though not entirely) been replaced by verbal violence, slander, and chicanery. Political machination was, of course, not new; but the parties brought with them new techniques. The achievements of the early electoral machinery, for example, have a modern ring. The extensive records at Hertford allow the reconstruction of voting person by person; and this shows a remarkable degree of commitment to the parties over time. Partisanship was becoming ingrained. Of those who voted at two successive elections, around two-thirds voted for the same party, leaving only a third of the electorate 'floating' and persuadable. The ebbs and flows of party success thus had something to do with how well the parties could influence this swayable section—and contests in Hertford, it should be remembered, were run so close that every vote was important. Victory had much to do with how well the parties got their voters to turn out, or how successfully they created new freemen, or how the local and national mood shifted.[40]

The political undercurrents to Spencer Cowper's trial had thus been swirling around the courtroom from the very start. Even selecting a jury had not been easy because of the degree to which political passions had permeated the town. When Judge Hatsell told the prosecution counsel, Mr Jones, that if 'any Jury man hath said anything concerning this Case, and given his verdict by way of discourse and shew'd his affection one way or other' it would disqualify him, Jones quipped 'then we should keep you here til tomorrow morning'. The political nature of the trial was also evident when Spencer brought down from London some important politicians to act as character witnesses. One of them was Sir William Ashurst, the Whig MP for London and its lord mayor in 1693–4.[41] In January 1690 Ashurst had been accused of having drunk a toast to 'our sovereign lord, or lords, the people'. His presence in court was a statement about the wider political importance of the trial which, he said, had 'made so great a noise all *England* over'. Another character witness was Sir Thomas Lane, a prominent Whig alderman of London, who will reappear later in the story.

It was also electioneering that had brought Sarah Stout and Spencer together in the first place. Sarah's father Henry:

> at all elections promoted the interest of the Cowpers, to the utmost of his power; through which a great intimacy was created between the families of the Cowpers and the Stouts; which did not expire with the death of her father [in 1695]; for her brother, by the father's side, continued his respects to that family, and spared no pains to espouse and carry on their interest, in order to their being chosen parliament men for that town... When they were in the country, some or other of them were often together, as well the young women as the men... And great pretensions of love and proffers of kindness were expressed by the Cowpers in general to the Stouts; and by this man, Spencer Cowper and his wife, to the deceased young woman.[42]

In 1698 the Stouts had thus been allies of, and electoral agents for, the leading Whig family the Cowpers; yet the following year, as a result of Spencer Cowper's trial, that alliance broke down and the Stouts turned towards the Tories. Not all Quakers defected; but the shift, which coincided with a resurgence of Tory power in the town and in the nation more generally, raises difficulties about where we should place the Quakers on the political spectrum. After all, William Penn, the Quaker leader with whom Sarah's parents and other Hertford Quakers were on good terms, had earlier supported James II's attempt to secure religious liberty for Catholics because he saw in it an opportunity to advance liberty for Quakers and all Dissenters. After the Revolution, Penn's political loyalty to the Williamite regime remained questionable. The Quakers, then, are the next group whose behaviour in Hertford merits further investigation.

3

QUAKERS

Understanding the Quakers, who emerged in the 1650s and flourished in later seventeenth-century Hertford, helps to explain how and
why the Cowpers and the Stouts were initially ideological bedfellows.
Quaker beliefs are also key to explaining why Sarah's death was so
deeply traumatic and destructive of that relationship, a breach that
contributed to the collapse of the Cowper's political fortunes in the
town. The trial meant that neither Sir William nor William Cowper
were ever re-elected to sit as Hertford's MPs. But investigating Quaker
ideas and values also helps with a larger story about the fracturing of
the Protestant Church in a reformation process that was still ongoing
in the seventeenth century. The Quakers offer an intriguing case study
of the challenges made to religious authority by Protestant groups and
of how threatened both churchmen and at times other Dissenters felt
in response. The Quakers illustrate what many at the time saw as the
disturbing nature of religious zeal and enthusiasm. And as an often
hated minority that was hostile to full assimilation with neighbours,
the Quakers were frequently prosecuted by the authorities and represented in negatively stereotypical ways. This chapter will outline the
prominence of the Stout family in the Quaker movement, the severe
persecution suffered by Sarah's father, and some of the Quakers'
expectations for her that she may have found difficult to meet. It
will also show how the Quaker movement posed important challenges to traditional belief and in doing so became part of debates
that helped to constitute England's early Enlightenment.

One of the major Enlightenment figures, Voltaire, was fascinated
by the Quakers. His *Letters on England* (1734), an attempt to spread
English Enlightenment to France, began with four chapters about
them—more space than he gave to all other branches of faith put
together. Voltaire had briefly fled to England in 1726, and to him
(on the look-out for ways of criticizing French Catholicism through
unflattering comparisons) the Quakers represented a curious but
simple, pure, unceremonial, un-priest-ridden, pacific, and moral faith,

even if he also found some of their manners comic. Voltaire may even have identified with the Quakers. Their claim to inner godly 'light' even echoed the vocabulary of a less Christian 'Enlightenment'; both challenged the world's assumptions with plain speaking, even if Voltaire was the wittier; and both weathered whatever scorn was heaped on them by contemporaries.

PERSECUTION

Sarah Stout left no autobiography, no letters. Nothing personal of hers survives. Had it not been for the trial, she would probably have been another of the faceless names of history. And yet it is possible to refract an image of her through the prism of her family, about whom a surprising amount can be recovered. The Quakers left a long paper trail, both a manuscript record of their own and a more public one, the result of frequent controversies in print, a medium that they exploited to the full. Sarah's parents were also very close to the national leadership of the Quakers. Her mother and father knew George Fox, who stayed with them on at least two occasions. Henry Stout wrote and published in support of William Penn, the founder of Pennsylvania, and was a friend of George Whitehead, who succeeded Fox to the national leadership. The Stouts were well connected and thus have left a mark on the records.

Sarah's mother, Mary Saunders or Sanders, had been maid to Oliver Cromwell's wife. Mary knew the Lord Protector well enough for him to tell her when he met Fox and for her to intercede with him on behalf of Quakers who were being persecuted.[1] In 1659, a year after Cromwell's death, she was one of 7,000 'handmaids and Daughters of the Lord' who petitioned Parliament against the imprisonment of Quakers who had protested against the 'oppression of Tithes' (clerical taxes), noting that parliamentarians had 'suffered more by these plundering priests than by the plundering Cavaliers'.[2] She may be the Mary Saunders who was arrested in Berkshire in 1664 and sent to a house of correction, having been seized by a vindictive self-appointed Quaker-catcher who sought to enforce the new laws against Quakers to full measure by rounding them up for imprisonment, using 'a Staff that had a Goad or some sharp Prick at the end of it' to jab at them until they were 'very sore and black'.[3] Certainly she became, if she was not already, a preacher empowered to spread the light.[4]

Her husband, Henry Stout, was probably converted by a female preacher in Ware and was 'the first called Quaker who suffered imprisonment in the Hertford goal...where his sufferings were greate, the prison windows being shut that he might not have the benefit of air or of the light of day'.[5] His 'sufferings' were indeed numerous. In 1659 he was fined £5 and imprisoned for seventeen weeks; and in the same year he was at a Meeting (the Quaker term for a gathering to listen to the spirit, a meeting that replaced a church or chapel service) that was violently attacked. The local magistrate, Sir Thomas Hewett, refused to intervene, allowing the mob 'to abuse them...wallowing them in the Mire, daubing others with Dirt, both Faces and Clothes, and filling their Hats therewith and clapping them on their Heads'. The hostile crowd flung 'such Showers of Stones, Dirt, rotten Eggs, Man's Dung and Water that few or none could escape the Marks of their Fury'.[6] The restoration of the monarchy only brought more intense persecution. Stout was imprisoned in November 1660, prosecuted in April 1662 and again in January 1664. Hertfordshire Quakers were particularly hated by Sir Thomas Fanshawe and his son (another Thomas), both of whom sat as MPs and took an active part in passing legislation against Dissenters in general and Quakers in particular. In July 1664 Parliament passed the Conventicle Act which increased the penalties for attending a non-Church of England service; and Hertford Quakers were among its very first victims. In August nine of them were convicted (despite a jury's attempt to release them) and ordered to be sent to the Caribbean colonies, though the sentence had to be commuted to seven years imprisonment when a ship chartered to transport them was repeatedly driven back by strong (the Quakers said providential) winds. The ruling of Judge Orlando Bridgeman in that case seems to have encouraged another set of prosecutions shortly afterwards and Henry Stout was among those indicted in this second wave, which produced remarkably similar results to the first. A verbatim account of the trial was later published by a Quaker and its extraordinarily vivid report of speeches not only reintroduces Henry Chauncy, acting as a judicial magistrate, but also gives an insight into the redoubtable character of Henry Stout, Sarah's father.[7] More importantly it highlights how religious and political freedoms were seen as inextricably linked, and how politicized religious struggles became.

The trial was something of a show. The jurors were hand-picked by the High Churchmen for their hostility to Quakers: 'only such made use of as were eminently disaffected to the persons that were to be tryed, and so far ingaged by prejudice, as resolved to find the Bills beforehand'. Chauncy acted as a (prejudiced) judge and was aided on the bench by Thomas, now Viscount, Fanshawe, the man who had helped enact legislation against the Dissenters. The latter could hardly contain himself. 'Your light is darkness, and a melancholly vapor of the brain', he told one Quaker who had tried to justify himself by appealing to the inner light of Christ. But Chauncy and Fanshawe had an uncomfortable time, for in defending themselves the Quakers showed a sharp awareness of their civil rights. When they disputed the terms of the law under which they were being prosecuted and denied that their religious meetings were seditious, Chauncy was forced into a mere assertion of judicial power: 'I must tell you all such meetings are seditious.' Undaunted, one of the Quakers, Robert Tyte, even read the law to the court to show that they did not break its terms and pointedly remarked 'I think thy self (meaning *Tho.* Vicount *Fanshaw* aforesaid) shouldst understand the intent of the Act, in regard thou wert one of the principal promoters of it in the House of Commons.'

When Henry Sweeting and Henry Stout were tried, Chauncy offered to drop charges if Stout and the others promised to cease meeting. Stout responded defiantly: 'I could rather offer up my life, as a sacrifice, then to engage to any such thing.' The prisoners protested to the court that they had met 'in the fear of God, for no evil end, but to worship him in spirit and truth', and not under 'colour and pretence' of religion, as the Act stated. Chauncy was unimpressed and wanted to move on, but Stout objected that the trial should not even be taking place outside Hertford's own town court. He claimed his rights as a freeman were being infringed: 'I conceive I am not to answer at this court, for any pretended offence, which is done within the corporation; but am accountable to that court, within whose jurisdiction I live . . . it is my just right and privilege to be tryed by the corporation and neighbourhood that knows me.' He then queried the power by which the mayor had committed him to the county prison, 'seeing by his charter he hath no such power and without his charter he is no more than one of us, or another man'. Stout proceeded to read out the town charter to prove his point. Like Tyte, he also argued that the Quaker Meeting was not, as the act stated, 'under pretence of religion', for his religion was deeply sincere: 'our intent is really to worship God, and nothing else'. Moreover, Stout pointed out, Charles II had, in no fewer than three declarations, promised 'That no man should be disturbed in matter of Conscience, provided they lived peaceably.' The court responded by telling him that he was being prosecuted not for his religion but so that 'you may not have any opportunity to contrive insurrections'. He had obtained an admission that he was being prosecuted for a seditious act that had not been proven to have taken place and hence denied any such intention: 'God knows we have no such design; but our design is to promote righteousness and holiness, and to reprove evil where ever we see it (although it be in the great ones of the world) and that we may live a godly life, in all honesty.'

Despite gaining the moral high ground, Stout, Sweeting, and his friends were all sentenced to be transported to Jamaica for seven years. Nevertheless, in passing sentence, Chauncy was noticed to have undergone 'a great change in his speech and countenance', in what, to the Quakers, was another providential sign of a guilty conscience. Even after his conviction, Stout remained defiant and once more commanded the floor:

> I remember I heard some upon the Bench speak very contemptuously of the Light. Now they that despise the light despise Christ, for the light is Christ, and was made manifest, to destroy the deeds of darkness, and to condemn sin in all its appearances; for he that is of God walks in the light, as God is light; whereupon they cryed, *That is true, that is true,* but would not endure to hear any further of that truth, but cryed *Take him away, take him away*; and so he had liberty to speak no more.

The Quaker author of the account left readers in no doubt about Chauncy's and Fanshawe's hypocrisy. The judge had twisted the law to oppress the godly: 'people may see the unjust proceeding of these *unrighteous Judges*, who pretend Law for their rule, in this matter, but practice none of it...O generation of Vipers, do you think to escape the damnation of Hell for your illegal proceedings?'

Perhaps because of the ignominious failure to transport the first wave of convicts, Stout and his Friends were not sent to the colonies to swell the ranks of labour for the sugar and tobacco plantations, but imprisoned in Hertford goal until 1672, when the king issued a new (but temporary) declaration of religious liberty. Not that incarceration had in any way dampened their faith. In 1669 Henry Stout and Sweeting (in whose house the very first Quaker Meeting in Hertford had been held in 1655) became trustees of a purpose-built Meeting House to be erected in the town. It still stands, the oldest such building to have remained in continuous use. Even as it was being raised, Mary Stout was being persecuted for attending Meetings—in

Figure 3.1 The Hertford Meeting House, built in 1670, is the oldest Quaker Meeting House in the world to have been purpose-built and to have remained in continuous use.

1670, as punishment, she had malt seized from her, which her imprisoned husband could do nothing to prevent.[8] Persecution was renewed in the 1680s. In August 1682 Henry Stout was indicted alongside many of those who would become the core of Cowper's supporters: Jeremiah Swift, Jonathan Smart, Joseph Barefoot, Henry Sweeting, and others, all for their Quakerism.[9] But by then the Quakers and other Dissenters were an established, even powerful, part of the community. An ecclesiastical survey in 1669 suggested that, in a town of only 1,500 adults, the Quaker Meeting numbered about 400 and that they were matched by an 'Anabaptist' (more probably a Congregationalist) one of similar size.[10]

The Quakers posed numerous challenges to conventional Christian beliefs and practices. As deeply pious people they did not seek to overturn religion, but to reformulate it. In doing so they helped contribute to a re-examination of the nature of God, how His will was revealed, and how best to organize life on earth. And in defence of their views they endured persecution throughout the Restoration period until James II's declaration of indulgence in 1687, though their 'sufferings' as they called them peaked in the late 1650s–early 1660s, 1670–1, and early-to-mid 1680s.[11] So what was the faith that inspired such defiance and resolution and in which Sarah was brought up?

The Quakers thought that the Bible was a useful, indeed sacred, guide; but they also believed that the light of Christ was not just a historical truth written in its pages. Rather, they saw it as a light living within all men as a continuing and illuminating presence. This 'inner light' was a source of revelation, and Christ could live in everyone. A number of positions followed from these simple but revolutionary starting points. One was that Christianity had become corrupted, both in doctrine and in its worship. Quakers believed that most Protestants neglected the inner light and ignored the redeeming power of the living Christ. They believed that men and women could live Christ-like lives on earth if only they would follow his ways and let him live in them. And if Luther was wrong in stressing original sin, so, they believed, was that other sixteenth-century Protestant reformer, John Calvin. Calvin had suggested that whilst some were destined to be saved after death, most people were reprobates, excluded from God's mercy, and that this predestination limited man's free will. The Quakers, by contrast, believed that God's grace was freely available to all. Calvinism, still adhered to by many Dissenters, thus did not, the Quakers were convinced, offer salvation.

It is true that many in the Church of England were also moving away from Calvinism, including the clerics in Hertford; but the Church of England was no spiritual bedfellow, for High Church hostility to 'Genevan' ideas were pushing in a very different doctrinal and ceremonial direction. Indeed, the national Church seemed to the Quakers to be a worldly rather than a godly institution and the parish church to be what Sarah's mother and her fellow petitioners of 1659 called a mere 'Steeple-House'.[12] Its clergy were 'hirelings' who put money and power before the love of God. Quakers therefore wanted nothing to do with such a church. They refused to pay the tithes that financially supported the clergy or to pay for the repair of churches; and they refused the fees customarily paid to clerics who officiated at baptisms, marriages, and burials. Indeed, they believed that these ceremonies were themselves corrupted; baptism was merely a 'sprinkling of children', an empty, godless, habit. The churchmen had put empty ceremonies above living revelation.

Hostile to Calvinistic Dissent, to the Church of England, and to the godless culture of the Restoration era, the Quakers appeared alienated from, and in conflict with, the world around them. This singularity seemed accentuated by the ways in which they lived and worshipped. Instead of attending formalized and ritualized worship, with set prayers, the Quakers held 'Meetings' at which Friends kept silent until moved by the inner light to testify to others. Strongly believing in the spiritual equality of everyone, they conceived that women as well as men could be moved by the spirit and should be able to preach. That spiritual equality also meant a refusal to recognize social hierarchy or show deference to earthly rank; Quakers refused to take off their hats to those deemed their social superiors, and addressed everyone with the familiar 'thee' and 'thou'. Rejecting formality, they also rejected worldly ways. They adopted a simple dress code. They rejected the need for baptism into their faith; rather, admission was a process of self-selection endorsed by the community of Friends. And without a clerical hierarchy they adopted highly participatory forms of self-governance. They also rejected oaths (as breaching biblical injunctions against swearing) and embraced pacifism after the Restoration, to show that they were not insurrectionaries (as Chauncy and others claimed), turning their back on the militaristic ambitions of the State. Intrinsically defiant of accepted norms, it is easy to see why Voltaire admired them.

SPIRITUAL WARFARE

Because they challenged contemporary society on so many accounts, the Quakers were often viewed by those outside the movement with deep suspicion, varying degrees of derision, and sometimes open and vehement hostility. Indeed, the identity of the Quakers is difficult to disentangle from the perceptions of their opponents. Friends spilt a good deal of ink responding to, as well as provoking, debates with those who disagreed with them. Over 500 pamphlets and books were published against them between 1650 and 1720.[13] Such an extensive printed debate at the local and national level raised important and wide-ranging questions that have a modern resonance: about how to respond to those who reject society's values; about the extent to which those who seek tolerance may themselves be intolerant of others; about the nature of religious fervour; and about how stereotypes are created. These issues were fundamental to the Enlightenment's concerns. One important bugbear of the Enlightenment was prejudice: not just prejudice against others, of the type shown against the Quakers, but also prejudice of the mind, the obstacles that prevented reason from prevailing. The Quakers are interesting in this respect since their inner light could be seen in two very different ways: either as a delusion, the product of an overheated imagination, or as a sovereign inner voice that was the highest form of authority. Quaker inspiration, which in its most intense form produced literal quaking and shaking of the body, forced contemporaries to think hard about what provoked religious zeal and delusion, whether there were natural or supernatural explanations for it, and how the condition could be contained or moderated.

Through the hostile polemic and satire of the Quakers we can glimpse more of their shock value, for it was not only Hertford's churchmen in the 1660s who found them offensive. The 1670s were wracked by bitter disputes between the Quakers and other Dissenters—in Hertford with the Independents, or Congregationalists as they were sometimes called. This group of Protestant sectarians took their name from their desire to form independent congregations gathered round godly ministers, with autonomy from the national Church. At first glance they seem to share much with the Quakers. Both groups sought freedom of conscience and liberty of worship, and shared a dislike for the national Church, which they both saw as overly formulaic, weighed down by remnants of popery, and lacking godly inspiration. But despite some common ideals, they also fundamentally and bitterly disagreed on a variety of issues, as a spat in Hertford in the 1670s makes all too clear. They quarrelled over Calvinism but also over the nature of the inner light that Quakers saw as fundamental to their faith. Indeed, the dispute shows how far the Quakers had travelled away from mainstream Protestant Dissent.

In 1673 William Haworth, the town's Independent minister, began 'Spiritual Warfare' against the Quakers, even though he had shared a cell with them during the 1660s persecution and had initially been 'tender' to fellow claimants of freedom of conscience.[14] The ensuing polemical campaign, in which Mary and Henry Stout played a full part, lasted five years and produced over a dozen pamphlets.[15] So, for most of her early childhood, Sarah grew up in a household as much at war with Dissenters as with the Church of England. A cynic might say—and the allegation was made at the time—that this was a turf war. Rival sects were fighting for and trying to police their communities in the aftermath of a declaration by the king in 1672 which gave a brief period of toleration for all those who refused to attend the services of the Church of England. Haworth was accused of being more interested in gathering his flock's money than their souls. Yet this would be to miss a more interesting and important contest over what religion and belief actually meant, for Haworth accused the Quakers of rejecting Protestant Christianity altogether.

Quaker hostility to Calvinism, a doctrine which Haworth still defended, was one source of conflict but another was the nature of religious truth. Whereas Protestants based their entire faith on the Bible, the Quakers seemed to Haworth and other biblical fundamentalists to devalue Scripture in favour of an inner truth. They seemed to displace the text that most Protestants accepted as the ultimate authority and means of knowing God's will. This was seen as a revolutionary but also heretical act. Once the Bible was no longer the ultimate arbiter of faith, and reliance was placed on the inner light of Christ and conscience, without the guide of a religious community or of a national Church, truth would simply become whatever (possibly misguided) individuals imagined it to be. This would risk placing individual 'fancy' and delusion over the word of God. To be sure, the Quakers did not want to destroy religion; indeed, they wanted a *more*

Figure 3.2 This polemical image from a 1701 work by Francis Bugg—a convert from Quakersim—shows the Quaker leaders stabbing a Bible. The centrality of Scripture as the source of divine authority was shared by the Independents and by the Church of England, even if they differed over much else.

intensely religious society and most of them saw no incompatibility between Scripture and the inner light. But the idea—even if only propagated by their enemies—that an inner belief was more important than either traditional institutions or Scripture had profound implications for the future. The displacing of the Bible as the sole or ultimate source of authority—for all manner of things—was a radical Enlightenment cause.

Thus although they disagreed on so many other issues, both churchmen and Dissenters could agree about the danger of the Quaker threat—which to them seemed remarkably like popery's placement of the authority of the pope and the Catholic Church over the written word of God. Quakers and Catholics, it was noted, also agreed on good works as a means to salvation (Protestantism had rejected this in favour of salvation by faith alone). The accusation was often made that Quakers and papists worked hand in hand.

In attacking the Quakers, Haworth spelled out the distinctions between his Independent congregation of Dissenters and the Quakers, even though by doing so he also highlighted his own sect's difference with the national Church. Haworth began his assault through the testimony of William Dimsdale, who had converted from Quakerism to join the Independents. The precise relationship of this Dimsdale to the Tory mayor is unclear; William was probably from another side of the family that had strong Quaker allegiance, a factor that may have helped John Dimsdale construct a Tory–Quaker alliance in 1699. What is clear is that William Dimsdale's allegations proved explosive and enduring; the pamphlet, which first appeared in 1673, was republished as late as 1690. He alleged that, as a Quaker, he had been 'stirred up to Ranting, to turn the grace of God into Wantonness and sin'.[16] Haworth made the most of this confession and of having made a recruit from the Quakers. In a lengthy introduction to Dimsdale's account, he sought to expose the Quakers' 'rotten opinions'. The Quakers, he said, had 'dethroned' Jesus and kept their followers in 'perfect Popish Slavery and Bondage' in the 'Spirit of Delusion'.[17] Indeed they were 'anti-Christian'. Elsewhere in print he accused them of worshipping a 'false and feigned Jesus', not the 'true and real Man in Heaven' but their own Jesus who they made a mere 'Quality in every Man'.[18]

John Crook, Henry Stout, and other Friends responded with *Rebellion Rebuked* (1673), to which Mary Stout appended a two-page remonstrance, denying that William Dimsdale had ever really been a Quaker (he had only been to Meetings ten times). The vehemency of the Quaker response to Dimsdale's apostasy helps to explain the similar reaction when Sarah Stout's alleged suicide offered their enemies another, fatal, abandonment of Quaker principles. Indeed, since Sarah's parents were key players in this earlier defence against an alleged apostasy, Mary Stout's later resolution to disprove the suggestion that her daughter must have abandoned her faith was entirely consistent with her earlier actions.

The Quaker response to Haworth nevertheless provoked a vitriolic 164-page reply that included a direct refutation addressed to Mary Stout. She was, he suggested, one of 'those Silly Women, that have been ever learning, but never yet came to the Knowledge of the Truth'. And he refuted her claim that the Quakers were honest, saying that 'of late they have much declined from Morality' and had 'Scarlet Errors of a deep dye' among them. Haworth accused Mary Stout of a 'narrow' outward belief 'that extends only to witness against some Pride in Apparel, against saluting with the Hat; and in the meantime can hug, embrace and kiss these Serpents, Crocodiles, Plague-Sores of Blasphemies' that her Friends advocated. God had left her to 'Delusion', for 'the Light within every Man is not the Lord' as she mistakenly believed. The Quaker leader George Fox, Haworth fumed, was 'bewitching' people like her into error and she risked being 'brought down to Hell'. Haworth also challenged the Quakers on their fundamental beliefs. He denied that Christ could be reduced to the inner light of men. For him the Scriptural Christ, as revealed in the Bible, was paramount. And he denied the Quaker stress on salvation on earth through a moral and godly life—for him these were signs of, rather than the means to, being saved after death. Indeed, Haworth thought the Quaker stress on good works was popish and he produced a lengthy comparison of the Quakers and papists. His enemies were, he suggested, spreading 'Gangrene, Leprosie, Plague'.[19] The phrase is redolent of the title *Gangraena* used by Thomas Edwards, Hertford's Presbyterian curate in the 1630s, in his 1646 catalogue of the heresies that had infected religion, though the irony is that Haworth was the spiritual heir to the Independents that Edwards had so bitterly attacked.

Mary Stout responded by arguing the importance of *living* a good, moral, righteous life rather than merely talking about it: 'it is not those that cry Lord, Lord, but they that do the things which he commands, whom he accounts his Friends'. True faith, she argued, purifies the heart and 'gives Victory over the World'. If people live well, she asserted, God could live in them. Rejecting the notion of enduring original sin conquerable only at death, Mary believed that there could be saints on earth, not just in Heaven. But although everyone had the light, it was not always listened to. Those that did listen, and followed Christ in 'the denial of Self' and the 'way of Holiness' became regenerated by 'a new Birth'. This was not easy, she admitted, for 'there is no Ease to the Rebellious Nature, which is in Enmity against God'. Cutting out sin 'Branch and Root' was a continuous struggle. But it could secure salvation. Mary thus explicitly rejected the Calvinist stress on faith alone, but denied this meant she was a papist. She also bristled at Haworth's chastisement: 'I am not to learn the Duty of my Place of thee', she told him. His exhortation to her to avoid spiritual pride was 'improper and impertinent'; he was nothing but a 'hypocrite' who needed to take his own advice about the need for humility.[20]

The dispute with Haworth was unseemly and bitter. One Quaker, Christopher Taylor, even railed at him in the street. But it represented more than a local spat. As Henry Stout said, it felt as though 'we have all this while waged War not only with W.H but with all the Independent Party in England'.[21] The dispute showed real tensions within the ranks of the Dissenters, who can all too easily be lumped together as a single group, tensions that were exploited by the Tories in the aftermath of Sarah's death in order to try to split the Quaker vote from the alliance of Whigs and Dissenters.

THE LUSTFUL QUAKER

Haworth depicted the Quakers in highly pejorative terms as anti-Christian, deluded, bewitched, ranting, proud, silly, hypocritically sinful, and popish. A series of printed visual images echoed his verbal caricaturing. They were doubly satirical because the Quakers themselves rejected the use of images, with Fox urging his followers to 'pluck down' such idolatry.[22] Such satires were not new, but they appeared in new numbers in this transformative period of press expansion and experimentation, and the large number of anti-Quaker prints suggests a very wide public fascination with the group. One image, somewhat ironically published in a book called *Work for a Cooper* (1679), depicts 'a Quaker that has a windmill in his Scull', with sails labelled Lust, Pride, Hypocrisy, and Covetousness, blown by the Devil. The image of the lustful Quaker was pervasive and it is clear that Spencer Cowper was, consciously or not, invoking these

He do's my business bravely

Needs must when the Devil drives.

Figure 3.3 A Quaker with a windmill mind, whose lust and hypocrisy is blown by the Devil.

associations when defending himself. His allegation that Sarah had made sexual advances towards him built on an association of Quakers (and before them, of Puritans) with hypocritical debauchery.

Another image reinforces this point; it shows a Quaker woman who is reprimanded (as Mary Stout was by Haworth) for not minding

Figure 3.4 A Quaker as lustful. The text echoes Haworth's condemnation of the Quakers for placing their inner light before scripture.

her housewifery; and her overheated state is said to make her 'hot about the tayle'. As in the previous image the Quaker has a Devil beside her, this time lasciviously leering and gesturing.

The interconnected idea that Quakers were hypocritical, devilish, and lusty was exploited visually and verbally. Thus a ballad, *Yea-and-Nay the Hypocrite* (c.1690), told the story of a Quaker who got his own sister pregnant. The 1675 short pamphlet *Mall and her Master* was accused of being 'grossly indecent' for its description of a Quaker master seducing his maid; and *The Quakers Art of Courtship* (1689, with three editions before 1710) explained the satanic nature of such lewdness, alleging that the Devil was disguised as a Quaker. It suggested that 'the Devil doth not only put on the Habit and Ear-mark of Friends; but sometimes their very Name too; and yet for all that, shall be a meer Devil still'. The satirical work catalogued the immoralities allegedly committed by Quakers and other Dissenters.

These included a Quaker woman hypocritically trying to seduce a non-Quaker 'well-featur'd Youth', urging him to give up the 'frothy carnal Way of the World', join the sect and relish 'the sweet Enjoyments that are to be had amongst Friends'. She boldly declares, 'Friend, I have a great yearning for thee, and wish I could prevail with thee to lay by thy overgrown Perriwig of Harlot's Hair, thy carnal Sword, thy painted habit, and become a Friend of the Light...for I am greatly moved towards thee.' The scenario of sexually and religiously suggestive Quakers is reminiscent of the one Spencer Cowper painted in court when revealing Sarah's suggestion to cohabit. In this printed satire of Quaker courtship whenever a Quaker woman enters a room with a bed, 'such a Lightness hath seized her Nether parts

Yea-and-Nay the Hypocrite:

O R,

A Brief Relation of a pretended Quaker near *Yarmouth*, who having lain with his own Sister, got her with Child, so that she brought him Two Sons at a Birth for a New-years-Gift.

To the Tune of *The Touch of the Times.*   Licensed according to Order.

Figure 3.5 A ballad showing Quaker hypocritical immorality.

that straightways Female Friend hath been overcome by the Weight of Affection'. And, echoing the image from *Work for a Cooper*, the tract claims that Quakers had heads that spun like windmills. The work itself then spins off into a lengthy fictional account of a Quaker's courtship, ending with a marriage ceremony that was merely a declaration of an intent to cohabit, similar to the one made in the letter from Sarah that Spencer produced in court.[23] Spencer Cowper was thus deliberately playing on the well-established notion that Quaker women were lusty, hypocritically disguising their designs under the

The London Quaker

Figure 3.6 Marcellus Laroon's depiction of a Quaker from a series of studies of working people called *London Cryes*.

veneer of their religion, and were prepared to flount the conventions of marriage.

England emulated the thriving Dutch market in visual prints, particularly after the Dutch invasion of 1688, in part because some artists worked in both countries. The prints reproduced here have a strong Dutch influence: Marcellus Laroon's father had come from Holland during the Restoration and his quasi-realistic *London Quaker* (Figure 3.6) seems discernible in Dutch-influenced satires depicting Quaker female preachers and their audiences. Figures 3.7 and 3.8 are by, or adapted from, the work of Egbert van Heemskerck, who came to England in about 1675 and, together with Laroon, helped to

Figure 3.7 A satirical print of a female Quaker tub preacher.

transfer to England the Dutch love of depicting groups of ordinary people in everyday, comic scenes. Van Heemskerck shows a gross and satirical, but at times sympathetic, fascination with the lives of the poor that invites the viewer into their world. The woman in Figures 3.7 and 3.8 is literally a tub-preacher, the term used to describe a Dissenting preacher of humble stock, and several of the Friends' faces, especially in Figure 3.8, are caricatures of deluded inspiration. Quaker women were thus depicted in these images as inverting the patriarchal order and mistaking inspiration for error, the result of an excess of emotion linked to their passionate and lusty natures.

Figure 3.8 Another version, with an even more exaggerated response from the inspired and quaking audience—see the old woman (top right) and man (bottom right).

Would Spencer Cowper's strategy of invoking the stereotype of the lustful and hypocritical Quaker woman pay off ? What would the jury decide about Sarah Stout's death?

The verdict was eventually returned after a long day in court.[24] When an exhausted Judge Hatsell tried to sum up for the jury his tiredness had clearly got the better of him. He confessed he found 'no certainty' in the conflicting scientific evidence that the court had heard about whether dead bodies floated or sank; and although the doctors had talked a great deal about the physical effects of drowning he told the jury that 'unless you have more skill in Anatomy than I, you won't be much edified by it'. He could find no motive for the murder, but neither could he see why Sarah, 'a person of a plentiful Fortune, and a very sober good reputation', should have killed herself, unless the letters did indeed bear out that she was lovesick and melancholy. But at that point his summary petered out, for he felt 'a little faint' and could not 'repeat any more of the Evidence'. The jury also seemed to be in haste. It took them only half an hour to agree that none of the accused was guilty.

Yet this was not the end of the affair, for three interconnected reasons: the dogged pursuit by Sarah's mother of a retrial, the print debate that raked over the rights and wrongs of Spencer's release, and the political fall-out in Hertford of the breach between the Cowpers and their former electoral agents. The first shows the tenacity and courage of the Quakers but also the obstacles facing a woman trying to wield the law, particularly against a family of able lawyers. The second shows the importance of print, particularly after the lapse of the Licensing Act in 1695, in denying 'closure' and its capacity to keep controversy in the public eye. The third highlights the importance of partisan divisions and the fusion of public and private lives.

In 1700 Mary Stout tried to launch an appeal in the Court of Chancery, but was frustrated at every turn by the legal tricks of the Cowpers. That she even began the process was a measure of her Quaker grit and conviction, for as a woman (and therefore barred from taking a legal action) she had to track down, and then make the appeal in the name of, Sarah's legal heir, her 10-year-old nephew, Henry. When the writ was eventually handed to Hertfordshire's undersheriff, Bostock Toller, he deliberately failed to execute it, apparently on the advice of (or pressure from) William Cowper, who was handling his brother's defence; and the Cowpers persuaded the young Henry and his mother to withdraw and then to burn the writ. Spencer even prepared a counter-petition, drafted by William, alleging that Mary sought maliciously and fraudulently 'to spin out a scandal'.[25] Their mother records in her diary how William and Spencer had debated for two hours what to do, pacing up and down, 'enough to make anyone giddy'.[26]

Yet Mary's complaint against Toller, for contempt of court, was upheld, landing him in custody. Then, 'having received no satisfaction for the blood of her Daughter', she petitioned the Lord Keeper, Sir Nathaniel Wright, for a new writ of appeal. The case for a retrial was heard by three other judges, one of whom, Sir George Treby, was a parliamentary colleague of Sir William Cowper's and fellow Whig; another was John Powell, one of the judges of the common pleas, who will again figure later in the book, since he presided over the Hertford witchcraft trial. Although Mary Stout's petition was rejected, Toller, who had called Mrs Stout 'a very busie, uneasie woman', was fined 200 marks (about £130) and imprisoned longer. Moreover, when summing up the judges' verdict the Lord Chief Justice Sir John Holt, who had heard the pre-trial evidence against Spencer immediately after Sarah's death and therefore knew the case well, launched a blistering attack on the Cowpers' attempt to frustrate Mary's counter-petition. He 'wondered that it should be said [by the Cowpers] that an appeal is an odious prosecution. He said he esteemed it a noble remedy and a badge of the rights and liberties of an Englishman.'[27] Had Holt been present earlier in the process (Powell had to deputize for him), the decision might well have gone against Spencer (and his co-defendant Marson) and a re-trial ordered.

Perhaps aware how close he was to further prosecution, Spencer simultaneously published a printed version of the case that his brother had composed, in which he outlined the legal reasons for the rejection of Mary's appeal as well as rehearsing the key defence made at the trial: the defendants' good characters, their lack of motive, and the lack of proof that a murder had even taken place, together with the charge that the Quakers were seeking to vindicate their sect and that a Hertford faction sought to pursue the case for political, electioneering reasons. Infuriated by Spencer's public declaration of innocence, Mary published her own case, refuting Spencer's explanation of how the writ had come to be burned, and dismissed his allegations of malice and political intrigue. In a poignant passage she said that the Cowpers would do well to consider 'if it were their own case, to have an only child murdered, and her reputation rendered infamous to posterity, whether nature and duty would not oblige them to use all means to make a discovery of the cause thereof? And whether they would not think it hard to have their own endeavours reflected on, and their utmost diligence accounted to be the cause of a party?' She took no pleasure, she protested, in the 'constant fatigue and considerable expence' of her cause. But convinced—with reason—that justice was being obstructed, Mary now petitioned Parliament. This certainly alarmed Spencer who complained to his mother that his father had done 'mischief' to his case by his 'continual provoking his enemies'. Spencer even asked her to intervene to 'persuade him to be silent and desist', at least until 'the danger was over'. She did so, 'but with no Effect more than to hear his outrageous desperate reply, which', she recorded in her diary, 'gave me disquiet and trouble Enough for that Day'.[28] Even so, the pressure worked. One MP was deterred from presenting the petition in Parliament, and even when it was eventually read, the Cowpers were able to stifle it. It seemed as if they had won.

Yet public interest in the case was too great to suppress easily, testimony to the interaction of private and public affairs. In the first age of party politics and a free press, scandal not only sold, it was becoming an intrinsic part of the political process. The dividing line between the public and private lives of politicians was being blurred. Spencer's case was now taken up by an entrepreneurial (and Dissenting) publisher, John Dunton, whose stock of improving, moral literature also fed off and profited from a prurient interest in the shocking. His new paper launched in 1701, *The Post Angel*, began to serialize Mary Stout's appeal case in a way that was highly damaging to Spencer's innocence. Dunton was adamant that Sarah had been murdered. He accused Cowper of lacking the courage to face another trial; and he claimed that Mary had 'MORE MATERIAL EVIDENCE than ever yet was made Publick'. Dunton also suggested that Charles Cox, one of Spencer's character witnesses, evidently had a guilty conscience about his part in the acquittal: Cox had fallen 'into a sort of a Distraction, and all the Time of the Tryal was mightily discomposed in his Mind ... and wou'd often tell the People about him, THAT HE HAD DONE A VERY BAD THING'. Having waxed lyrical about murder as a violence against God, Dunton argued that by bringing her appeal 'the Widow Stout, in endeavouring to find out her Daughter's Murtherers, does a Publick Good to the Kingdom, (besides clearing her Daughter of the Scandal of being her own Murderer)', and he suggested this would not be the first time that 'Persons who have been charg'd and acquitted of Murder, have afterwards been found guilty of it'. Dunton knew how to entice an audience. In the next issue he declared that he possessed 'SECRET and *Material Things relating to the case that give so great a Light into the Cause of that Gentlewoman's Death*, as are not yet proper to be publish'd: And therefore, tho' they are now in my Custody, I'm under an Obligation not to Publish 'em, till further Leave, which I believe I may have time enough, to insert 'em in my next *Post-Angel*.'[29] He went on at length about how the secret would be safe with him until the right time, but whether he really had anything substantial is doubtful, for he never published it.

Dunton was not the only one to keep the case in the public eye through the promise of new revelations. A pamphlet, which must have been written either by Mary Stout or with information supplied by her, also offered new details and ascribed to Spencer a possible motive that had seemed missing at the trial. The work, *Some Observations on the Tryal of Spencer Cowper*, went through two editions, in 1701 and 1702, suggesting ongoing public interest in the trial and its mystery. The tract made it clear that Spencer Cowper had, like her other suitors, been interested in Sarah's wealth. Henry Stout had made Sarah the executrix and main beneficiary of his will, even though he had a son alive and Sarah was his youngest daughter. What had perhaps been intended as a kindness to his favourite child proved a curse; and in the short term it provided her with a dilemma. The choices available in the financial world of the 1690s had become incredibly complex, the result of a 'financial revolution' that had created new ways in which the public could invest its money. The creation of the Bank of England in 1694 was one such project. Until then the State had relied on a small number of very wealthy private individuals to loan money. Now, private individuals with much less money could pool their wealth and lend it to the State in return for interest guaranteed by receipts from taxation. The investing public therefore acquired an 'interest' or stake in the State and in the war they were helping to finance. This early form of capitalistic behaviour, it can be argued, also helped to give the public a louder political voice. Another option available to Sarah was the fledgling stock market, though it was surrounded by allegedly unscrupulous and lying dealers, known as stock jobbers.

Sarah had thus been in need of financial advice and Spencer was in a position to give it. In court the prosecution had done little to establish any motive for Spencer to murder Sarah; but there had been plenty of speculation about his financial dealings with her. Indeed, even during the trial he had felt it necessary to defend himself against allegations of having embezzled and misappropriated her money. Because of 'all the Slanders and Stories' about it, he offered the judge 'a full Account of all that ever was in that Matter'. According to his version Sarah had asked him to recommend to her 'a Security for £200 if it came in my way'. In other words she wanted him to invest the money for her. He recommended that she invest by loaning it to one of his clients, in the form of a mortgage—a transaction not yet available from banks, though the idea of a 'land bank' had been mooted. He had told the court that he 'never was otherwise concerned with her in the receiving, or disposing of any of her Money; nor had I ever any of her Securities for Money in my keeping; and I defie any Adversary I have to shew the contrary'.

That was the challenge taken up in *Some Observations on the Tryal*. It explained that the full facts had not been revealed at the trial because the Quaker refusal to swear oaths had prevented Mary Stout from giving evidence to the court.[30] The tract claimed that, in the course of three visits to London, Sarah had told Spencer about her financial affairs and that he had 'proffered to do her all the kindness that lay in his power' to help her to find the best return on her money. He promised to 'be as careful in it as if it were his own concerns' and make the transactions for her free of charge. She accepted. When she returned to Hertford her mother asked her if she was sure she could trust Spencer; 'she said, Yes, she believed that he was a very honest man'. As a result her mother also gave money for Spencer to invest. A month or so later, Spencer and his wife came to the town; and Spencer began visiting Sarah 'two or three times a week'. Once Sarah had collected the debts owed to her father, about £1,000, Spencer told her that he had found the perfect investment, 'so great a bargain that he would buy it for his own use' if she did not want to take it up.

Thus began a financial intimacy that perhaps became something more. One evening Spencer came to visit the Stouts in Hertford even though he was 'not at all expected to lodge there', for he had not done so (out of propriety) since her father died in 1695. After an hour's conversation he admitted that 'he was destitute of a lodging', so she 'in civility' invited him to stay. On leaving he 'very much importuned' her to come to stay with him, and refused to go until she agreed. Had he used such intimacy to fleece her? Some time after that a friend of Sarah's saw her with only two guineas which, she joked, was 'all the money that I am now mistress of'. At the time of her death, Spencer was alleged to have a great deal of Sarah's money unaccounted for. Yet, in the pre-trial hearings, 'when her mother asked him before the then lord chief justice Holt what money he had in his hands of her daughter's? he said, None'. On the night of her death, Mary had left her daughter to speak alone with Spencer so that they could talk about the money. 'What discourse they had is not known; but sure enough it was very different from, and inconsistent with, what he rendered it to be at his trial.' Certainly he presented her with a receipt for her to sign, which she refused to do, 'which plainly shewed her dissatisfaction and that there was more due to her'. Her mother heard the door 'clap...and never saw her alive' again.[31]

Figure 3.9 A print, from around the turn of the century, satirizing the pursuit of money. It was published along with verses from Robert Gould's 1693 poem 'The corruption of the times by money'. This argued that Satan invented money 'to corrupt the mind' and seduce mankind into vice and deceit. It also suggested that it made mankind pursue worldly rather than spiritual advancement. The 'smooth-tongu'd flatterer' was, as the image shows, a principal danger.

With the case remaining a high-profile one, the Tories were determined to exploit the scandal for political ends. The breach with the Quakers was significant and the sheer notoriety of the family in the aftermath of the trial damaged the Cowpers' electoral fortunes.[32] At the next election, in January 1701, William Cowper refused to stand and Sir William lost his seat to Charles Caesar. Caesar was a Tory and, after the accession of George I, a leading Jacobite, seeking the restoration of the Stuart line out of conviction that the direct line of inheritance could not be altered. The Cowpers now faced, in Caesar, an opponent of local eminence, able to take advantage of the disaffection evident among at least part of the town's Quaker community. The 1701 overthrow of the Whigs was also the product of the long-standing Tory gerrymandering. Over 40 per cent of the voters were new.[33] But the Whig vote was also shaken at local and national level. Overall, in Hertford over a fifth of those who had voted Whig two years before swapped their allegiance, and Quakers were more reluctant to vote for the Whigs: Sarah's half-brother even sided with Caesar. It is true that the alienation of the Quakers was not total: in March, Quaker leader Henry Sweeting was at the forefront of those petitioning against Dimsdale and the corporation for their illegal manipulation of the franchise against the inhabitants.[34] Yet the result of the trial did mean that for the foreseeable future the Cowpers' reputation in Hertford was seriously compromised and that they had to work behind the scenes rather than contest the seat themselves. Indeed, a Cowper did not represent the town at Westminster again until the late eighteenth century.

The Tories Caesar and Goulston were able to consolidate their hold. In January 1702 the House of Commons even upheld the Tory faction's right to poll honorary freemen. Only in 1705 did the Whig fortunes rally a little in Hertford, when Parliament reversed that decision and replaced the Tory Richard Goulston with Thomas Clarke, who had Cowper backing. William Cowper thought this 'a fair step to deliver a poor town from the manifest oppression and wrong from those who should have protected them'. Even so, John Dimsdale spat his venom, as Sarah Cowper put it, at William Cowper, by telling him 'contemptuously' that he 'would toss him in a blanket, with more such like Bugg words'. Sarah thought Dimsdale might be officially reprimanded for his words against an officer of the State (her son was now Lord Keeper), fined, and 'oblidg'd to meddle no more at elections', but that was wishful thinking.[35] If anything the Dimsdales' grip on local power tightened over the coming years. In 1706 Dimsdale became mayor again and in 1708 even stood for Parliament with the support of the county's Tory leader Ralph Freman. Perhaps overreaching himself, he trailed last in the poll, and this encouraged Spencer and William Cowper to use their legal expertise to try to loosen Dimsdale's grip further. In November 1709 Lord Chancellor Cowper (as William had by then become) upheld a complaint from Leonard Dell (who had helped to drag Sarah Stout's body from the water and who had also been assaulted by Dimsdale's son) and other inhabitants. Dell and his allies successfully alleged that the corporation had failed to distribute money to the poor from the rents on land bought from the Crown. Spencer Cowper had acted as counsel for the town's poor. In 1713 the corporation, including the two John Dimsdales, appealed to the House of Lords against the 1709 ruling, but lost their case.[36] The two families locked horns again in an electoral contest as late as 1715, when Spencer gave evidence to Parliament of the Dimsdales' electoral malpractice. In 1721 the Whigs (though not the Cowpers directly) finally regained the Hertford seats, a reflection of the growing party stranglehold on power under George I, but the struggle to regain influence had been a very long and hard one.

Indeed, the longevity of the influence of the 1699 trial was remarkable. Perhaps because he remained a public figure, becoming an MP in 1705 and even a judge in 1717, Spencer's trial held an enduring fascination. At least four editions of it were printed in 1699, together with a one-sheet summary rushed out just two days after its conclusion, suggesting considerable public demand. In 1703 it was included in *An Exact Abridgement of all the Tryals . . . in the Reigns of the late William III of Glorious memory and of our present Gracious Sovereign Queen Anne*. This seems to have guaranteed it a place in the new eighteenth-century genre of collections of 'state trials' which were published from 1719 onwards, though its inclusion was unusual because it had been a local prosecution not of direct relevance to the State.[37] One such collection, in 1735, suggested 'that it was one of the most memorable Trials in our Age, and the World to this day divided in their Opinions concerning the Innocency of the Prisoners'.[38] The trial's continuing ability to divide and lure a reading public was exploited in 1733 when it was chosen to launch a new newspaper, the *Penny London Post*, which serialized it, and again in 1751 at the start of the *London Morning Penny Post*.

Spencer's crime evidently continued to fascinate the publisher John Dunton and his readers, since in 1706 he published yet another attack on Sarah's murderer. In it Dunton imagined tying Sarah's murderer to the gallows and whipping him. The 'Ruffian' should be taught 'what Lashes he must expect', for 'be he never so Rich or Great' he deserved 'not only Whipping but Hanging'. He was 'such a First Rate Sinner that all the Severities of Human Justice are, in this case, Impotent'. He should be flogged until he was 'out of Breath (I mean til he has none left)' and imprisoned in a dark prison, lit by a pale lamp, containing the 'dead Carkass which he has deprived of life...with all the wounds gaping and the face writhed into all the Postures of Terror and Amazement...the Ghastly looks of the Dead Body...and the Dimness of the Light wou'd make it look the very Emblem of Hell'.[39] Not surprisingly, given this degree of public interest and condemnation, Spencer found it hard to live down the scandal associated with his name. It was said that as a judge he found it difficult to look other lawyers in the eye, especially when their cases too closely resembled his own. And in 1728, a few days after Spencer's death, a ballad by Charles Beckingham revived the story, depicting Sarah as a betrayed mistress spurned by a cold-hearted rake, Lothario.[40] A verse riposte reasserted the allegations of suicide and conspiracy.[41]

Spencer's trial and the collapse of the Cowpers' power in Hertford were not the end of the family's and town's divisions and debates. The rest of the book will track two more trials. The first, at which Spencer Cowper was now prosecutor rather than the accused, and at which his brother presided, was the trial in 1710 of Dr Henry Sacheverell. This parliamentary impeachement, which took place in Westminster Hall, became the most notorious prosecution of the early eighteenth century. The second trial, influenced indirectly by the Sacheverell trial, was the last conviction of a witch in England, a trial held in Hertford in 1712. These episodes, and the context in which they occurred, will uncover further layers of England's early Enlightenment. They will raise issues about the role of women, marriage (including bigamy), and morality; the science of religious delusion; the decline of belief in the power of the Devil and witchcraft; and changing ideas about the justification for suicide.

4

MORAL PANIC AND
MARITAL AFFAIRS

The next three chapters follow the fortunes of the Cowper family, and of the wider national culture, in the decade after Spencer's trial. They pick up a number of themes that have already been touched on, but also place these in a wider context. We move from the hidden but turbulent desires underlying Spencer and Sarah Stout's relationship to the more general moral crisis that seemed, to many of their contemporaries, to be engulfing society. The late 1690s and early eighteenth century saw something of a panic about a tide of immorality and vice. This in turn seemed to spring from an anxiety about the growth of deism (the rejection of the Christian God whilst maintaining that there was a God, evident in reason and nature), atheism, irreligion, and indifference to all religious guidance. Challenges to the power of the established Church seemed to shake the whole edifice of morality and accepted codes of behaviour that had been supported by it.

Society faced a paradox, arguably a key liberal dilemma when any established authority is attacked and the precise consequences of such an attack are unknown. Religious freedom had been granted in 1689 to allow men and women to find their own way to God; but it could also allow them to find Hell, to wallow in sin, or to reject conventional belief systems and in the process undermine any sense of communal unity. It might be overstating the case to argue that it was in the seventeenth century that this challenge was faced for the first time but it is not much of an exaggeration. The sixteenth-century Reformation had been one in which the Bible occupied centre stage. There was plenty of disagreement about how to interpret Scripture but at least there was a shared biblical framework within which such disagreement took place. In the two revolutions of the seventeenth century, however, this consensus was under threat. During the mid-century revolution the growth of sectarianism had led to a moral panic and a dread, particularly acute in the late 1640s and 1650s, that religious freedom led to atheism and irreligion.

The later seventeenth century saw the return of such anxieties and fears just as, if not more, strongly. During the Restoration era and particularly after the Revolution of 1688–9 contemporaries seemed to be in a world in which old religious and biblical values were under threat or even scoffed at, in which a shared mental universe seemed to be in danger of fracturing or already to have been destroyed. Religious diversity shattered the notion that there were shared assumptions—as we have seen, the Quakers seemed to their enemies to have created a new code of behaviour. But perhaps even more troubling to many was that core religious and moral values seemed not only to be disputed but also under direct assault from the forces of freethinking, deism, and atheism, which attacked the notion of religion as it had been traditionally understood and which seemed to be gaining considerable momentum in the wake of the Toleration Act and the freedom to print.

The Cowper family once again seemed to exemplify these tensions. Hostile to the established Church and open to a variety of different religious ideas, Sir William Cowper epitomized the stereotype of the freethinking Whig; his sons were less openly anticlerical but were certainly committed to freedom of worship. And there was an apparent correlation between their pursuit of religious and sexual freedom. Spencer was not the only son with a roving eye, for his brother also acquired a scandalous reputation as a bigamist. Certainly he had two illegitimate children, and carefully kept letters from them amongst his papers; and contemporaries thought that he advocated polygamy. Until restrained by the strengthening codes of polite behaviour (but also by their political responsibilities), the brothers seem to exemplify an unbridled and predatory masculinity. In this they emulated their father, who had a reputation as a lecher. Their apparently unbridled behaviour threatened to undermine the institution of marriage. Sir William ruled his wife with a ferocious temper, allowing her few liberties, and Sarah Cowper in turn viewed their marriage in terms of slavery—a word that had both political and social application. The Whigs insisted on political and religious liberty; but, from Sarah's perspective, they denied her freedom. Whilst she shied away from seeing her husband's behaviour as representative of the oppression of her gender as a whole there were others who did make that connection and exploited the discrepancy in Whig attitudes. Sarah's diary reveals the strains within one marriage; but the institution as a whole seemed also to be struggling to contain wider social, religious, and political changes.

Integrating religious and social history by studying the family and morality requires us to take both belief and behaviour seriously. A religious crisis set the framework for the moral one. Before turning to morality in the Cowper household, therefore, the religious ideas reverberating around it have first to be sketched. Doing so will also illuminate a key Enlightenment concern with reason, since rethinking religion had profound intellectual consequences. The Cowpers thus show the importance of linking the private and the public, of integrating social with political, religious, and intellectual history; and their story helps us to join the Puritanism of the seventeenth century to the Enlightenment of the eighteenth.

RETHINKING RELIGION

At first sight the disagreement between Sarah Cowper and her husband, Sir William Cowper, appears to be a straightforward conflict between religious orthodoxy and heterodoxy. Whereas Sarah regularly attended Church and outwardly showed her conformity to it, Sir William spoke 'sharply against the Church and priests' and, in a show of his freethinking, made a point of inviting the whole gamut of religious opinions to his table.[1] On one uncomfortable occasion for Sarah, four men of very 'Various Opinions' were present: 'a Latitudinarian, another for the Church, a papist, and a preaching Anabaptist'.[2] Yet in fact Sarah's beliefs were less straightforward, and Sir William's even more unorthodox, than this simple dichotomy suggests.

Some insight into Sarah's views can be gleaned from her diary. Over and over again, her entries lament how much she missed the company and ideas of Martin Clifford, to whom she had become exceptionally close in the 1670s when the Cowpers lived near the Charterhouse, a London school where Clifford was Master. Clifford had been no orthodox member of the Church of England. He was secretary to the dissolute libertine and freethinking duke of Buckingham, one of the most notorious rakes in Restoration England. And Clifford shared Buckingham's tolerationist and rationalist views about religion. Indeed, if we recover Clifford's views, we get a set of rather surprising ideas for Sarah to have admired—and admire she did, since she felt it necessary to assert that her friend had been 'no Contemner of Religion'.[3] Certainly not everyone in the Church held such an indulgent view of him. Clifford's *Treatise of Humane Reason* (1674) was said by the bishop of Ely to make 'every man's private fancy the judge of religion'.[4] The bishop was not the only one to be shocked. The annotations made in one copy now in the New York Theological Library by an anonymous reader suggest that Clifford's book was seen as heretical and atheistical.[5]

By his own admission Clifford placed a very strong emphasis on reason, boasting that on his spiritual quest he had 'no other Guide ... but my own Reason'. Sounding rather like a Quaker (and he explicitly defended the sect), he believed that every soul 'hath in it self as much light as is requisite for our travel towards Heaven' and needed no other 'Authority'. But whereas for the Quakers this was the light of God, for Clifford it was the light of reason. Clifford saw no danger to society in every one seeking their own version of 'reason' and thereby creating a plurality of religious standpoints: such 'variety of opinion' had not been destructive to ancient societies, such as Greece, he said, where 'every man enjoyed his own Opinion with more safety and freedom than either his Goods or Wife'. Indeed, he suggested that Christianity, and even the Protestant Reformation, had led to 'Blood and Confusion' by displacing this pagan allowance of every man to follow his own judgement. It was not the use of liberty that was dangerous 'but the appropriating it for ourselves only', 'the tying *infallibility* to whatsoever we think Truth, and *damnation* to whatsoever we think Error'. Unity was destroyed 'not so much by them who differ in Opinions as by them who will not allow of such a difference' and rather than follow 'authority' men should follow reason. Reason would dictate, he said, that Christianity was the path to follow; but there were 'a thousand several waies' to Heaven. God, he asserted, does not ask us to find the truth; but to seek for it, since we do not know for certain what truth is, nor would he punish those who erred as a result.[6] Clifford had thus advanced a highly rationalist view of religion, in which the light of reason was divine and more valuable than the artificial confines laid down by the religious establishment. Remaining sincere to one's reason was more important than following the dictates of any one Church.

Sarah never went anything like as far as this and for much of her life remained a devout adherent of the established national Church. For all her admiration of Clifford, she held to a view of religion that sought to buttress Christian morality and piety rather than to explore the diversity of ways to salvation. The other Churchmen she admired (such as John Tillotson and Simon Patrick, two future bishops) were indeed rationalists but they were also moderates who worried about a

Church undermined by immorality, irreligion, infidelity, and enthusiasm. She, like them, was convinced that 'in this Degenerate Age... Christianity seems to decline' and needed defending through the established Church.[7] Indeed, Sarah was particularly shocked by John Toland, the most controversial of the writers who advocated a purely rational and anticlerical religion. She was once, as she recorded in her diary, in Toland's 'Company where he did Vent such incredible Stuff that he seemed to out-lie the Devil'.[8] She barely resisted a temptation 'to have given him a Box in the ear' and sarcastically called him 'our celebrated author', a reference to his publication in 1696 of *Christianity not Mysterious*, in which he advocated a Christianity that was barely recognizable to most of his contemporaries.[9] Indeed, the book was ordered to be burnt. It sought to strip away anything that was mysterious or superstitious, for 'the true Religion must necessarily be reasonable and intelligible', accessible to all. Mysteries, Toland argued, were enthusiastic fooleries. He denied that miracles were anything more than the extraordinary: 'whatever is contrary to reason can be no miracle... the celebrated Feats of *Goblins* and *Fairies*, of *Witches*, of *Conjurers*, and all the *Heathen Prodigies*, must be accounted fictitious, idle, and superstitious Fables; for in all these there appears no End deserving a Change in *Nature*. Besides, they evidently contradict our Idea of God, and quite subvert his Providence.' Miracles were no more than clerical tricks.[10] Toland instead placed reason at the heart of Christianity; anything that was above reason was a mystery and had no part in rational Christianity. Mystery was 'the distinguishing Mark of the false or *Antichristian* Church'. Reason did not make revelation useless, Toland argued, but it was the way in which man could comprehend revelation. Reason was the 'candle, the guide, the judge he has lodg'd within every man that cometh into this world'.

Whereas the seventeenth century had identified 'conscience' as the guide, the early eighteenth-century radicals were replacing this with reason. But perhaps even more shocking was Toland's vehement anticlericalism at a time when the Church already felt it had lost considerable authority after the dislocation of the 1640s and 1650s and then the Toleration Act. He blamed the clergy for deliberately making religion mysterious in order to increase their own power: Christianity, Toland asserted, had only became mysterious 'through the craft and ambition of priests and philosophers'.

Sarah's hostility to Toland makes it unlikely that she was the owner of four rather remarkable manuscripts in the Cowper family papers, for they outlined a deist religion even more strongly than Toland had done.[11] Toland, publicly at least, always defended the Gospels, and revelation, and explicitly counted himself a Christian: 'The only religious Title therefore that I shall ever own, for my part, is that most glorious one of being a *Christian*.'[12] Indeed, even if they did manage to shock many Churchmen, deist writers were restricted by what they could say in print. William Stephens wrote, in 1696, a history of the growth of deism, giving a refutation of revealed religion; but he prefaced it (as well he might, given that he was an ordained minister) with a profession of his belief in the veracity of Scripture. It is true that Stephens was able, obliquely, to attack the 'mysteries' insisted on by the Church that confounded plain sense; that he stabbed at the 'Church-mens wrangles' that he said put people off religion; that he objected to the Church's demand that men surrender their reason to its authority; and that he even accused the High Churchmen of encouraging deism by prostituting the Church to their party. But he did not aim to set out a coherent deistic system, and indeed professed to write against the deists. To do anything else publicly was extremely dangerous. In 1697 an Edinburgh university student, Thomas Aikenhead, was executed for saying in coffee houses and drinking dens what were deemed to be blasphemous thoughts about divine revelation.[13] But writers were much freer in manuscript, which was seldom prosecuted, to develop an alternative belief system and the deist manuscript treatises among the Cowper family papers show precisely this freedom of thought. Indeed they show a daring break with orthodox belief.

The treatises were written by James Boevey who has almost disappeared from historical view.[14] We do, however, have a lively character sketch of him by his friend John Aubrey who depicted Boevey as a multilingual merchant and lawyer of Dutch extraction, only about five feet tall, with strikingly black curly hair and beard, and very sprightly hazel eyes. He was 'a person of great temperance and deep thoughts, and a working head, never idle'. His restlessness made him a prolific writer. Aubrey knew of thirty-nine manuscript volumes in 1680 and there were more by his death in 1696. The range of his writing was encyclopaedic. Boevey's early career sparked thoughts about trade, wealth, the law, and negotiation. And his other treatises touched on much more philosophical topics: education; conversation, talking and writing; reputation; servants; subserviency; love and marriage; the art of discerning one's self; moderating desire and grief; the diseases of the mind; discord and concord; friendship; and 'religion from reason'. Aubrey also informs us that he was 'a great lover of naturall philosophie'.

In 1693 Boevey reworked a vindication of Nicholas Machiavelli, the early sixteenth-century writer who was notorious both for his non-scriptural morality of politics and for his advice about how to create and maintain a strong republic.[15] The piece had originally been published in November 1642 under the title *The Atheisticall Politi-tian*, so, assuming that Boevey was also the author then, he had used Machiavelli to attack both monarchy and the Church at the outbreak of the Civil War.[16] His tract marked a turning point in the hitherto negative reaction to Machiavelli in England, since Boevey argued that Machiavelli had correctly represented the nature of princes and the corruption of religion. In 1693 Boevey omitted and softened passages that were deeply critical of princes, to make the work less anti-monarchical—the theme of tyranny was no longer so relevant in the wake of the Revolution of 1688–9. But about the same time, in 1694, Boevey wrote four manuscript volumes on deism which are among the Cowper papers: 'The Deists' Reflections on Religion'; 'The Deists' litany', 'The Character of Deism'; and 'Deists Reflections upon Biggottism'. They are complex pieces, significantly influenced by the early seventeenth-century work of Lord Herbert of Cherbury, but the contours of Boevey's arguments are worth briefly sketching, for he wrote with a freedom and vigour that is striking and he serves to show the challenge faced by conventional religion.

It is true that Boevey believed that there was a God and that he also attacked atheism. There had to be a prime mover, he said, a 'first and eternal cause of all things, which is that which men mean by the name of God'. But Boevey's God was not the God of the Bible, and his Church was certainly not the established Church of England. This was in part because, having written biographies of both Confucius and Mahomet, he was aware of competing global religions that also claimed truth: 'there have been many faiths, or Religions, all of them pretending to Divine Inspiration, so that a man may find one in Europe, another in Affrick, and a third in Asia and perhaps a fourth in America or the West Indies. From which consideration a man can hardly prefer the Arguments drawne from his owne Native Soile in the defence of the Religion used there.' If reliance on local custom was insufficient to guarantee truth, so too was reliance on the revelations and dogmas asserted by most organized religions. The truth, he insisted, was simple and universal, 'engraven upon man's heart by the most High God and ever was accounted as certainly true in all

Ages, among all the Nations of the Earth'. Man could thus 'by the strength of his owne facultyes distinguish inward things from outward, certain things from uncertain, Divine things from Humaine'. Or, more poetically, truth was 'written by the finger of God in the inward Court of Conscience'. And conscience was none other than reason. This led, in Boevey's formulation, to a simple, rational religion, 'that which men may know and should be obliged unto by the meer Principles of Reason, without the help of Revelations'. And this in turn meant stripping religion to a non-Christian set of basic principles of belief:

> The Universall, the true Catholick Articles of Religion are these vizt that there is a supreme God. That a cheife Worship is to be given him. That the best Worship of him consists in Piety, virtue and Charity conjoined with faith in ye love of God. That if wee transgresse or fall from the Rules thereof, we must repent Cordially and turn to the right way. That there is both rewards and punishments here & hereafter. The great points of Religion we leave to be from hence derived, even from a Mans Reason. We should have no Article of faith exhibited but what may be discernible by their own light.[17]

Salvation was thus available to all from a very simple set of doctrines discernible through reason.

Although Boevey rejected a Christian God, he did advocate a wise and providential God who 'presided over and governed all things'. This included nature. It was no chance, he said, that the human body had over 600 muscles, 284 bones, and about 100,000 different parts; nature was proof of God's existence and of his providence. Providence was very important in Boevey's system of belief, since he thought that men did not have an absolute liberty: 'Man is governed by the secret force of a Deity, being not at his own liberty till he hath gott out of the Body and out of this World.' But Boevey's sense of providence was very far from the Calvinistic providential predestination proclaimed by Hertford's Independent minister, William Haworth. According to Boevey, God's will governed everyone, not just an elect few. Indeed he thought Calvinistic predestination a pernicious doctrine that removed hope; mankind did have free will, within the parameters of God's naturally ordered universe. Providence, for Boevey, seems to have meant a divine beneficence, an ordering of the world for the best. Thus his God was also just, infinite, immutable, omnipresent and omnipotent, and fundamentally good: 'the idea of absolute perfection must be essentially good', he wrote, in words that anticipate the German mathematician and philosopher Gottfried Leibniz's more famous formulation about the best of all possible worlds.

Moreover, Boevey's God did not need worship in the same way that the Christian God did. We should, said Boevey, love, trust and revere God; but 'the best way of Worshipping the Supreme Deity consists in Piety and Vertue, conjoyn'd with faith & love of God', rather than in formalistic, ceremonial Church worship. There was still a requirement to worship (Boevey wrote a whole volume of prayers) and system of rewards and punishments in the afterlife, but the latter were based on how an individual had behaved towards his fellow man, on his virtue and charity, as much as on his obedience to God.

Boevey hated wrangling over theology—what he called 'polemical divinity'. Men should 'trust rather to his own rational faculties in matters of salvation than to the implicit faith imposed by the Priests'. Indeed, in his volume against 'biggottism' he was very scathing about 'priests' of any kind and came close to developing a history of superstition which saw all organized religion as a conspiracy of counterfeiting, tyrannical, greedy, intolerant, and bigoted clerics who were intent on suppressing reason. During the course of his diatribe against such priests he suggested that they deliberately played on the fears, passions, and ignorance of the common people to magnify their own power, using miracles, inspiration, and prophesies as 'crafty' tools to hook the unwary. Boevey filled almost a hundred pages luridly cataloguing the horrors and errors of 'biggottism'. And in this he more than justified the anticlericalism that High Church polemicist Charles Leslie said was intrinsic to deism. The deists, Leslie concluded in 1696, wanted to be free from 'priestcraft' and to have 'their Judgments freed from the Slavish Authority of Precedents and Laws, and matters of Truth, which they say ought only to be decided by Reason'.[18]

Deism was seen by critics as a short step to atheism, the rejection of God entirely. Deism stripped belief to its non-biblical core. By removing the Christian underpinning of belief in God, the deists risked removing belief in God altogether; for if knowledge of God rested solely on reason or nature, what if reason or nature dictated that God did not exist? Anxiety about atheism was, of course, not new and had been growing since the mid-seventeenth-century revolution. But it was on the rise again in the 1690s because many worried that the Toleration Act of 1689 could lead to irreligion rather than freedom of religion. Indeed, the High Church Tory polemicist Charles Leslie attacked deists in 1696 for being in league with the Quakers and the Devil against the Church.[19]

Boevey's manuscripts constituted what the Church considered to be blasphemy, irreligion, and anticlericalism. His tracts may have belonged to the anticlerical and freethinking Sir William Cowper or to his son William. But their existence among the Cowper family papers is significant for another reason. Deism was associated not just with atheism but also with another threat to the Church and the way of life it inculcated: immorality. The rejection of conventional Christianity led, it was alleged, to the rejection of conventional morality. Freedom of conscience led to freedom of morals. Once again the Cowper family seem to embody a larger set of issues, for both father and sons acquired reputations as loose-livers; and the link between their alleged immorality and their religious unorthodoxy was no accident. Freethinking and loose-living were, to their critics, two sides of the same coin. So the Cowpers' possession of deist material and their sexual indiscretions conform to the contemporary association of the irreligious and the immoral.

Boevey's deist ideas were shared by a minority. But even so there was a more general shift in thinking about God that was producing a change in the moral landscape. Calvin's Reformation of the sixteenth century had been a moral reformation as well as a purely doctrinal one; but Calvinism was going out of fashion and its moral code was also being eroded. Ralph Battell, son of one of Hertford's ministers, thought Calvinism a 'vulgar error'. Geneva, Calvin's adopted town, became for the High Churchmen a pejorative label associated with rebellious fanatics. Thus whereas Calvin and his followers had seen God as choosing only a few for salvation, his critics (and here, for once, the Quakers and Church of England were in agreement) stressed a God whose grace and salvation extended to all repentant sinners. To some, this merciful God could become an indulgent God. As Charles II told Burnet, he 'could not think God would make a man miserable only for taking a little pleasure out of the way' and his partner in promiscuity, the earl of Rochester, similarly doubted that 'so good a Being as the Deity would make him miserable'. The challenge for Churchmen who were not rigid Calvinists, then, was whether and how to inculcate strict morality without Puritan ideology.

These changes in perceptions about the character of God reflected a larger debate about the centrality and certainty of Scriptural rules and hence also about biblical morality. What moral certainty and value system, sufficient to require everyone's assent, was to be found if biblical authority was displaced or even rejected? Was morality merely a human invention and not an absolute and unchanging truth, asked Edinburgh student Thomas Aikenhead in 1697, shortly before his execution the following year for a series of blasphemous outbursts that included ridiculing the Scriptures, which he described as being 'stuffed with madness, nonsense, and contradictions'?

It is not surprising, therefore, to find in the late 1690s a wave of concern about morality. Royal proclamations were issued against immorality in 1698 and 1699 and then again in 1702 and 1703; legislation was aimed at blasphemy in 1698 and against vice and immorality in 1699 (a bill which William Cowper opposed); and a pamphlet assault was launched against the perceived immorality of the stage. Indeed, the years 1697–1701 were the 'high point of the moral reform movement', and included the foundation, in 1699, of the Society for Promoting Christian Knowledge.[20] It was in part a desire to stem the tide of irreligion and atheism that led to the creation, after 1689, of societies for the reformation of manners. Their campaign, particularly strong in the burgeoning metropolis of London, relied on pious informers to prosecute sexual laxity, especially prostitution, and in the first decade of the eighteenth century over 1,000 men and women a year were convicted. But the reformers faced an uphill task. According to one pamphleteer, 'the common Degeneracy in this Age and Nation is become such as is hardly to be parallel'd in any History' and 'a strong and habitual addictedness to unlawful Pleasures' led to 'Atheism and Infidelity'.[21] Infidelity of belief and sexual infidelity went hand in hand.

The restraints on selfish behaviour, on rampant individualism, on worldliness, seemed to the reformers to have been taken off. Moreover, the Church courts had ceased to function for much of the 1640s and 1650s. Although they were revived in 1660, they focused much less than before on moral cases and after 1689 the Church of England lost its monopoly over Church attendance. If the established Church was deprived of some of its armoury to enforce morality and there was no longer an obligation to listen each week to its religious advice, asked many Church-goers, what restraints were there to the erosion of traditional ways of life? The early eighteenth century faced the question: how could liberty be prevented from degenerating into licence and an atomistic world? This question led to a re-examination of the implications, possibilities, and extent of the Revolution of 1688–9 and its consequences. The Whigs and Dissenters had to think through how far their political and religious revolution extended in social and moral directions, and Tories and High Church-men had to decide how much to accept. As a result, ideas about sexual morality and familial relations came under particular scrutiny. The revolution in Church and State thus also had a broader cultural impact; and in turn, cultural change had an impact on how the revolution was viewed; for, as we shall see in the next chapter, the sense that cultural change had gone too far fostered a High Church Tory attack on revolution principles as a whole.

RETHINKING MARRIAGE

The institution of marriage was one of the battlegrounds for the conflict over morality. This was inevitable because marriage was central to social, sexual, religious, economic, and political life. The ideal, advocated in a mass of 'advice' literature, and aimed primarily at the better off, was one of mutual care and affection between husband and wife, but not equality: the wife was expected to exercise power only within the household and then only over children and servants rather than over her spouse. Patriarchy, or the rule of male authority figures, prevailed in both the private and public spheres. Just as the Jewish patriarchs of the Old Testament had ruled over and led their people, so early modern husbands were princes of their households and, for Tories at least, princes were fathers of their country. The idea of a 'natural order' reinforced patriarchy, both in the sense that God had made men superior to women but also, as the revered ancient philosopher Aristotle had argued, that the household was the first natural unit of political society: families had heads, and when family heads came together to form society they chose a single family head, a monarch, to rule over them. Long-held ideas about the family therefore governed not only the relations between the sexes but also most other aspects of early modern life. The sixteenth-century Protestant Reformation had generally enhanced rather than reduced the importance of the family. Reformers wanted a godly Reformation free from what they saw as vice and immorality, and that strength-ened their commitment to the family and traditional patterns of gender and sexuality. Protestantism stressed order and hierarchy within the family as well as within the State. Thus the institution of marriage remained relatively unchallenged.

It is, of course, easy to exaggerate both the stability of marriage and the power of patriarchy. Amongst those less well off, marriage was sometimes a precarious institution—much to the concern of the Church and State authorities that sought to prosecute those who strayed outside it, particularly if they produced illegitimate children. Patriarchy also had anomalies: it subjugated men, such as male servants, as well as women, whilst wives were sometimes empowered to act outside the household—in the market place, for example—and, especially in gentry households, even to exercise rule over those within it. It is also true that the Reformation had already led to some revision of attitudes. Although they had received little sympathy among the reformers as a whole, the early Anabaptists had questioned conventional ideas about monogamy, arguing that the Bible justified polygamy. With marriage no longer seen as a sacrament, ideas about divorce had also begun to change. In 1653 England temporarily adopted civil marriages. So it would also be wrong to argue that everything suddenly changed for the generation after the Revolution of 1688–9. Attitudes to marriage changed slowly. Even at the end of the eighteenth century Mary Wollstonecraft was still railing at the institution of marriage and lamenting the double standards that allowed men liberty and women slavery. She discerned a misogyny even in the writing of those who claimed to be spreading Enlightenment.

Yet because marriage was such a centrally important institution, and because it was political, religious, moral, and economic in scope, it was necessarily affected by the changes in those spheres ushered in by the Revolution of 1688–9 and the family was one of the sites in which such changes could be discussed.[22] The period around 1700 was a moment when marriage seemed in something of a state of flux and when the grounds for morality came in for a good deal of serious rethinking. In other words, marriage was part of a *system* of thought and a pattern of behaviour. Changes in any one part of that system and pattern necessarily had consequences elsewhere. The customs and traditions of marriage and sexual propriety were questioned in the late seventeenth century in ways that left a long legacy, even if they did not lead in a linear fashion to 'modernity'.

A key factor unsettling conventional attitudes was the attack on the political ideology of patriarchy. The Whigs argued that kingly power was *unlike* the power exercised by a father and that royal authority should be seen in terms of a *contract* between freely consenting individuals. This had important ramifications for how people thought about familial and marital relations. If political authority did not flow from nature or the law of God, then why did it follow that men naturally had rule over their wives? Similarly if political authority was man-made and artificially constructed by a type of contract, and breach of contract could lose a prince his kingdom, should husbands not lose their wives when they behaved like tyrants and breached the marital contract? These questions were ones that had to be answered by both Whigs and Tories; but interestingly, as we shall see, it was often Tory critics of Whig ideology who often exploited the dilemma, even if only to embarrass their opponents. In doing so they developed ideas about the freedom of women from subjection even if they did not articulate them as a coherent feminist ideology.

Political debate also had an impact on morality because each party was convinced that the other was redefining good and evil to suit their partisan purposes. What was liberty to the Whigs could be licence to the Tories. The cultural civil war between the parties was thus also a war over language and its meanings. Partisanship led to rival inter- pretations of words and concepts, including moral ones, especially since vices were, as we saw with the image of the genealogy of fanaticism, deliberately associated with hated ideologies in order to delegitimize them. As poet laureate John Dryden noted, Whig and Tory made vice and virtue relative values, and dependent on the eye of the beholder. In such a world, morality could be distorted by partisan polemic and trickery. For example, most Whigs (including the Cowpers) came to see the duke of Marlborough, the commander of the armed forces in the war against France, as the public-spirited saviour of the nation; to others, mostly Tory, he was rapacious, greedy, corrupt, and self-interested. Partisanship thus undermined moral absolutes. Personal morality and virtue were, perhaps inevitably in an age of fierce competition for public electoral support, increasingly seen through a political lens. Political opponents exploited the sexual indiscretions of their rivals. Thus the Tories delighted in exposing the Cowpers' tangled love lives. The press, liberated after 1695 from pre- publication censorship, washed this dirty laundry in front of a national audience; not only did such prurient literature sell, it also made individual indiscretions synonymous with the party. The private, then as now, was public and political. Perhaps in part as a conse- quence of this vulnerability to invasion and exposure, privacy became more prized.

The political capital to be had from exposing indiscretions may also have contributed to another trend that had important implications for how morality was regarded. This was a heightened awareness and dislike of hypocrisy, one of the recurring themes of this book. Anxiety about the growing prevalence of hypocrisy was perhaps inevitable in a world of partisan politics, for each side was convinced that the other consisted of tricksters intent on covering their true designs in order to deceive the people into supporting them; and a partisan press meant that there were usually two versions of every story, only one of which could be true. But hypocrisy in the religious and moral sphere rendered politicians particularly vulnerable. To many Tories there seemed to be a disparity between the Whigs' pretence of piety and their impious or immoral behaviour; between their pretence to uphold the Church and activity that seemed to undermine its core values; and between their political ideology of freedom and their private tyrannies. Exposing such vice and hypocrisy was therefore a public duty. But as a result of this process, the nature of vice and hypocrisy was also being destabilized and reformulated. If the vice of a fellow partisan had to be forgiven for political reasons, did the vice cease to matter? Or, more radically in the formula of Bernard de Mandeville, could private vice in fact be public virtue? In a poem first published in 1705 and subsequently revised over the next ten years into a provocative tract, Mandeville argued that private vice was actually what oiled the wheels of a burgeoning market economy: the indulgence of vice employed many, either in producing luxury goods or in the services that their enjoyment demanded.[23] But for vice to be virtuous, many of the Church's teachings against self-indulgence and against the pursuit of self-interest had to be challenged.

These larger national shifts and tensions are again evident in the local context. The Cowpers and the Hertford Quakers illustrate the ways in which shifts in and debates about marriage and sexual morality could lead to familial strife and public scandal. Sarah Stout's ideas about cohabitation, revealed at Spencer's trial, can be placed in the context of a swirling debate among Quakers about marriage that nearly tore Hertford Friends apart, a debate that illustrates the restraints on the Dissenting imagination for social change. Her own inclination to worldly pleasures, conflicting with the strict demands of her faith, seem to have driven her to a state of guilty anxiety and melancholy, perhaps (if Spencer Cowper is believed) even to suicide. The strife among the Quakers was echoed, in different ways, behind the doors of Hertford Castle. Indeed, the Cowpers seem to sustain Lawrence Stone's claim that 'in the period between about 1680 and 1710 the country, both high and low, seems to have lost its moral moorings. Story after story, whether about the making or the break-ing of marriage, provide evidence of an abnormally cynical, merce-nary and predatory ruthlessness about human relationships.'[24] Sir

William Cowper's marriage to Sarah was clearly one in crisis; Spencer married without his mother's consent (and possibly against her wishes), a source of ongoing tension in the family, and may also have preyed on Sarah Stout; and William, whose first marriage turned sour, kept a mistress (who he may also have married bigamously) and was said to have written in defence of polygamy. Even with both 'wives' dead, William continued to act oddly: he married his third wife, Mary Clavering, in secret. What follows is an attempt to explore each of these relationships in turn, since they are all highly revealing of the tensions evident in the institution of marriage and of the challenges to conventional notions of morality.

THE QUAKERS, MARRIAGE, AND MORALITY

By the standards of the day, the Quaker attitude to marriage was highly unusual. Wanting nothing to do with the 'steeple worship' of the established Church, they had abandoned customary forms of marriage entirely. Instead of a minister conducting a marriage, the Quakers merely required a declaration that two Friends had joined— the announcement of cohabitation that Sarah advocated in her letter to Spencer. Of course for most Quakers that decision should be driven entirely by the inner light and not by lust, and should be one approved by the local Quaker community. The Quakers had thus pared marriage down to its most basic form, though to critics it appeared little more than concubinage. There were nevertheless deep tensions even within the Hertford Quakers about marriage and patriarchy; and in 1678 a furious row erupted. The problem was not the Quaker requirement that Friends should only marry Friends—a restriction that may have been one element of Sarah Stout's frustrations twenty years later—but how Friends sought permission to marry. That issue in turn sparked larger questions about how the Quakers organized themselves and whether the leadership could restrict the dictates of any individual's inner light.

In 1678 Quaker leader George Fox recommended that Friends wanting to marry should first seek the approval of the Womens' Meeting before the Mens' Meeting. Fox did not believe in total social as well as religious equality: a woman, he said, should not, like a 'whore', diverge from the instructions of her husband or father, and mothers were to instruct their children 'in virtue, in holynesse and godlynesse'.[25] But—and this may reflect his own marriage to a woman socially superior to him—his ruling inverted the normal social order and conventions. Fox made things worse by some rather pointed remarks about his Hertford Friends, comments that fused his views on marriage with a dispute, about his authority over the Quaker movement, that had been rumbling for most of the 1670s. Visiting Hertford in 1678 Fox reproved two of the local Quaker leaders by alleging that 'under a pretence of Liberty of Conscience All manner of Looseness & wickedness would hide it selfe'. He added fuel to the fire by giving an inflammatory example to support his case. He attacked, John Story, who had publicly split from Fox's leadership, claiming that Story allowed 'Whores & Rogues, Drunkards & swearers' to be present at Meetings. The occasion for this alleged immorality had been a 'wedding' at which the couple went 'to drink & eat some cake & cheese'. The groom had also drunk a toast to Story and doffed his hat, crimes which seemed to Fox to smack of wicked old ways of worldly decadence and deference. By linking the Hertford Quakers to Story Fox thus implied that they were disloyal. He had used the marriage question to couple the issue of moral and spiritual decadence with challenges to his own authority. A local storm erupted, in which Fox was supported by Henry Stout who wrote to all Quakers that the new system of regulation on marriage was God's 'heavenly will'. Fox made the whole thing worse by trying to claim that he had never said anything against Story, prompting both sides in the dispute to accuse the other of lying.[26] The matter was only resolved in 1680 when a compromise agreement about permission to marry was reached. Although it was no longer made obligatory to seek permission from the Women's Meeting, those who wanted were free to do so. At the same time it was decreed that Hertford women who wanted to preach—Mary Stout being chief among them—were to be tolerated without 'interruption, molestation or reflection upon them'.[27]

The dispute—which must have overshadowed Sarah Stout's formative years—showed how a debate over marriage had the capacity to act as a lightning rod for matters of authority, freedom of conscience, the role of women, and morality. It was this last issue that increasingly preoccupied Quakers during Sarah Stout's lifetime, in part because the first generation grew worried that the second lacked their spiritual fire. The Quaker youth seemed vulnerable to worldly snares and hence to immorality.

John Crook, a respected Quaker elder who was by the late 1690s living in Hertford, issued a printed letter from there to 'All that

Profess the Light', in which he attacked worldly immorality.[28] Having outlined the spiritual struggle that he had himself gone through—'earthquakes in the heart', in his memorable phrase—he went on to advise the Quaker youth to examine themselves to see if they had come by their faith only by the dead hand of tradition. In recent times, he noted, 'many come amongst us, that in outward appearance may seem to be of us ... but walk as if the gate of entrance into the Truth, was grown wider, and the Path and the Way thereof, broader than it was at the beginning'. He therefore condemned worldliness: the only 'comely attire' and 'beautiful garments' that Friends needed were ones of spirituality and they could do without perfumes and pleasant walks. In a postscript, added at Hertford on 11 September 1696, he warned them to 'take heed of the Friendship of this World, lest you become Guilty of Spiritual Whoredom and Adultery before you are aware of it'.[29] The year before Sarah's death he published another letter from Hertford, urging Quakers to 'learn well the Doctrine of Self-denial'.[30]

Yet self-denial in 1698 was a very hard thing for second-generation Quaker Sarah Stout. She was wealthy and her money and status brought her constant temptation. By the turn of the seventeenth century Britain's trade was booming, with increasing imports to London of fine silks and calicoes from India. Sarah frequented a local shop that sold such new 'India goods' and bought some 'for a Gown', though she failed to have it made up, telling the shopkeeper 'I believe I shall never live to wear it.' How could she, when the Quakers adopted simple clothing? And did she really receive 'some songs' from London from an admirer, as was claimed at the trial? Her family later denied that she had ever sung a song in her life, and Quakers believed that music stole hearts from God. But it is not unlikely that Sarah was precisely the sort of young woman who worried Crook. We learn, from testimony at the trial, that she 'did not love to keep company with Quakers', and entertained friends at night in the summer house in the Stout's garden 'now and then with a bottle of wine'. After her guests had left she 'us'd to make her Mother believe that she went to Bed' but instead crept out through the garden and could be gone all night. She also visited London where a dazzling array of pleasures was on offer.

All the evidence suggests that she was fighting an internal struggle between the moral code of the Quakers and the temptations of the world. Certainly she found herself harangued for her worldliness by a Quaker preacher. When Theophilus Green, who had been a servant in

Oliver Cromwell's house with Sarah's mother, preached in Hertford he 'directed his Discourse to her, and exasperated her at that rate, that she had thoughts of seeing no body again; and said, she took it heinously ill to be so us'd'. Green warned her not to 'fall inwardly' away from God.[31] No wonder, according to William Cowper's wife Judith, Sarah sometimes 'seem'd to dislike her' religion. Paradoxically then, Quakerism was both liberating for women (as Mary Stout's preaching and capacity to pursue the law shows) but also, in worldly ways, restrictive. Sarah was not the only young Quaker woman to feel constrained. In January 1683 Sarah Russell of Chalfont St Peter, in neighbouring Buckinghamshire, admitted that although she had attended Women's Meeetings and resolved not to marry an unsuitable man, her resolution had failed her. After her marriage she was 'ashamed to look on' any of her Friends and, repentant, 'desired with tears that Friends might not cast her off'.[32] The price of straining to conform to Quaker morality seems to have been, in some cases, anguish and guilt; it may possibly, for Sarah Stout, have been suicide.

SARAH COWPER AND THE SLAVERY OF MARRIAGE

If we turn from the Quakers to the Church of England, and from the Stouts to the Cowpers, we find a similar tale of tensions over marriage and morality, though they were different ones. Tensions are abundantly evident in the pages of Sarah Cowper's diary, which runs from the time of the appeal against her son Spencer's acquittal, through to 1716, the second year of George I's reign. The diary is important in a number of ways. First, it chronicles the very real strains within a late seventeenth-century marriage, the type of evidence normally only obtainable in divorce proceedings, and which, since this marriage remained outwardly intact, would otherwise have been lost. The details about Sarah's mistreatment by her husband highlight the helplessness that many women must have felt trapped within a loveless marriage. Second, the language Sarah used to describe Sir William Cowper's mistreatment of her was highly politicized, echoing many of the keywords used in the Cowpers' Whig ideology. By deploying it, she not only sought to expose Sir William's hypocrisy but also the real limitations in the revolutionary ideology that he espoused, limitations that help to explain why the Revolution of 1688–9 did not translate into a more socially radical revolution and hence why, for all its language of freedom and rights, Enlightenment writers remained deeply ambivalent about the subordination of women. Sarah's language can be linked to that of female authors who were re-examining the inequalities of marriage, including Mary Astell who has been hailed as a 'proto-feminist'. Like Sarah Cowper, Mary Astell's religious beliefs infused her attitudes to politics and the relationship between the sexes, further confirmation of the need to see the interconnections between religion and gender.

Sarah Cowper was not an easy person to live with. She was huffy, sanctimonious, and sometimes paranoid and withdrawn. She confessed to having 'a Natural Bitterness and Severity'.[33] But the entries in her diary make it difficult not to sympathize with her plight, for to describe Sarah's relationship with Sir William as bad would be an understatement. If she was difficult, he was impossible. 'I do from my Soul believe him to be the most difficult humour to live at Ease with this world ever afforded', she lamented shortly after she began the diary.[34] In 1702 she made the painful calculation that she had lived with Sir William 'almost 14000 daies and from the bottom of my Soul do believe I never past one without Something to be forgiven him'.[35] Three years later she concluded, 'Never met two more Averse than we in Humour, passions, and Affections: our Reason and Sense, Religion or Morals agree not.' They bickered constantly and she thought that 'his Tongue Cuts like a Sharp Razor'.[36] The marriage seemed without much love at all. When in 1701 she wrote a letter to Sir William (her first ever!) she found herself at a loss how to sign off: 'The Common form of Words y^r loving, Affectionate etc I omitted, and said y^r most ffaithfull Consort, w^c Sure I am was perfectly true.'[37] Things came to a head in 1702 when she refused to accompany Sir William to Hertford for the summer, 'the first time (I may truly say) that ever I design'd to Contradict his Will'. Their separation brought two more letters from Sir William which totally perplexed her. Absence, or a fear that a total breach was imminent, seemed to have made him temporarily contrite, for one letter was 'fraught with kind expressions' and the other protested that he was sensible of his great faults, that he had 'failed very much' in showing her 'good Intentions', but that he 'never Did or Spoke any thing Designedly to Disturb' her peace or quiet.[38]

At first glance, then, Sir William and Sarah seemed to live out *The Unhappy Marriage* on the right-hand side of Figure 4.1, published in about 1690 as a satire on marital discord. Certainly the 'heavy burden' of matrimony was increased, as in the image, by the disagreements between husband and wife. On closer examination, however,

Figure 4.1 The political overtones of the image are suggested by the physical similarity of the couple in 'The Happy Marriage', on the left, to King William and Mary, and by the subtitle indicating that the state was happy when hearts were united.

the print depicts another stereotype: the shrewish wife or scold who beats or chastizes her husband, usurps his place (swapping his wig for her cap) and is devilishly jealous. Sarah certainly reproved her husband, and clearly Sir William did believe her tongue was too sharp; but she was always successfully subordinated by him, by threat of force if not by word. During one quarrel (provoked by her waking him too early) 'He swore—damn me for a Bitch I did hector him, he wou'd fell me to the ground.' In all their disputes, it was usually Sir William's will that prevailed, even when this meant humiliating Sarah. Indeed, Sir William seems to have wanted her to behave like the submissive wife depicted on the left of the image, who 'serves' her spouse to 'give him contentment'. The print was typical of a mass of advice literature that provided an idealized version of how women should behave. In 1701 Sarah came across such a book outlining 'the Duty of Wives'. She reflected that she had 'discharg'd the Negative part punctually well, not being guilty of any thing forbidden', but added that she had not been able to perform 'some positives such as

Education of Children, governing the House and Servants' because that power had been 'taken from me by him who shou'd have invested me with it'.[39] She was all too aware of the disparity between the ideal and reality.

Besides an incompatibility of temperament, Sir William and Sarah held very different views about household government. Gentry wives could exercise considerable authority within the house, particularly over servants; but Sir William took all this on himself and, to Sarah's intense annoyance, then failed (at least in her eyes) to exercise proper oversight. This was, she complained, one 'never-failing subject of our disagreement'.[40] She could 'by no means be reckon'd Mistress of the Family, but...one beset with a small Mobb of disorderly Wretches' who passed as servants.[41] Sir William failed to punish what Sarah saw as the misbehaviour of their servants, on one occasion re-employing a coachman she had dismissed. When it came to the servants, in her view, Sir William gave liberty, even licence. There were times when she felt physically threatened by them, convinced that they were trying to poison her. Indeed, she thought her 'ill-governed Family' (family here meaning the household as a whole) was 'an Emblem of Hell'.[42] She had 'a House and Servants without Authority or Command'.[43] In resenting what she saw as her servants' insubordination she was not alone. Mary Clarke, wife of another Whig MP, complained in 1696 that 'the most troublesome and vexatious parts of my life hitherto have been occasioned by the turbulent spirits and ungrateful temper of servants, who are designed and thought to be kept for ones ease, but it does not prove so to us in this ungrateful age'.[44] A print depicting the 'AGES RARITY or the Emblem of a Good SERVANT' (1682) showed what perhaps both Mary Clarke and Sarah Cowper held to be the ideal servant: a man with long ears for hearing orders but with a bridled mouth making him incapable of answering back. Defoe was still puzzling over the 'insolence and unsufferable Behaviour of SERVANTS' in 1724.[45] Chafing at living out one stereotypical ideal, that of the good and submissive wife, Sarah nevertheless hankered after the stereotype of the submissive and obedient servant, an irony that eluded her.

The ideal of marriage and an orderly, hierarchical household is nicely set out in another print from 1685, *The Husband's Instructions*, depicting the male head of the household, surrounded on one side by his seated (and hence important but submissive) wife, his family and his servants. The text below the image enlarges on the respect that the servants owed their master, and which the wife owed the husband. A good wife was to be mild, never upbraiding her spouse, but she in turn ruled over her children. The print also shows the way in which such relationships were politicized. 'A Family well Govern'd is like a Kingdom well Rul'd', proclaims the motto above the master's head; and his love and care of his children are compared to 'that of the KING's over his People'. Good servants and children were good subjects. The timing of the print's publication is not coincidental. In 1680 Sir Robert Filmer's *Patriarcha* set out the patriarchal nature of political authority and the work was republished in 1685. Filmer argued that God had given Adam lordship over the world and that his power had been passed down through the patriarchs to kings. He also argued that political inequality was *natural*. This integration of political, gendered, and social authority took very literally the time-honoured metaphor of the king as the father of the nation. For Filmer, the kingdom and the household were as one and natural and patriarchal subordination worked hand in hand.

Filmer had written his tract in order to counter the challenges to royal power in the reign of Charles I. The publication of his work almost half a century later was testimony to how useful the doctrine was to the High Church Tories who sought to resist Whig attempts to bar or unseat the Catholic James from the throne. If James was a divinely appointed and natural patriarch, then the Whigs had no right seeking to remove his authority. To do so would be to overturn the natural and divine order.

Social and familial relations had of course always been political; but Filmer's work threatened to take their politicization to a new height and the Whigs got to work refuting Filmer's political and religious arguments. Both John Locke, England's most important early Enlightenment philosopher, and Algernon Sidney did so, the latter losing his head in 1683 for what he said in his manuscript attack on Filmer. But, in refuting Filmer's ideology the Whigs had also necessarily to engage with the social implications of their critique, for if they denied that there was the equation between household government and kingly authority, as indeed they did, then they had to explain why it was that fathers still exercised authority over children and households, and indeed why the gentleman could claim the profits of his servants' labour. Moreover, by deploying the notion of a contract to legitimize the limited transfer of power from citizen to ruler, Whigs also had to explain the limits to the rule they enjoyed over wives to whom they were similarly contracted. Whig theorists, such as Locke and his friend James Tyrrell, did indeed allow women greater autonomy because, as Tyrrell put it, even after a marriage contract the wife 'never so absolutely submitted her will to his, as not to reserve to her self the faculty of a rational woman'. But what, then, were the boundaries of female liberty?

One answer to this knotty problem was, for the Whigs, to be found in the idea of property. One reason for disliking Filmer's patriarchalism had been that it seemed to make individual property rights vulnerable to the patriarchal monarch who had 'dominion' over all. The Whigs, on the other hand, wanted to assert the legal right to property; it is significant that William of Orange flew a banner proclaiming 'Liberty and Property' when he sailed for England in 1688. So, the Whigs argued, if property rights were to be upheld, then conventional marriage and household structures had to prevail. In England at this time married women could not legally hold property. If women were given sexual freedom, the inheritance of property would also be thrown into turmoil, for the paternity of children would be in doubt. Besides, unlike the type of power monarchs exercised over subjects, parents did have a *natural* power over their children, Locke argued, until reason grew sufficiently strong in them for them to act in their own right. Property and reason, two Whig rallying cries, justified political revolution, but also, when buttressed by constraints of nature and contract, the continuing subordination of women and children, curbing that other revolution principle of liberty from slavery.[46]

Nevertheless, the anti-patriarchal Whig arguments did give critics of male tyranny a highly charged and evocative vocabulary in which to express themselves. Sarah Cowper was all too aware of this, regarding it as hypocrisy in her husband that he did not extend his political beliefs further than it suited his interests. She duly turned the political language of 'slavery', used by the Whigs in their ideological challenge to the arbitrary rule of the Stuarts, against Sir William. In other words, although the Whigs seldom took advantage of the rethinking of the nature of social and gender subordination made possible by their refutation of Filmer and the Stuart doctrine of patriarchalism, they did create a language through which the perceived abuse of social and gendered authority could be castigated and reproved, a language that it was difficult to refute without provoking the accusation of hypocrisy.

Sarah used politicized language to describe her husband. She called him 'imperious' and noted the discrepancy between how he treated her and his political and religious views: 'Tis marvellous to hear him talk how much he is for Liberty... when at the same time there is not a more absolute Tryant', she fumed. Her application of Whig political language to her own case, and her mixing of the public and private realms, is also evident in her reflection on the election of a new Speaker of the House of Commons in 1701, which had gone against the king's wishes:

> To have a right and Title to power and Government without the Exercise is a hardship and greivance Equal to Slavery. I Speak it from Experience in the low and little Sphere I move in as a Wife and Mistress, where Servants presume to use me with the utmost Contempt of my Authority which I must endure without hope of redress.[47]

Sarah claimed that she had been 'kept as a Concubine not a Wife', since whereas the latter administered the affairs of a family, a concubine was 'not to meddle with them', a view perhaps reinforced by Sir William calling her a whore.[48] The idea that she had been enslaved and the consequent politicization of her thoughts about her own domestic relations are again apparent in a comment in 1702, when musing on a book she had been sent. *The Several Orations of Demosthenes to Encourage the Athenians to Oppose the Exorbitant power of Philip of Macedon* (1702) was intended to rouse England to oppose French power when war broke out again that year but Sarah's reaction was to apply the political lesson to her own private circumstances: 'a prospect of Slavery is less formidable to mee, who have all my daies lived a Slave. For the definition of that I take to be, one who is oppressd by a Tyrannick power, and Arbitrary Will Contrary to Reason and just Government. Now I have suffer'd so much from that, as come what will, it can scarce be worse with mee.'[49] Not surprisingly, after Sir William's death in 1706, she forbade herself to remarry, penning a reminder in her diary: 'Lead your Life in Freedom and Liberty, and throw not your Self into Slavery.'[50] She described her widowhood as 'a state of Liberty'.[51] Yet Sarah was no feminist. She had little conception of the slavery of women in general but rather of the miseries of her own particular condition, and she accepted her fate with Christian fortitude rather than rejecting it entirely.[52] For sure, the long periods she spent alone with her books were a cry against her condition, but they were a strangled, internalized form of protest.

Sarah's politicized language echoed that of Mary Astell, extracts of whose *Some Reflections upon Marriage* (1700) Sarah copied into her diary. Astell was musing on the disastrous marriage of the duchess of Mazarin, who had become Charles II's mistress; and lamented the physical, mental, and cultural restrictions on women trapped in unhappy marriages. Astell, too, talked of women being enslaved by men and saw the hypocrisy of the Whig position, as epitomized by the Whig hero John Milton, who had argued against monarchical tyranny but who had tyrannized his wife: 'how much soever Arbitrary Power may be dislik'd on a Throne, Not *Milton* himself wou'd cry up Liberty to poor *Female Slaves*, or plead for the Lawfulness of Resisting a Private Tyranny'. Thus the Whigs allowed for a right of resistance against a tyrant on the throne but not a tyrant in the house. Through such comments it is possible to see how the rhetoric of slavery could be turned more systematically to question the subordination of women. Judith Drake's *Essay in Defence of the Female Sex* (1696) did generalize the tyranny of men over women and compared the condition of the latter to the 'Negroes in our Western Plantations', whose numbers were at this time increasing enormously, an analogy that was to be repeated almost a century later in Mary Wollstonecraft's more famous *Vindication of the Rights of Women* (1792).[53]

Astell and Sarah Cowper, unlike Wollstonecraft's secular and even anticlerical outlook, were united by a deep sense of allegiance to the Church of England, even if both (but especially Sarah) felt reservations about the nature of its leadership. For them, defending either themselves or women more generally from the misogyny of men was couched within, even empowered by, their religiosity. This was also true of Mary Chudleigh who wrote *The Female Advocate* (1700) to refute a wedding sermon given by a Nonconformist minister, John Sprint, who had sought to curb 'imperious wives' by stressing their subordination to their husbands and their natural inferiority.[54] Chudleigh saw Sprint as 'as an Instrument of Oppression and Tyranny' who sought to preach women 'into Slavery and Chains' and define obedience as 'servile Subjection'. Using the word 'slave' a dozen times she argued that 'Tho Women are for the Comfort and Benefit of Men, yet that's no reason why they should be their most obedient Slaves and Vassals.' She utterly condemned Sprint's enslavement of wives: 'This is a Tyranny, I think, that extends farther than the most absolute Monarchs in the World.'[55] As with much of the early Enlightenment, innovative thinking could occur within what seems a traditionally religious framework rather than a rejection of its restrictions.

Astell and Cowper—and indeed many Quaker authors—were also linked by a belief in the importance of education or learning as a means of carving out a legitimate role for women. Indeed they were part of a wider late seventeenth-century concern to extend female education, evident in the writing of others such as Damaris Masham,

Bathsua Makin, and Hannah Woolley. Astell asserted intellectual equality, advocating a form of Protestant nunnery that could nurture the minds and souls of women who chose not to marry. For such women, as for many other Anglicans, education more generally was part of a campaign to instil Christian morality at a time when the Church was under attack; for Dissenters, such as the Quakers, education was also a means to keep their followers firm. There is a good deal of truth in the observation that 'Seventeenth-century pro-woman writings emerge less as declarations for female individualism, and more as manifestos for a national reformation in morals and manners.'[56] It is this wider concern, shared by the Churchmen, that explains the prominence of Hertford Tories in the administration of Hertford school (no doubt sharpened for the Dimsdale faction by a desire to ensure that young minds were not led astray by Dissenters) as well as Sarah Cowper's charitable donations to it. Indeed, the town built a huge and imposing new 'blue coat' school, where there was provision for girls' education as well as boys.

Even so, religion was not the only factor shaping ideas about gender and education. Judith Drake seems to have shared the High Church views of Astell and of her husband, the polemicist Dr James Drake, who was prosecuted in 1705 for lamenting the death of the Church of England at the hand of Dissenters.[57] Certainly religion was important to her, for her belief that 'all Souls are equal, and alike' nourished her defence of women. Yet Drake stated at the outset that she did not intend to make a religious argument in defence of women and offered a far more secular argument than Astell, one based on ideas about the nature of the human mind and the power of women to civilize men through their sociability. Thus whereas Astell disputed John Locke's *political* ideas, Drake took advantage of his *philosophical* argument that 'there are no innate Ideas, but that all the Notions we have are deriv'd from our external Senses, either immediately or by Reflexion'. From this, she believed, it followed that only 'the tyranny of custom' had produced inequality between the sexes. She also drew on science, no doubt influenced by the work of her doctor husband. Anatomy, she argued, showed that between the sexes 'there is no Difference in the Organization of those Parts which have any Relation to, or Influence over, the Minds'. Indeed, she believed men's limited horizons were in part the result of their having imbibed useless learning from the Greeks and Romans. Better education was to be had, she thought, in the informal world of female sociability. For, in the company of women, men had to present good manners and civility, rather than the bitter hostility they reserved for the political arena. Thus whereas Sarah Cowper frequently lamented in her diary that she found polite society rather nauseous because the conversation she encountered was so petty, bitchy or insincere, Drake thought female conversation was civilizing—an idea at the heart of many of the eighteenth-century Parisian salons. She did not press a case for women being involved in politics, though her own intervention could be seen as such; rather that the non-political nature of women could moderate the political passions of men.

The women discussed here indicate that there was no neat correlation between Whig political views about liberty and the adoption of ideas that gave greater freedom of action to women. Rather, Sarah Cowper, Mary Astell, and Judith Drake seem united by a devotion to the Church. It is possible to see how the retreat from conflict adopted by Sarah Cowper, the women's intellectual refuge advocated by Astell and the civilizing nature of Drake's women, for all their shared politicized language of freedom from tyranny and assertion of equality, did not break free of patriarchalism, since that was not really their objective. Undoubtedly the ferment of political and religious ideas made available to them a language in which to express their sense of constraint; but the emancipation they desired was often very personal and limited and although they were all politically minded they did not seek female entry into party politics. All this, however, contrasts markedly with the very political use made by one woman of William Cowper's unusual marriages.

WILL BIGAMY

Early in 1710 Jonathan Swift's Tory periodical *The Examiner* nicknamed Cowper 'Will Bigamy'. When defending his brother Spencer at the latter's murder trial in 1699, William Cowper was indeed seemingly married to two women. He had married Judith Booth in 1686 after a clandestine courtship, and for a while the relationship seems to have been successful. A decade later, however, things had turned sour. Despite bringing £5,000 to the marriage (swallowed up by the family's debts) Judith had to live with William's parents because of their straitened finances, and relations between Judith and her mother-in-law Sarah Cowper were often strained. Sarah blamed Judith's 'bitter resentments' for spoiling her relationship with her favourite son.[58] And as William's legal career took off he spent more time away from home. Perhaps resentful of her husband's freedom, Judith began to voice suspicions about what William was doing with it. In 1695 he complained that she was 'importunate' and he clearly resented her demand that he be 'accountable' for his time, a request which he regarded as an intrusion on his 'reasonable liberty'.[59] But Judith's suspicions were well founded. It is quite possible that by then he had already begun his affair with Elizabeth Culling, the daughter of one of the Hertford Whigs, since she bore him a son in 1697 and a daughter three years later. And some sort of marriage ceremony may have taken place.

At first sight, William's unorthodox marriage seems to suggest an alternative, less shackled way of thinking about morality and sexuality, implying a much more self-conscious pursuit of freedom from convention. William might thus be said to exemplify the fashionable male sexual freedom of the later Stuart period, a muscular masculinity that seemed to have broken free of Puritan shackles. Exploring whether this was really the case requires us to piece together his actions and views, and relate them to a wider context. At the end of this process Cowper's dramatic break with convention will appear much less revolutionary than it initially appears; indeed, it was probably his Tory satirist, Delarivier Manley, who was genuinely more mould-breaking. Nevertheless, Cowper's double marriage and the scandal it provoked allow us to explore the ambiguous, uncertain, and seemingly fragile morals of the day. The debates that his case bring together—about sexual freedom outside of a conventionally monogamous marriage, about libertinism, and about freethinking— were to resound through much of the Enlightenment. Indeed, it is probably not coincidental that one of the most furious debates in the eighteenth century about the legitimacy of polygamy was sparked by Martin Madan, who had married Spencer Cowper's daughter.

The best contemporary introduction to William Cowper's alleged bigamy was the scandal novel, *The New Atalantis*, written by Delarivier Manley, part of which has already been quoted in relation to Spencer Cowper's story. Manley began her account by archly praising William's natural abilities:

> His memory was good, so was his luck; to these were joined a great deal of wit, a volubility of tongue, ready sentiments and a most plausible address, religion in pretence, none in reality. He held it lawful for a man to attain by any methods, whether pleasure or riches. He was violent in the pursuit of both, quitting his interest for nothing but pleasure and his pleasure for nothing but interest.

Though he 'lived civilly' with his wife, Manley suggested, he really hated her and his amorous intentions soon focused on the 'very agreeable' Elizabeth, who lived in the Cowper household as a companion for Judith. Elizabeth was, Manley alleged, virtuous and pious, and accordingly 'set a value upon her chastity'; she had nothing of 'an amorous constitution, nothing of the native coquet; all was regular, all was cool and innocent'. So when William 'resolved to proceed in undermining that seemingly invincible chastity' he had to use all his cunning and charm. Had he been truly in love with her, she suggested, he would have desisted; but William was 'a friend to none but himself', the epitome of a self-seeking, duplicitous and callous Whig. He found himself desperate to have her:

> [Talking] every day with a young handsome woman was impossible for him to do without desiring of her. The little freedoms that were permitted, inflamed him. He could not pass her without trembling; when he did but touch her hand, his blood flushed in his face. Sometimes he would ravish a kiss in the way of play, but then he was lost in pleasure. He took all occasions for those pretty liberties.

Elizabeth was flattered by his attentions. She 'thought her self obliged by these distinctions; they even created a sort of gratitude, which warmed it self to tenderness. She was pleased to see, to hear him; his company seemed more diverting than others. She knew no harm in it, she thought no harm.'

William's passion was brought to a head when a rival appeared on the scene. According to Manley's account, Elizabeth and her young suitor were going with Judith and Sarah Cowper to the opera—a form of entertainment that had only recently become popular in London—when William, who had not been expected to go because he had work to do, leapt into the carriage, squeezed himself next to Elizabeth and 'without knowing what he did, pressed her knees with his, till he pained her'. Surprised but submissive, Elizabeth said nothing:

> The story of the opera chanced to be of a woman that had married a second husband, her first yet alive, although unknown to her...The play was wrought up with all the natural artifice of a good poet. [Elizabeth] who did not often see such representations, became extremely moved at this. Her young breasts heaved with sorrow, the tears filled her eyes.

This outburst of sympathy encouraged William and gave him an opportunity to woo his mistress under the eyes of his wife. For while Judith mocked the stage heroine's 'sensibility of the soul', William praised it, an early enthusiasm for the sensibility more associated with much later in the eighteenth century. On the journey back home, he again ensured that he pressed himself against Elizabeth and at supper the subject of conversation turned to the plot of what they had just seen. Judith argued that the stage heroine had been right to kill herself because "twas impossible she should live without being infamous and consequently detesting her self'. But William took a very different and bold view. Using all his barrister eloquence he began to justify 'the lawfulness of double marriages'. He admitted that:

> in all ages, women had been appropriated: that, for the benefit and distinction of children, with other necessary occurrences, polygamy had been justly denied the sex since the coldness of their constitutions, the length of time they carried their children and other incidents seemed to declare against them; but for a man who possessed an uninterrupted capacity of propagating the species and must necessarily find all the inconveniencies above-mentioned in any one wife, the law of nature, as well as the custom of many nations and most religions, seemed to declare for him.

William (according to Manley) argued that a barren wife should yield to a fertile husband's second marriage, and that the Jews of the Old Testament 'not only indulged plurality of wives but an unlimited use of concubinage'. Jacob, after all, had twelve sons by two wives and two concubines. Indeed, 'the Turks and all the people of the world but the Europeans still preserved the privilege'. And then came his masterstroke: countries that tolerated polygamy and concubinage were in fact *more moral* than Europe: 'their manners in all things are less adulterated than ours, their veracity, morality, and habit of living less corrupted: that, in pretending to reform their abuses, Europe had only refined their vices'. This notion was to be the central theme of Montesquieu's infamous *Lettres Persanes* (1721), which held up the Persian harem against the vices of Europe. And whilst (in Manley's reconstruction) William went on to condemn promiscuity, he argued that if more than one woman was 'appropriated to one man, they were so far from transgressing, that they but fulfilled the law of nature'. Indeed 'a young lady ought never to oppose those good inclinations she might find in her self towards a married man because she was gratifying at one time both her passion and her duty'.

Yielding at last to his argument, Elizabeth at last 'consented to marry him', for while she 'could admit of polygamy', she 'would not hear a

Figure 4.2 William Cowper in 1695.

word of concubinage'. William hurriedly arranged a mock marriage, in which (Manley alleged) Spencer Cowper dressed up as a French protestant minister—a Huguenot—disguising himself further with a wig and 'speaking à la Française' with plum stones in his mouth, in order to conduct the bogus and secret ceremony. Spencer then disappeared in a coach, leaving his brother with his second 'wife'.

One night some time later Judith Cowper caught her husband kissing Elizabeth, who 'proved with child'. Understandably outraged, Judith 'lost her usual moderation' and gave vent to 'tears, grief, rage, reproaches'. But rather than give her up, William gave Elizabeth her own house where she could have the baby and where he could visit her without hindrance. Elizabeth, for her part, thoroughly convinced that polygamy was lawful, seemed unperturbed. Indeed she bore William another child. Not that two women were sufficient, Manley claimed; for William contracted a venereal disease from one of his other women, and passed it on both to Elizabeth and Judith. His inconstancy broke both women's hearts; indeed, the shock and the disease killed first Elizabeth and then, later, Judith. William now appeared to show remorse, though Manley doubted whether it was genuine, for her death 'left him at full liberty to pursue without control his amours and his ambition'. This 'wandering star' was only fixed by his third wife, Mary.

Manley's novel did contain a good deal of truth about William, as both his mother Sarah Cowper and his daughter (another Sarah) reluctantly conceded in their diaries after they had read it. In July 1709, very soon after its first publication, William's mother copied out large sections of Manley's story relating to both her sons, concluding that although there was 'more Scandalous Stuff than I can believe to be True; yet withall so much as may justly be acknowledg'd the due punishment of those that Do Ill'.[60] She recognized that Manley had embellished the story—'the Main Matter is but Old Dirt grown So Dry it may not Stick if it be not Mixt with New Stuff'—and was inclined herself to put most of the blame on 'Betty', who had had a 'Soul harden'd in Wickedness' and 'an impudent Face of Brass' to live in such 'open adultery', claim to be William's wife and bear him children. Betty's motto, she noted, was that 'every one had some Fault and she had but one'; but Sarah thought that the fault of 'robbing another woman of her Hus[band]' was 'a Swinger'.[61] And when Elizabeth died in November 1703 Sarah was shocked that she had been buried 'Close by the Ewe tree' in the parish Churchyard 'for which Fancy I can imagine no other reason unless it be to Suggest this Motto, Where I lost my Virginity I lay my Body'.[62]

William's daughter, Sarah, reading Manley's tale some twenty years later, also had to admit that the stories had 'some foundation of truth'. She was nevertheless more inclined to point out Manley's errors than her grandmother had been and tried, even in her diary, to vindicate her father. He had never tricked Elizabeth with a false marriage ceremony, Sarah claimed, and Manley's allegation that her father lacked religion was wrong: he 'had a great deal of Religion & the highest veneration for Vertue of every kind'.[63] She also claimed that her father had been punished for his youthful indiscretion by the fate of his two illegitimate children by Elizabeth Culling.

It is true that both offspring had led wayward lives and caused their father pain.[64] William's relationship with his illegitimate son, 'Bill' Culling, had been strained, as a dream that he recorded and sent William shows. In it (and surely also in reality), Bill lived the life of a rake, indulging in 'swearing, whoring, Drinking & all manner of vice'; but a vision, later identified as personifying both 'Discretion' and his father, tried, unsuccessfully, to divert him to a more virtuous life. Although in the dream Bill 'abused' the vision and turned away from it to resume his idle life, he did eventually see the error of his way and by the end of the dream was put back on the path of good behaviour. Whether that was wish-fulfilment is not known. Certainly Bill had his own illegitimate son, to whom he left money in his will, suggesting that a proclivity to lust was in the genes. Mary Culling, William's illegitimate daughter, seems to bear this out. In 1720 she ran off with a ne'er-do-well, despite assuring her father that she would never marry secretly without his permission. Perhaps she knew too much of her father's story for his remonstrating to carry much weight. We know all this because letters from both children remain among William's papers; it is as though both he and posterity needed a permanent reminder of his earlier transgressions.

William's scandal was public knowledge. William's mother noted the publication of Daniel Defoe's poem *Reformation of Manners* (1702), which included an attack on William's bigamy.[65] More devastating in the local context, a 1697 satire of the Cowpers used William's sexual immorality to try to loosen his family's electoral grip over the Dissenters in Hertford. It was clear that the Tories wanted to depict the Cowpers as unfit to serve as the town's MPs, not least because they were libertines. Sir William was described as a 'burning letcher' who thrust his sexuality on the town. A Quaker (a thinly disguised Henry Stout) and other Dissenters who gathered for the fictional conversation were shocked by the birth of William's illegitimate child and Sir William's glorying in his son's 'gallantry'. The child was said to have caused a breach between William and his mother, and between William and his wife who was said to be furious: 'she frets, storms, teares off her hair; is in that Rage and Fury, as if newly put into Bedlam'. The pamphlet also suggests that Culling's family deeply resented William's unorthodox relationship with Elizabeth, even to the extent of threatening Sir William with a duel and his son with prosecution. A mock charge was drawn up:

That the Eldest Son of a Baronet, a Man in the sacred Bonds of Wedlock, a Learned Counsellor, a grave Senator, a Sworn Friend, a pretender to all Virtue; suspected of no ill or base design &c But being a true Chip o' th'old Block, a Lewd Young Fellow, of Spruce, Natural Parts, innocent as a Serpent; Forgetting all Friendship, Fidelity and Religion; Not having the Fear of God before his Eyes; instigated by his own Carnal Inclination, did either in Hertfordshire, Yorkshire or at London, Insinuate, Court, Delude, Intice, Steal, Carry away and Dishonour a Young, Fair, Beautiful, Lovely Creature, the Top and Glory of her Family, a fit Wife for a Prince, Losing her one of the best Matches in the Country, with a Settlement of a great Estate, and destroying her Vertue, Good Name and Fortune, Which (if true) not all his Wit, Wealth, Honour, Life nor Death can repair.[66]

JUSTIFYING POLYGAMY

Just as there was some truth in Manley's fiction and in the imagined conversation of an election tract, so there may also have been something in the rumour that William defended polygamy. Jonathan Swift suggested that Cowper had drawn up a defence of bigamy 'with intention to publish [it] for the general good'.[67] A manuscript in the British Library, on which someone has written 'probably alluding to Lord Cowper', does indeed provide such a justification.[68] It takes the form of a letter written by a lawyer clearly relishing a difficult brief, in which an outline of a defence of polygamy is offered. The author claimed that he wanted to promote the public good and to force 'all ingenious men to a modest acknowledgement of a vulgar error' in thinking it unlawful. This was done by arguing that marriage, for Protestants at least, was not a sacrament; that polygamy was not incompatible with piety; and that whilst polygamy in women was not to be tolerated, and monogamy might be preferable for men, 'yet Polgyamie is not bad in itself'. There was, it was claimed, no biblical injunction against it and was common practice amongst the Jews and Romans. Yet the authorship of this piece, though uncertain, does not seem to have been Cowper. On the back of the letter, heavily scored out but just legible beneath the ink, is the annotation 'Dr Loftus', presumably Dr Dudley Loftus of Trinity College, Dublin, who Jonathan Swift had also attacked in 1688 as a bigamist.

It is also possible that Martin Madan might have had access to William Cowper's papers when he wrote his lengthy defence of polygamy, *Thelyphthora*, in 1780–1. Madan, an evangelical minister better known today for his role in popularizing Church hymns, was Cowper's nephew-in-law. He was also chaplain of the Lock Hospital for the treatment of venereal disease and he recommended polygamy because he believed it would be better for the many women who found themselves seduced or forced into prostitution. His arguments were similar to those in the British Library manuscript. Thus Madan also insisted that it was only Catholics who believed that marriage was a sacrament; that intercourse therefore joined men and women in marriage; and that the Bible did not condemn polygamy, which was thus a practice 'allowed, owned and even blessed' by God. The condemnation of polygamy, he suggested, was merely human, not divine; it might even be the work of 'SATAN'.

A Protestant argument in favour of polygamy was not new. The early Church reformers had, as Madan suggested, had to rethink the nature of marriage once it had been downgraded from the Catholic sacrament of the medieval period. But as one historian puts it, 'between about 1680 and 1750 the campaign for polygamy was in full swing'.[69] Certainly, if Cowper did not himself pen a defence of polygamy, there were those on the Whig side who did in the late seventeenth and early eighteenth centuries. Charles II's lack of a legitimate heir had played a large part in focusing attention on the issue in the 1670s and early 1680s and Gilbert Burnet, who was to become a bishop after the Revolution of 1688–9, duly wrote a defence of polygamy as a possible solution to the king's marital problems. So too did two men who had served the commonwealth regime of the mid seventeenth century. One, Henry Neville, wrote a satirical fantasy, *The Isle of Pines* (1668), in which one man populates an entire island with four wives. Another, William Lawrence, argued in 1680 that marriage was merely an imposition by a power-hungry Church. His stance was part of the wider hostility to 'priestcraft' that characterized a good deal of Enlightenment thought. Lawrence insisted that 'carnal knowledge and not ceremonies make marriage'.[70] The political problem of Charles's lack of an heir, leaving the Catholic James in line to succeed him on the throne, thus added urgency to a re-examination of the nature of marriage and prompted several Whigs to advocate polygamy.

Such attitudes were thought to go hand in hand with a disregard for religion and morality. In 1696 Charles Leslie, a cleric who was a prolific author for the High Church Tories and a hammer of both Dissenters and deists, wrote *A letter of advice to a friend upon the modern argument of the lawfulness of simple fornication, half-adultery, and polygamy.* These sins, he said, were the result of men 'having their appetites unbridled by any Restraint or Discipline of Religion'. Lust, he argued, was the stubborn Devil in us; and polygamy was the liberation of that Devil. He attacked the 'thin beaux' of his day who covered their ignorance and delusion with 'cobwebs' of reasoning. He particularly disparaged the argument that the Old Testament allowed polygamy, for, he claimed, Christ had restored monogamy. Much the same argument was to be found in another tract published the following year, though its title suggested a hint of salaciousness, *God's judgments against whoring, being an essay towards a general history of it, from the creation of the world.*

That same year, 1697, another cleric, John Butler, scandalized many when he went into print not against polygamy, as a clergyman might have been expected to do, but apparently in favour of it. A decade earlier Butler's wife had refused to sleep with him—alleging cruelty to her and her sons by him—and Butler sought solace in the arms of his maid, Mary Tomkins, claiming he 'had not the gift of continency'. According to his wife's version of events, Butler had already committed adultery with his servant, who bore him four children. Before the case could be heard at an ecclesiastical court Butler published a vindication of his actions in which he claimed that 'honest concubinage' was allowable as a 'case of necessity' when a wife had deserted her husband. He also argued that his own conscience was a good enough judge of his actions and that his behaviour was 'Lawful in the sight of God'. As he warmed to his own defence, he widened his argument into a general defence of polygamy. Again arguing from the evidence of the Old Testament, Butler asserted that 'God did plainly allow of a lawful Concubinage' and that whoring and adultery were far worse sins. It had only been the popish corruption of religion, he argued, that had removed concubinage from the Church's customs. But Butler soon found that the Protestant Church was equally intolerant of his ideas. A London grand jury found him guilty of writing and publishing what 'may prove very destructive to divers Families, if not timely suppress'd'. His case may also have eased the passage of the 1698 Blasphemy Act, since he had also imprudently asked whether Jesus' 'Conception and Birth were stain'd with Fornication or Incontinency, because perform'd out of marriage?'

Butler's case and pamphlet prompted howls of protest from those who sought to shore up the institution of marriage. One cleric, John

Turner wrote a *Discourse on Fornication* (1698) to refute Butler, arguing that fornication was contrary to God's will and that polygamy was unlawful. From fornication, he suggested, men fell 'into Atheism, Profaneness, Blasphemy, and an Universal Scorn, and Contempt of God, and Religion'. He also felt it necessary to add an appendix devoted to attacking the false 'Modern Distinction between Whoredom and Concubinage'.[71] The issue of concubinage was also taken up directly in another, anonymous, response to Butler, *Concubinage and Poligamy Disprov'd* (1698). Butler was accused of writing 'an Apology for the Modish practice of keeping a Miss' and of 'making every man a Judge in his own Cause' irrespective of the restraints of law or of religion. There was not, it was claimed, 'the least Vestige of Concubinage to be found in the New Testament'. The author went on to recommend fasting, praying, cold baths, and bleeding as ways of cooling overheated passions. Butler's proposal that concubinage—legalized mistresses—represented a remedy against whoredom and adultery was condemned as 'ridiculous'; besides its impropriety, the tract noted, it was impractical, for there were not enough women to go round and women in polygamous marriages would remain sexually unfulfilled, thereby pushing them into adultery.[72] Refuting this barrage of criticism, Butler composed a reply, *Explanatory Notes upon a Malicious Libel called Concubinage and Poligamy Disproved* (1698), in which he posed as someone who had been slandered, listing over one hundred lies that had been levelled against him. He did, however, backtrack and claim that he had not justified polygamy per se but only concubinage under necessity, when legal monogamous marriage could not be had.[73]

The 1690s seemed particularly prone to such scandals.[74] In 1693 Mary Stoakes was convicted of marrying two men and the court heard that she had a further two husbands; moreover, she had been convicted on another bigamy charge only six months earlier and had stayed with one husband only a single night. The court judged her 'an idle kind of a Slut', primarily interested in fleecing her husbands for whatever money she could get from them. The same year a shoemaker with seventeen wives was also condemned to death for his crime. And in 1699 a fraudulent faith healer, John Paydon, was convicted of polygamy, his deceit spreading through all areas of his life. But cases of bigamy also seemed rife in Anne's reign in the 1700s. Indeed there were three spectacularly public instances of bigamous or adulterous marriages—the press becoming a powerful means of self-vindication and attack in such cases.

One concerned John Spinke, an apothecary who was well used to going into print, against commercial rivals, to attack their quack remedies for venereal disease and to proclaim his own superior products. In 1711 he found himself having to explain in print, at quite extraordinary length, how he had found himself tricked by the woman he married in 1705. His wife, Elizabeth, had pretended to be the widow of Sir John Williams, claiming to have lived with him eighteen years and to have borne him eight children. But it soon became apparent she had told him a tissue of lies; indeed, she had never been married to Sir John but merely been his mistress, before becoming a London whore, continuing some sort of relationship with her pimp, or 'BUM-Gallant' as Spinke called him, even while she was married. Elizabeth had only promised to reform herself when Spinke threatened to send her to the London lunatic asylum, Bedlam. In 1707 they had tried to make a new start but she was an inveterate liar and matters soon deteriorated again. Within a few days she had begun claiming again that she was a baronet's wife and that Spinke himself kept whores. He in turn claimed that she began to use sorcery against him, carrying his urine to a White Cross Street cunning woman in order to cast spells on him. But when he temporarily imprisoned her in a mad-house, she got her pimp to raise a mob at his door and release her. In October 1707 they drew up articles of agreement to live separately, allowing them to live with whoever they pleased and for two years this rather unusually modern marriage worked. But she then tried pressing him for money and applied for a divorce on the grounds of his cruelty. She was well used to litigation, having been involved in as many as thirteen defamation cases against neighbours. But, hurt financially, Spinkes had had enough. He had her committed, and then published his side of the story.[75] It is a rather sordid tale symptomatic of the callousness and deceptions that seem quite common in marital relations at this time. Spinkes had only married her for her money; and she had in turn exploited him.

This was also the conclusion of the trial in 1705 of Robert Fielding for bigamy. Fielding, nicknamed 'beau' because of his rakish lifestyle and good looks, had already been twice previously married and widowed when he began to court Barbara Palmer, duchess of Cleveland, with an eye to recovering the fortune he had squandered. Cleveland had previously been the mistress of Charles II, during her marriage to the earl of Castlemaine, and consequently was well provided for by royal largesse even though she had been discarded by the king. At the same time as wooing her, the predatory Fielding also had designs on a young, rich widow, Anne Deleau. Fielding sought the help of Charlotte Henrietta Villars, Mrs Deleau's hairdresser, offering her money in return for getting his prize. But Villars tricked Fielding. Knowing that Deleau would not voluntarily consent to marriage with a rake, Villars arranged for a poor widow, Mary Wadsworth to impersonate Deleau; Fielding did not see through the deception and on 9 November 1705 they were married by a Catholic priest. Undeterred by this commitment, Fielding also married Cleveland a fortnight later. Of course, Fielding was furious when he found that his first marriage was a fraud. He beat Mary Wadsworth and threatened Villars not to say anything about the marriage. But Villars went to Cleveland to reveal Fielding's bigamy. Fielding's marriage to Cleveland was in any case in crisis; he had beaten her too, and begun a sexual relationship with her granddaughter. Understandably, Cleveland began proceedings against him, securing his conviction in 1706 and an annulment the following year.

The third case of notorious bigamy was that of Delarivier Manley, who had written the scandal novel against the Cowpers and other Whigs. There was a connection between Manley and Cleveland, both wronged bigamists, since Manley had at one time been taken up by the notoriously fickle Cleveland as a favourite and then dropped. She had her revenge by satirizing Cleveland in the *New Atalantis*, describing her as 'querilous, fierce, loquacious, excessively fond, or infamously rude'. Manley's own story was not much less sensational than that of her former patron. At the age of thirteen, Manley had been persuaded by her cousin and guardian, John Manley, who was twenty-three years her senior, to marry him, bigamously. She later said he was 'so perfect a libertine that he never denied himself the gratifications of any of his passions' and she soon fell pregnant. It was only then, it seemed, that she discovered that he was already married. In order to quieten her conscience about the double marriage John Manley showed her 'a famed piece that was newly wrote in defence of polygamy and concubinage, by one who was afterward Lord Chancellor', in other words the piece said to have been written by Cowper. If that was true, it may certainly explain some of Manley's pique against William. Manley nevertheless left her husband—the year before he became a Tory MP—and joined the house of Lady Cleveland. But Cleveland dismissed Manley, ostensibly for an affair with her son; and in 1696 Manley began an affair with John Tilly, governor of the Fleet Prison, who was nevertheless temporarily inside it because of corruption charges. Tilly was himself already married but this time bigamy was avoided only because the pair simply cohabited for many years (during which time she bore him three children) until Tilly's penury forced him into marrying for money. According to Sarah Cowper, Tilly initially provided for Manley's subsistence but then cut her off, and Manley's antipathy to the Cowpers began when Spencer acted as lawyer for Tilly, who refused to pay her food bill.[76]

Such a plethora of highly visible bigamy cases was more than a manufactured press campaign; it served to underline the case that a moral crisis, affecting marriage and the relations between the sexes, had changed the cultural landscape, from the Puritan repression in the 1650s to one of cynical and manipulative permissiveness. Yet it was this catalogue of scandal that also provided grist to the mill for one of the victims of bigamy, Delarivier Manley. The first volume of her *New Atalantis*, which was full of the immoralities of leading Whig politicians besides Cowper, appeared in May 1709. The title of the work played with Francis Bacon's Utopia, *The New Atlantis*, published posthumously in 1627, perhaps because in it Bacon had described at length a ceremony celebrating the family, the institution now threatened by the voracious appetites of the Whigs.

MANLEY AND *THE NEW ATALANTIS*

Manley's *New Atalantis* needs some explaining. After all, her own private life seemed as scandalous as those she wrote about. Was a bigamist in a good position to condemn another bigamist? Was she not guilty of the same hypocrisy she affected to despise in others? Was there not some irony that the success of the *New Atalantis* enabled her to edit *The Female Tatler*, writing in the persona of Mrs Phoebe Crackenthorpe, which professed to aim at the 'Reformation of Mankind' and to give women conversation 'somewhat above mere Tittle-Tattle' and hence, ironically, to 'stifle a World of Scandal and Detraction'?[77] Why, then, pack her novel with just such material?

Manley might not have been as hypocritical in her treatment of William Cowper as she first seems. She was clearly the victim of a bigamous marriage rather than its instigator. Her case was similar to Elizabeth Culling's not William Cowper's, a parallel she may have felt very keenly, for in her story she made Elizabeth become William's ward, even though she knew that not to be true, presumably because it heightened the resemblance to the breach of trust committed by her own guardian. She was acutely conscious of the double standards that allowed men normally to indulge in acts that they condemned when committed by women. As she put it in her memoirs, 'what is not a crime in men, is scandalous and unpardonable in women'. And unlike Elizabeth Culling, who had been provided for by Cowper, Manley had eventually rejected the bigamous marriage and been forced to make her own very uncomfortable way in the world. Moreover, the hypocrisies of marriage were not her primary theme, for she was writing as a political partisan as well as, perhaps as much as, a woman. The main target of Manley's satire was probably the Marlboroughs, the greedy but highly talented couple who were at the heart of the government and who had ensured Cowper's rise through the legal ranks. William acknowledged the role that Marlborough and his close ally William Godolphin had played in his promotion to Lord Keeper in 1705; and Marlborough and Godolphin were, at the time Manley's story was published, supporting a Whig government that she wanted to undermine. Her Tory inclinations were shortly to qualify her to edit *The Examiner*, the most famous and deeply polemical paper of its day, taking over from Jonathan Swift, who praised her sense and powers of 'invention'. She had become one of the very first women to earn her living as a journalist, but she did so as a partisan in the conflict between the parties.

Manley's politicization of immorality became very apparent when the anti-Whig bias of the *New Atalantis* provoked a Whig writer, John Oldmixon, to write a satire in a similar vein of Tory immorality and hypocrisy.[78] One of those he attacked was Charles Caesar, the Tory who had profited most from Spencer Cowper's trial when he had became MP for Hertford in 1701. Caesar was infamous for his ill-treatment of women, notorious (as Sarah Cowper noted) 'for lying with other men's wives'.[79] He had kept a married woman, Charlotte Pershall, as his mistress and even settled part of his estate on her; but when he grew cold and tried to reclaim it she harassed him with a lawsuit (in league with a 'notorious gamester', James Ashburne, who she repaid with sexual favours). In Oldmixon's hands, Caesar's dissolute life and rampant hypocrisy became useful anti-Tory propaganda to counter the impression created by Manley that immorality was a Whiggish monopoly. Oldmixon attacked Ceasar as 'a Beau without Beauty, a Bully without Courage, an Orator without Eloquence, a Critic without Learning, a Satyrist without Wit' and chronicled his sordid affairs with married women whose husbands he bought off. Turning from gallantry to politics only as a temporary refuge from venereal disease, Oldmixon suggested, Caesar distinguished himself as a Tory MP by his 'Pertness and Forwardness, which were mistaken for boldness and wit'; but, imprisoned in the Tower in 1705 for an outspoken attack on Lord Treasurer Godolphin, he reverted to type, making his jail a venue for 'women and wine'. Oldmixon then recounted graphic details of Caesar's affair with Charlotte Pershall and his simultaneous political wooing of the leader of Hertfordshire High Church Tories, Ralph Freman, whose unattractive sister Mary had a very attractive £20,000 which Caesar coveted. But Caesar's mistress nearly spoiled things when she revealed their affair to Mary Freman, his future wife, and it was only with 'much ado' that Caesar bought off Charlotte to clear the way for his marriage.

Oldmixon no doubt embellished his story, just as Manley had done: the timing of the marriage in his version does not fit the facts, and he exaggerated Mary's wealth. Even so, the rival versions of Whig and Tory hypocrisy that were peddled and embroidered by Manley and Oldmixon were testament to how far scandals had become part of political life and a staple of the press, as well as how easily fiction blended with fact. Where once the indiscretions of monarchs and courtiers had provided political gossip now the newly liberated press exposed the private lives and hypocrisies in the ranks of politicians who were, with the rise in Parliament's importance, more intrinsic to the system of government. Such exposés were ironically made by partisans in order to undermine their rivals, even though (as today) such mud-slinging may have only served to make the public more cynical about *all* those who professed to serve them.

The political implications of Manley's project led to her arrest in October 1709, on the publication of the second volume of the *New Atalantis*. At the same time, the government apprehended John Morphew, an important publisher of Tory propaganda, and the printer John Barber, with whom Manley had been living and who helped produce *The Examiner*. In order to have these two released, Manley admitted her authorship and was released on bail. Even though many restrictions on the press had been lifted in 1695, Manley could, if the government could muster sufficient evidence, face charges of sedition, treason, or libel. She later gave an account of her questioning by the government in her semi-fictional autobiography. Her motive in writing the book, she had told the Whig Secretary of State Lord Sunderland, had been 'to examine the defects and vices of some men who took a delight to impose upon the world by the pretence of public good whilst their true design was only to gratify and advance themselves'.[80] Less plausibly she told the government that any resemblance her characters bore to real people must merely be the result of 'inspiration', to which Sunderland replied that though her inspiration was good 'her writings were stark naught'. Sunderland seems to have suspected that she was working in league with the earl of Peterborough and a Tory clique that aimed to bring down the Whig government.[81] But eventually the government dropped the prosecution. The truth was that her case had been displaced by one of far greater importance and one in which the Cowper brothers would again figure prominently: the trial of Henry Sacheverell.

That trial, the subject of the next chapter, has to be seen in the wider context of moral crisis that has been outlined here. Of course, anxieties over moral decay were nothing new and punctuated the sixteenth and seventeenth centuries. What was new was the structure within which the crisis operated, and which shaped it: the loss of the Church of England's monopoly over the religious culture and of the power of its courts to regulate immorality, an attack on political patriarchalism, the rise of freethinking and libertinism, a free and market-driven press that could expose as well as revel in immorality, and a politicization of vice. Within this broader context, tensions were played out at the familial level, over roles within marriage, over the institution of marriage, and over personal immoralities and hypocrisies. Of course anxieties about these were not merely limited to High Churchmen; Low Churchmen and Dissenters shared concerns that irreligion and immorality were growing and initially the reformation of manners movement of the late 1690s and early 1700s seemed almost ecumenical in its scope. But the polarizing High Church rallying cry of the 'Church in danger', and the politicization of immorality, made it increasingly difficult for them to share the same platform. As a result moral instruction was, ironically, pushed into the hands not so much of the clergy as the periodical writers, especially Addison and Steele whose papers were specifically designed as secular sermons, witty instructions about how to navigate the new world of temptation with a degree of virtue.

5

FANATICS AND FALSE BRETHREN

In 1709 Dr Henry Sacheverell preached a firebrand, High Church sermon attacking the Revolution of 1688–9 and the principles underlying it. The following year he was prosecuted for it, in what proved to be one of the great set-piece trials of the eighteenth century and the focal point of a political crisis. The trial unleashed the worst violence on the streets of London since the civil wars and sparked one of the largest print controversies of the eighteenth century. Such a reaction was testament to the enduring strength of popular allegiance to the Church that Sacheverell claimed was being undermined. Both William and Spencer Cowper played significant roles in Sacheverell's prosecution. Spencer was one of the team of lawyers, known as the 'managers', who set out the case against the doctor; William, as Lord Chancellor, presided over the whole process and delivered the verdict. William's house was accordingly considered a target for the rioters who took to the streets. Reactions to the trial can be gauged through the diary of Sarah Cowper; the letters of William's sister-in-law, Ann Clavering, who attended the trial; and the visual satires and print of the time. They help to tell a story about the contested legitimacy of political violence, the proper relationship between Church and State, religious tolerance, the nature of fanaticism, freedom of speech and of the press, and the political dangers of hypocrisy and deceit.

Sacheverell's trial poses interesting questions for us, as well as for his contemporaries. One of his prosecutors said that he hoped the trial would be 'a noble precedent to excite our posterity to wrestle and tug for liberty'.[1] Although few any longer share his passionate concern about the survival of the national Church, and hence we might be bemused by the extreme emotion he generated, the prosecution of a troublesome fundamentalist cleric and the capacity of an inflammatory religious statement to ignite popular fervour have plenty of more modern parallels. Sacheverell's trial does indeed raise important issues about political, religious, and civil liberty. Parliament prosecuted Sacheverell for his attack on religious toleration, but, with hindsight, probably encouraged more expressions of intolerance in his defence than if they had let him alone. The trial thus asks us to question how far we should tolerate those who preach intolerance and grant them free speech. To his critics Sacheverell was intolerant and wanted to suppress those who disagreed with him; but to his admirers his trial was itself a form of censorship, an attempt to gag a whole way of talking and thinking. Sacheverell's trial also raises the question of how far clerics and religious leaders should comment on political matters. To his critics, Sacheverell was abusing the pulpit for political ends and his 'priestcraft'—the secular power exerted by religious leaders—was a danger to the State. To his friends, however, it was not Sacheverell but the Dissenters who posed the threat because they used religious meetings for political purposes. It was, after all, the fear of sedition that meant that the 1689 Toleration Act insisted that Dissenters should meet behind *open* doors. Sacheverell also raised a timeless question about whether and on what grounds an established government can be resisted and overthrown, for his attack on 'revolution principles' forced a heated debate about the resistance used in 1688 and more generally about the right to resist a tyrannous monarch or State.

Perhaps most pertinent to modern concerns are deep-seated anxieties that Sacheverell raised about hypocrisy and trust in politicians. In the sermon for which he was prosecuted, *The Perils of False Brethren*, the doctor had asked whether anyone could trust those who seemed to be able to shift or abandon their opinions in order to pursue power and self-advancement, those who apparently believed in nothing but their own gain, or who covered their ambitions with professions of goodness and friendship? This, of course, had been the question lying behind Manley's satire of the Cowper brothers, for she had depicted Spencer and William as men who were indifferent to religion, pursuing nothing but their own interest and lusts. The party system and the growing importance of public opinion seemed to have heightened anxieties that politics was a game of deception and manipulation of the public. But Sacheverell went one stage further than satire, and demanded action against the unholy alliance of the duplicitous and the evil. In doing so, he posed a question about how best to deal with a threat to a cherished way of life: moderation and conciliation, on the one hand, or zeal and steadfastness on the other? His resoundingly firm answer was the latter; and in doing so, he questioned whether moderation is a virtue in the face of the destruction of what is held dear. Sacheverell posed a challenge to what we would now say were fundamental tenets of liberalism—free speech, toleration, consensual government, and moderation—and the extent to which we should expect politicians to be free of hypocrisy. As one historian has put it, 'Sacheverell may have been a mean man, but the debate he aroused was no mean argument.'[2]

SACHEVERELL AND HIS SERMONS

Henry Sacheverell was an overbearingly confident High Church clergyman. He was brazenly ambitious, vain, irrepressible, flashy, histrionic, capable of putting a case strongly, but not subtle enough to argue cleverly; a noisy firebrand who delighted in preaching sermons full of 'heat, passion, violence and scurrilous language'.[3] Two sermons, in particular, were the focus of the charges brought by Parliament against him. At Derby on 15 August 1709 and again in London on 5 November (the day celebrating deliverance from the Gunpowder Plot and from James II's tyranny, since it marked the date of William III's landing in Britain in 1688) Sacheverell had used the pulpit to condemn the Revolution of 1688–9. The second of the sermons, on which most attention focused, had in fact first been delivered at Oxford, where Sacheverell was out to make a name for himself, in December 1705. He had delivered it shortly after the failure of a third attempt in Parliament to ban the practice of 'occasional conformity', by which Dissenters qualified themselves for political office by occasionally taking Communion in the established Church. Indeed, by attacking 'the fanatics and other false brethren' in 1705, Sacheverell had clearly been waving a red rag to MPs who had resolved, five days earlier, that the Church was in 'a safe and flourishing condition' and that anyone who suggested otherwise was 'an Enemy to the Queen, the Church and the Kingdom'. The sermon had not, however, been published at that time and Sacheverell's remarks escaped wider public notice. But when the Derby sermon was printed in October 1709 and the London sermon followed it into print (despite an official refusal by London's governing body to sanction its publication) the Whig government decided to act against him and to bring a prosecution, not just in an ecclesiastical court but in Parliament, through a procedure known as impeachment.

Sacheverell's sermon was as violent on paper as it had been when delivered in church. It began by uncovering a 'conspiracy' of the 'most unheard-of Malice' that could only have been 'Hatch'd in the Cabinet

Council of Hell'. Sacheverell remembered not just the Catholic Gunpowder Plot of 5 November but also another key date in the political calendar, the execution of Charles I on 30 January 1649, the anniversary of which was a pretext for High Church bombast against Dissenters. Sacheverell thus repeated the High Church cliché that there was a conspiracy against the Church and State from a confederacy of 'Popish and Fanatic enemies' who were equally dangerous. This much was conventional. But he went on to argue that they were joined by another group, 'the false brethren' of the sermon's title.[4] As in the early days of Christianity, he suggested, the Church stood in danger from its 'pretended friends and false brethren'; her priests were ridiculed; and her altars and sacraments lay 'prostituted to hypocrites, Deists, Socinians [those who denied the Trinity of God, Christ and the Holy Spirit] and Atheists'.

Sacheverell wanted to unmask all those who subverted the Church. He fumed against those who derided it as being 'nothing else but Priestcraft and Popery in Masquerade' and lambasted those who sought to explain their faith 'in the New-fangl'd terms of Modern Philosophy' which, he said, in reality gave up Christianity to scepticism and atheism. He attacked the lukewarm, those who were really of no religion, 'a secret sort of reserv'd Atheists' who were interested in 'nothing but getting money and preferment'; and the holier-than-thou false saints who, under the pretence of conscience, committed 'the most abominable Impieties and justif[ied] Murder, Sacriledge and Rebellion'. In other words, he attacked the Low Churchmen and Dissenters. Alongside these religious traitors, he also defined a second group of 'false brethren': those who shook the State, the Whigs. Since the Church supported the State, and vice versa, those who undermined belief in the Church's maxims of non-resistance and obedience necessarily weakened the State. 'The Grand Security of our Government, and the very Pillar on which it stands', he thundered, 'is founded upon the steady belief of the Subject's Obligation to an Absolute and Unconditional Obedience to the Supreme Power, in all things lawful, and the utter Illegality of Resistance upon any pretence whatsoever.'

A key part of the sermon was thus an attack on the legality of resistance. The doctrine of obedience, Sacheverell lamented, had been displaced by ideas about the 'Right Liberty and Property of the PEOPLE' who, it seemed, could cancel their allegiance at will and call their sovereign to account. In condemning resistance Sacheverell had to make the case that the Revolution of 1688–9 had not, in fact, involved resistance at all. The invading William, Sacheverell claimed, had 'solemnly disclaimed the least Imputation of Resistance'; and he pointed out that the House of Commons had burnt a pamphlet by Charles Blount who had argued that a conquest had taken place. Sacheverell likened those who defended the principle of resistance to those who defended 'the horrid Actions and Principles of Forty One', in other words the 'Republican faction' who had brought about the Civil War. The 'New-fangl'd Notion of Self-Defence', Sacheverell claimed, would justify 'all the rebellions that ever were or can be'; and would reduce the monarch to 'the breath of his Subject's nostrils, to be blown in or out at their caprice and pleasure'. The government, he urged, should suppress such dangerous ideas with the sword and condemn them through Church and Parliament. This meant tackling the academies run by Dissenters that taught 'all the Hellish principles of fanaticism, regicide and anarchy'. They abused the freedom granted by the Toleration Act of 1689 which, he claimed, had never been intended to 'cherish such Monsters and Vipers in our Bosom' who would 'rend, distract, and confound the firmest and best-settled constitution in the world'. In short, Sacheverell argued for a conservative reading of the 1688–9 Revolution and a condemnation of the principles of resistance and rebellion that he asserted were intrinsic to the Dissenting cause. He believed 'the English government can never be secure on any other principles but strictly those of the Church of England'.

But that Church, he claimed, was in great danger, and in the second part of his sermon Sacheverell laid open the threats facing it. The national Church, he argued was undermined by those who wanted to make it a 'heteregeneous mixture of all persons of what different faith soever', a soup of Protestants, 'Jews, Quakers, Mohometans and anything', all allowed entry by a policy of 'moderation and occasional conformity'. Such an enfeebled and incoherent institution, he warned, would fall prey to 'universal scepticism and infidelity', thereby ensuring the triumph of popery which had been working so long to defeat Protestantism. But the danger to the State was no less great. Republican notions amongst the Dissenters would end in rebellion, just as they had done in 1642: 'the old leaven of their forefathers is still working in their present Generation' and their 'poison still remains in this brood of vipers to sting us to death'.

In the final sections of the sermon Sacheverell analysed the sins committed by the 'false brethren' that he had earlier identified. Prominent among them was the appalling hypocrisy and deceit of those who subordinated their principles to self-advancement and material gain. Such men were ready to 'fall down and worship the very Devil himself for the riches and honours of this world', and they set up 'an Universal Trade of Cousenage, Sharping, Dissimulation and down-right Knavery. For what dependence can there be on a man of no principles? What trust in equivocations, evasions and lies?' Yet such men, Sacheverell warned, were crafty: they covered their treachery with 'plausible pretences of FRIENDSHIP, whereby they are capable of doing much more mischief than a bare-fac'd and professed enemy'. The false brother was thus a dangerous self-contradiction, 'maintaining an irreconcilable war betwixt the outward and inward man', a mixture of 'inconsistency and nonsense' whose habitual hypocrisy would undermine all religious faith. Such hypocrisy was ultimately self-defeating, Sacheverell hoped, for the turncoat would 'meet hypocrisy with hypocrisy' and they would be left keeping company 'with hypocrites and unbelievers, with all liars, that have their part in the lake which burns with fire and brimstone, with the Grand-father of Falsehood, the Devil'. Instead, Sacheverell encouraged sincerity. First, the false brethren should 'throw off the mask, entirely quit our Church of which they are not true members'. Second, Churchmen must stand firm and united, and senior clerics should 'do their duties by thundering out their ecclesiastical anathemas', proscribing the lukewarm as well as the seditious, and promoting men of conscience and courage. Courage was all the more necessary, he warned, because the defenders of the Church were now in a war against 'the rulers of darkness in this world, against spiritual wickedness in high places'.

Sacheverell had issued a clarion call to the defence of the Church, which he depicted as under attack not only from professed enemies (the Dissenters and their allies the papists) but also from those who pretended to befriend it—the moderates, the Low Churchmen, who wanted toleration or to comprehend Dissenters within the Church of England, and the politicians and prelates who helped them. He trot-ted out most of the rallying cries and maxims that the High Church Tories had used since the civil wars: 'forty one is come again', 'the Church in danger', 'Church and State', 'all dissenters were republican rebels', Puritan tyranny and hypocrisy, 'Geneva' Calvinists in league with the papists, 'low church indifference'. Sacheverell pulled all the emotive and highly charged levers he could, wrapping them all up in a giant conspiracy theory that tapped popular fears and prejudices. And he had the nerve, or effrontery, to attack head-on the legitimacy of the Revolution of 1688–9 and the current leadership in Church and State.

Manley's *New Atalantis* had satirized Lord Treasurer Godolphin by his nickname Volpone, acquired because of his craftiness; and when Sacheverell condemned false brethren as 'wily Volpones' he levelled a calculated blow against the chief minister, whose career reflected precisely the suppleness of principle that Sacheverell abhorred. Godolphin had begun his political life siding with the Tories and ended it at the head of a largely Whig ministry. So Sacheverell's attack was also a fundamental questioning of the whole drift of politics and society since the Revolution, a shift, as he saw it, towards atheism, irreligion, republicanism, hypocrisy, and self-advancement. His solution was to reverse the tide of tolerance, to root out those who were not vigorous in their adherence to their principles or who could be labelled as hypocrites, replacing them with zealots of his own stamp.

THE TRIAL

In his sermon Sacheverell had protested that he spoke only from a 'hearty Zeal for the Honour and Safety of our Excellent Church and Constitution', and hoped none would take offence. But on 13 December 1709 Spencer Cowper seconded John Dolben in making the first complaint in Parliament against Sacheverell's sermon. The following day the Commons voted to impeach the doctor and, by way of adding insult, requested the queen to show a mark of favour to his Low Church rival, Benjamin Hoadly, who was already the bogeyman of the High Churchmen.[5] Spencer was again at the forefront of the prosecution when he was appointed to the committee to draft the charges—the 'articles of impeachment'—against Sacheverell. These, made public on 9 January 1710, accused the doctor of a conspiracy of his own, 'to create Jealousies and Divisions amongst her majesty's subjects, and to incite them to Sedition and Rebellion'.[6] He had done this, it was alleged, 'with a wicked, malicious and seditious Intention to undermine and subvert her Majesty's Government and the Protestant Succession'. The specific articles against Sacheverell accused him of asserting:

there had been no resistance at the Revolution of 1688–9

the toleration of Dissent enacted in 1689 was 'unreasonable' and 'unwarrantable'

anyone who defended the toleration was false to the Church

it was the duty of the clergy to 'thunder out' against Dissenters

the Church of England was in 'great Peril and Adversity' under the present government, just as it had been under Charles I

the government was helping 'the Destruction of the Constitution'

there were 'false brethren' in office who sought to undermine Church and State.

Sacheverell was also accused of being a 'publick Incendiary' who had sought to 'keep up a Distinction of Factions and Parties', and stir them to violence. He had abused his position as priest, perverting Scripture in order to make his case, and had 'most grievously offended against' the public peace, the rights and liberties of the people, and the laws.

On 12 January Lord Chancellor William Cowper asked Sacheverell, who had by now been in custody for a month, to respond to the charges laid against him. Sacheverell recruited a set of first-rate Tory lawyers, led by Sir Simon Harcourt, a former Attorney-General, and together they concocted a feisty reply that included an unrepentant reassertion that resistance was never legal. This was presented, in the presence of a large crowd that had gathered to hear it, on 25 January. But in the long period before the trial finally started over a month later, the Whig position weakened dramatically at Court and the duke of Marlborough, the target of so much of Manley's satire, saw his authority fatally wounded. Outraged that Queen Anne had given the command of a regiment to the brother of Abigail Masham, his wife Sarah's rival for the queen's confidence, Marlborough had insisted that Abigail be removed from court; when the queen refused he stormed off to the Continent. With Godolphin's credibility already damaged by Sacheverell's 'Volpone' jibe, and Marlborough sulking, the Whig government that they nominally headed began to look shaky. To shore up their position Lord Chancellor Cowper was one of those who hurried to reassure the queen that he had never intended to force the queen to part with her (Tory-inclined) new favourite, Abigail Masham.

Sacheverell's trial took place in Westminster Hall, appropriately enough the venue of his hero Charles I's trial in 1649.[7] Indeed, several prints were made depicting the doctor holding the portrait of Charles, to drive home the parallel between the two Church martyrs and to echo Sacheverell's invocation of the king's memory at several key points in his controversial sermon. The flood of portraits was swelled further by means of the relatively new technique of mezzotint—a

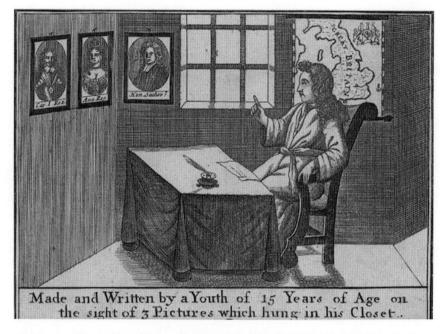

Made and Written by a Youth of 15 Years of Age on the sight of 3 Pictures which hung in his Closet.

Figure 5.1 A youth in his study gazes admiringly at three Anglican heroes: Charles I, Queen Anne, and Henry Sacheverell.

quick way of producing a print that had the additional advantage of achieving paint-like shadows and texture. So desirable did a print portrait of Sacheverell become that pirate copies were soon made. As Figure 5.1 shows, portraits of Sacheverell (hung alongside two royal defenders of the Church, Charles I and Queen Anne) became objects of private devotion.

Demand for seats at the trial was also high, from women as well as men. In part this reflected a peculiar charm that Sacheverell had over women, who avidly collected his portrait. A ballad told the story of one woman who fell in love with Sacheverell during his prosecution and Sarah Cowper noted in her diary that he had 'become the Toast of Such Ladys as Strenuously adhere to the Doctrine of Non:Resistance. To accomadate their Full Petticoats 24 Inches of Seat is allow'd to Each Non:Resisting Female as Comes to this Audience and 'tis Thought there will be no Small Appearance, for the Criminal 'tis said, is a Hansome Bonny preist.'[8] Ann Clavering, the lively sister of William Cowper's new wife, Mary, was nevertheless one woman definitely not under Sacheverell's spell (she spikily remarked that most of the clergy were 'imps of Lucifer'), but even she got up at 4 a.m. every morning to secure her seat for the three-week trial, that eventually began on Monday 27 February.[9]

After the charges against Sacheverell had been read Lord Chancellor Cowper invited the prosecution to begin. In one of the opening speeches, Anthony Lechmere set out the Whig notion of the original contract between king and people, and of the people's right and duty to resist when the executive power broke it. Next day, six speakers, including future prime minister Robert Walpole, tackled the first article, which centred on the legality of resistance and hence on the lawfulness of the Revolution. Sacheverell was accused of wanting to undermine loyalty to the queen and to promote the cause of the Pretender—the exiled Stuart heir of James II, who 'Jacobites' saw as the lawful king. Walpole and the other Whigs sought to imply that Tories were crypto-Jacobites who really sought the restoration of the Stuarts. In place of Sacheverell's conspiracy of Dissenters and Low Churchmen, the Whigs outlined a conspiracy of High Churchmen and Jacobites. Yet the Whig managers had a difficult line to steer between, on the one hand, justifying resistance in the past and, on the other, denying that they were advocating it in the present.

The boldest speech was made by the military hero, General Stanhope, who stated very clearly that the legitimacy of all authority rested on the consent of the people, and that contract—or 'compact' as he termed it—was essential both to securing this and to legitimizing any resistance. This discussion of original contract, the consent of the people, the supremacy of law, and a right to resist to defend the original contract from the invasions of the executive power owed a good deal to the ideas of John Locke, whose *Two Treatises of Government* had been written to justify resistance against Charles II. Published in 1690 it adopted a position of natural rights to argue along precisely the lines followed by Stanhope. Locke, not surprisingly, was something of a hero in the Cowper household: Sarah's diary contains a long eulogy to him on news of his death in 1704.

Locke's heir, Peter King, also led the charge on the second article, about toleration, in which he was eloquently seconded by Spencer Cowper. Spencer accused the doctor of a direct assault on the Toleration Act of 1689, a law which he said had united the people after years of division caused by High Church 'intemperate Zeal' against Dissenters. Spencer's task was relatively easy: he had merely to repeat the doctor's bombast against the Dissenters and then castigate it as intolerant bigotry. He described Sacheverell's depiction of Dissenting and Low Church hypocrites burning in Hell as 'a most dreadful Unchristian Sentence, a sentence so barbarous, so astonishing that he was at a loss to imagine how it could enter the Mind of Man to conceive it'.[10] Spencer's slick delivery both impressed and disgusted one Tory observer who noted that he spoke 'with so fine & deliberate a Cadence, & so soft & engaging a Tone, that I had not time to mind the Sense of his Speech, only that he maintained that Religion had nothing at all do doe with the State'.[11] Under his smooth words was a steely determination to divide (as Locke had done) the realms of politics and religion, and to make faith a private and not a public concern insofar as it was consistent with public order and community. Spencer also warned that violence was imminent. Perhaps having seen a raucous mob that had supportively accompanied Sacheverell's coach to the trial that morning (and shouted loudly when his brother William's coach overtook it), Spencer predicted that Sacheverell had sown seeds of sedition 'and the fruit to be expected was civil discord and confusion, unless some Remedy was apply'd to prevent it'.[12]

That evening Spencer's warning came true. A crowd of over 1,000 accompanied Sacheverell back to his lodgings and elements of the mob smashed the windows of the most important and newest Dissenting Meeting House. The London authorities—headed by a Tory to whom Sacheverell had dedicated his sermon—did nothing. The following day, Wednesday 1 March, a crowd of about 3,000 hung around Westminster waiting for the day's proceedings to end, entertained with a print depicting an imaginary prizefight between the Low Church champion Benjamin Hoadly and the High Church Sacheverell, an indication of how visual propaganda was becoming peculiarly important in this dispute. The print was probably *The Modern Champions*, which on the copy reproduced as Figure 5.2 carries the date on which its owner, the book-collector Narcissus Luttrell, acquired it, just a few days before the trial opened.

The image shows Sacheverell, fictionalized as 'Jehu Hotspur' on the right with his 'second' Dr Francis Higgins (another High Church firebrand), and Hoadly as 'Balthazar Turn-Coat' on the left, with his second, Dr Daniel Burgess (a leading Dissenting minister). Hotspur brandishes 'hypocricy' at Hoadly; and Hoadly in turn thrusts 'Perkin' at Sacheverell, an allusion to the Pretender and hence to the charge of Jacobitism that was levelled against the High Churchmen. In the text—omitted here but printed under the image—Sacheverell fought Hoadly with accusations of 'toleration', 'rebellion', 'moderation', 'regicide', and 'anarchy'. Hoadly's weapons were the counter-charges

Figure 5.2 *The Modern Champions,* an image that may have helped to spark rioting.

of 'non-resistance', 'passive obedience', 'superstition', 'jacobitism', 'tyranny', and 'persecution'. The print thus nicely conveys the power of emotive words in polemical disputes and encapsulated the three-week trial in a simplified form that can only have encouraged the mob to think about translating the paper battle into reality.

The insults shouted at Lord Chancellor Cowper on his way home that evening were a foretaste of much worse to come.[13] Some had come prepared, with crowbars and axes, and stripped Burgess's Meeting House of all its wooden furnishings, including the pulpit, piling the spoils onto a bonfire to the accompanying chant of 'High Church and Sacheverell'. Another image, this time an illustration from a book, captures the scene (Figure 5.3).

The armed mob then moved on to attack the Independents' Meeting House in New Street, burning its contents in Holborn, one of the main routes in and out of the City. After one more such episode part of the crowd moved towards Cowper's house in Lincoln Inn Fields but then switched course, to wreck another Meeting House in Drury Lane. In the meanwhile Cowper had hastened to the Secretary of State and told him of the danger that a fire lit by the mob posed to his house.[14] Troops were at last despatched to quell the unrest and they did so, remarkably, without any loss of life, though not until

Dr Burgiſes Theater

Figure 5.3 The crowd that destroyed Dissenting Meeting Houses considered attacking Lord Cowper's house.

about 3 a.m. and not before six Meeting Houses in all had been wrecked. There were nearly 100 arrests and 30 were later convicted of riot; a further 3 of treason. It was London's worst riot since the Civil War; and was not matched until the Gordon Riots of 1780, when another loyalist mob took to the streets and similarly targeted buildings of symbolic value.[15]

So when Spencer was given another chance to speak 'in the same elegant way of delivery' at the trial on 10 March he was able to claim that his own prediction of civil unrest had already come true. Sacheverell's sedition, 'calculated to seduce and delude the Rabble had, even during the continuance of the Tryal, produced an actual Rebellion; in which several places of religious Worship (. . . represented by Doctor Sacheverell as necessary to be destroyed) had been accordingly pulled down and burnt'. And Spencer delighted in the irony that all this violence had been at 'the Instigation of one who would be thought an Advocate of Passive Obedience'. Violent language had produced actual violence; the doctor had incited religious hatred and provoked the mob to action. Spencer was also 'very smart upon the whole sermon' which he called a 'bitter Invective against the Toleration'.[16] In Sacheverell's eyes, Spencer said, toleration undermined civil society: it led to 'Schismatical Impostors, Enthusiasts, Hypocrites, to a Mungril union of Sects, to Fanaticks, Rebels, Traitors, Atheists, Deists, Tritheists, Socinianists, to the Principles of Fanaticism, Regicide and Anarchy, to Monsters and Vipers . . . to Jews, Quakers and Mahometans, in a word, to all false Brethren'. But for Cowper, toleration was not as dangerous as those who opposed it. He argued that Sacheverell lacked moderation and 'even Christianity itself'. And he concluded by saying that it was the Revolution of 1688–9 that had created 'the future Expectation of a Protestant succession; the Religion, Laws, Rights and Liberties of the British Nation'. For Sacheverell toleration and revolution were vices; for Spencer Cowper they were virtues.

Sacheverell's defence team then had the tricky task of justifying his general case that resistance was always illegal and of trying to clear him of having condemned the Revolution of 1688–9. They did so by arguing a contradiction. On the one hand they argued that no resistance had been used at the Revolution and that non-resistance was part of the Church's history. On the other, they also argued that Sacheverell's doctrine did, silently, allow for resistance in cases of necessity. Moreover, they argued, there really was, as the doctor had claimed, a tide of irreligious and blasphemous print. To prove as much, extracts from recent publications, united in their hostility to 'priestcraft', were read out. The 'black catalogue' included some shocking comments. William Stephens's *Account of the Growth of Deism* (1696), for example, which had seemed to support the deism it ostensibly condemned; Edmund Hickeringill's doubts that the Bible was infallible or always divinely inspired; Charles Blount's argument in *Oracles of Reason* that reason was 'able to furnish us with enough to be happy'; and the earl of Shaftesbury's claim in his *Letter Concerning Enthusiasm* that 'nobody trembles to think that there should be no god, but that there should be one'. An array of anticlerical literature was cited: John Toland's *Christianity not Mysterious*, Daniel Defoe's attacks on High Churchmen in his periodical *Review*, and fellow journalist John Tutchin's anticlericalism in his *Observator*.

Sacheverell concluded his defence by speaking very well, asserting that the motive behind his impeachment had been 'to procure an eternal and indelible brand of infamy to be fixed in a parliamentary way on all those who maintain the doctrine of Non-Resistance, and to have the clergy directed what doctrines they are to preach and what not'. Unrepentant, he reiterated that the Church was in danger; indeed, 'in greater danger it is now, than since Christ had a Church upon earth'. And he pleaded for compassion, with such eloquence and emotion that there was much weeping in court. He had, he said, been 'made a gazing stock' and a 'spectacle to the whole world' for a long and very public trial. And he ended on a suitably pious yet pointed note: he beseeched God to deliver all men from 'false doctrine, heresy and schism, from hardness of heart, from contempt of His word and commandment, from envy, hatred and malice, and all uncharitableness'.

The scene then shifted to the House of Lords, who were the judges of the case. Before they could deliberate, however, William Cowper, as Lord Chancellor, had to head off an important legal challenge that threatened to derail the whole trial. He was asked 'whether by the law of England, and constant practice ... the particular words supposed to be criminal must not be expressly specified' in the indictment? The articles, which his brother Spencer had helped to draft, had failed to quote a single passage from Sacheverell's sermon. There followed a hunt for precedents; but only one, from 1628, could be found to support the Whig case that stating the precise words was unnecessary in an impeachment, and even that had never been formally entered into the parliamentary record. After a clamorous debate, Cowper and his fellow Whigs only narrowly secured a vote that this was sufficient.

'No bear garden was ever more noisy', observed Cowper's relieved sister-in-law.[17] With that hurdle jumped, the way lay clear for Sacheverell's conviction; clear that is, except for a marathon peers' debate on Sacheverell's guilt, which took twelve hours to conclude on 16 March, largely because so many Tories who had joined the Revolution in 1688 felt it necessary to explain why they should now vote for a man who condemned it. Even then it took another day to vote on all the articles of impeachment and a further day to decide how the verdict was to be delivered. It was only on Monday 20th that Lord Cowper formally asked each peer to declare his verdict and ended with his own, on the side of the majority: guilty.

The Tories nevertheless snatched victory from the mouth of defeat. The Whigs had wanted to punish Sacheverell with imprisonment, a fine, and a ban on preaching. A harsh punishment as a deterrent to others had, after all, been part of the rationale for trying him in Parliament rather than the lesser law courts. But, catastrophically, and amidst scenes of great confusion, they could only persuade peers to agree to a much milder, tokenistic, sentence. Sacheverell was ordered not to preach for three years and his two offending sermons were to be burnt by the common hangman. No wonder, then, that Cowper, when giving the judgment to Sacheverell on 23 March, pointed out the 'extreme tenderness' that it showed a man of the cloth. After all the effort of prosecution, the end result was laughable, though few Whigs found it so. Ann Clavering thought that the ministry of which her brother-in-law was a member had not only been 'insulted' but was now also 'insupportable'.[18] She rightly predicted that the weakness of the punishment augured political change: by the end of the summer the country would get a Tory government.

For the six months following the trial the country was gripped by a most extraordinary frenzy, producing a series of State convulsions, a medical metaphor that was used by Sarah Cowper in October 1710, when she reviewed the fevered State:

> Were the Body Politick to be phisick'd I Shou'd venture to prescribe to it after the Same Manner. It may be Thought absurd to Propose a Diet for yᵉ allaying of populer Commotions and National Ferments. But if in Such a Case, people were to Eat Nothing but Water:Gruel for a Fortnight, it wou'd Abate the Rage and Animosity of Parties; and not a litle Contribute to yᵉ Cure of a Distracted Nation.[19]

'Never before did I Discern So great, So general a Frenzy, possess Human-kind', she noted at the end of the year.[20] The first convulsion was the widespread and wildly exuberant popular rejoicing at Sacheverell's light sentence. Bells were rung, drums were beaten, bonfires lit (with effigies of Hoadly and even of King William burnt on them), toasts were drunk, Dissenters were threatened and windows were smashed. Then, from March, there was a fevered nationwide campaign to bombard the throne with expressions of High Church Tory loyalty and doctrine. In Hertford the Tory corporation produced a polemical 'address' to the throne that attacked the 'factious, anti-monarchical and rebellious notions' that stalked the land, one of ninety-seven such Tory addresses, most of which used similarly high-flown language to drive home an association between the Whigs, republicanism, atheism, and rebellion.[21] A counter-address, from the 'principal inhabitants and freemen' of Hertford in turn suggested that the 'persons truly dangerous to your Majesty and the Protestant succession are those who traduce the honour and justice of the Revolution; those who seditiously suggest the Church to be in danger'.[22] Lord Cowper ensured that this address was presented at Court but it was one of only fifteen to express a Whig standpoint. A third national fit happened in the spring when the doctor went on tour of the West Country and Midlands to receive the adulation of the admiring crowds, which numbered many thousands. Indeed, it was compared to a royal progress, in which the monarch journeyed round the realm basking in popular applause. Both the addresses and the 'progress' were intended to show the queen the popularity of the High Church Tory cause and hence to encourage her to break with the Whig government and to call a new election.

This, then, was one of the longest and most exuberant election campaigns in British history. And when the elections were finally called, for October and November, the Tories achieved a landslide victory amidst turbulent scenes. Sarah Cowper noted that 'Tis amazing to hear of the fraudulent practises and Corruption, Riot and Outrage Comitted att the Election of Members for Parliment; Under pretence of Loyalty and Defence of High-Church.'[23] These elections were, bar one, the most contested in the eighteenth century, with more seats being actively challenged than ever before. Robert Walpole, who had been one of the managers of the prosecution, found himself pelted with mud and stones (spoiling his fine laced coat) when standing for Norfolk, an experience that might be said to have had an important psychological impact on him, for when in power 1720–42 he sought to reconcile the Church to his Whig ministry rather than attack it. Spencer Cowper, as another member of Sacheverell's prosecution, was also a marked man. He would not return to Parliament

See him Surrender up the Purse and Mace,
That Harcourt may Supply Ld Cowp_s Place.

Figure 5.4 To celebrate the decline of the Whigs in the wake of the Sacheverell affair a pack of playing cards was produced, each card depicting a different scene in the doctor's drama. Here William Cowper resigns as Lord Chancellor, to make way for Sir Simon Harcourt, who had led Sacheverell's defence. The card is a good example of a new genre of topical visual print. Cowper's name is abbreviated in order to avoid prosecution, even though it was clear to everyone who was being depicted. Both print culture and censorship are discussed later in the chapter.

until after the accession of George I. And although Robert Harley, the new prime minister—a term that was first applied to him rather than Walpole—was keen to retain Lord Chancellor Cowper in office, William resigned both out of loyalty to his Whig colleagues and because he was convinced the new regime would work only by 'Trick and Shuffling'.[24] Whig and Cowper fortunes were on the wane.

HYPOCRISY

As the mother of two of its key participants, Sarah Cowper had a vested interest in the trial and its aftermath, so we should not, perhaps, expect her diary to record an impartial reaction. Nevertheless her comments are deeply revealing, not least because Sarah was, as we have seen, a devout churchgoer for whom the 'Church in danger' slogan might be expected to have had some appeal. After all, her attachment to the Church had been one of the main bones of contention with her husband. Yet, quite the reverse, she was vigorously hostile to Sacheverell, increasingly alienated by an overwhelming sense of his hypocrisy. Ironically, the attribute that the doctor wanted to pin on the Whigs (and Manley had wanted to pin on her sons), hypocrisy, was the one she was convinced was most applicable to Sacheverell himself. She believed that he was part of the problem, not the solution, for he was, like those he attacked, using religion for political and selfish ends.

For a start, Sarah Cowper thought Sacheverell's stance on non-resistance was both dangerous and inconsistent. The 'notion of unlimited submission', she noted on the second day of the trial, would put 'it into the power of the Prince, if it be in his intention, to destroy the Subject'.[25] Sarah then summarized the whole of the Whig prosecution in her observation that:

> Submission and Obedience to Governers is Certainly the Doctrin of the Gospel; and is as Certainly the Dictate of that Reason which first Shew'd Men the Necessity of Government. But to make Obedience of Such a Nature as to Destroy the End of Government which was Certainly the Good of the whole Society and to leave no Room for Self Defence in any Case is no part of Reason or Christianity. The Sense of the Nation was otherwise att the late Revolution.[26]

And she was horrified by the hypocritical actions of the mob that gutted Burgess's Meeting House and burnt its contents in front of her son's house: 'are these ye Effects of Passive Obedience? Sure this is Resistance', she exclaimed. Whoever paid the mob, she believed, 'wou'd Raise an Army to Oppose when they Can. God Save The Queen.'[27] Indeed, she became increasingly convinced that the restoration of the Stuarts lay at the heart of the High Church design, quoting approvingly some anti-Jacobite verse that claimed:

> Tho Loyalty and Church is the pretence,
> Inherent Birth-Right is the Secret Sense.
> And Restauration is the Consequence.[28]

Sarah was convinced that it was Sacheverell and the High Churchmen who were destroying true religion by failing to preach its fundamentals. Even the pagan writers of classical antiquity, she thought, had more piety. Socrates, Cicero, and Seneca had at least tried to inculcate a sense of divine providence and perfection, the immortality of the soul, and an afterlife of reward and punishment; but the High Church parsons, she argued, undermined these great thoughts. Failing to adore God, she insisted, they focused instead on 'a little Trash of words and sophistry'.[29] The pulpits were equally full of nonsense and 'non-resistance'.

Indeed, she found the clergy to be utter hypocrites:

> Sagacious Persons will Easily look under the Mask and see thro' all fine pretensions, and will quietly Discern the Absurdity of Telling the World that we beleive one thing when we Do the Contrary. He that wou'd know what a Man Beleives, let him attend rather to what He Does, than to what he Talks. It were Really better upon Some Accounts that Such men Shou'd abandon their profession, than keep on a Vizard which Serves to no Other purpose but to Scare Others from Religion.[30]

The idea of a mask hiding a sinister hidden truth was, as we have seen, a familiar one: used against the Cowpers, and the Whigs and Dissenters more generally, it was also here turned against the High Churchmen. This theme of clerical hypocrisy was one to which Sarah Cowper returned again and again. Thus on 5 May she noted (paraphrasing Bishop Burnet's printed speech about the Sacheverell trial):

> There is a great deal of Impiety and Infidelity Now Spread thro' ye Nation; and a great part of it is founded on the prejudice those persons have att ye Clergy and att the publike Worship of God. They see Clergy-Men take Oaths, and Use all prayers both Ordinary and Extraordinary for the Government and yet in their Actings and Discourses, and of late in their Sermons they Shew Visibly that they look another Way—from

whence they Conclude, They are a Mercenary Sort of people without Conscience.[31]

It is true that Sarah agreed with Sacheverell on one point: she, too, saw the Church as a 'Beseig'd Citty hemm'd in on all Parts by the Impudence of Atheism, the Insolencies of Popery and the Turbulency of Faction'. There was, she feared (perhaps reminded by her own sons' actions):

> an almost Universall Degeneracy and Inpenitence among Us. The Sinners of this Age are grown Impudent and appear with a Whores forehead forsaken of all Modesty; turning the World of God it self and the most Serious Manners of Religion into Raillery. Such Clamarous Sins are almost come to be the Garb and Fashion, and to be accounted the Witt and Gallantry of these Times![32]

But far from siding with Sacheverell, she turned her back on him and the 'Detestable Villains' who abetted him. She 'never felt so Bitter Zeal against any, as These Cheverell Miscreants: who make me that was a Staunch Church:Woman become one of the Staggering Party'.[33] As she pithily put it, 'Sacheverel's High Church has brought me from Low Church to be of No Church; Except the Christian.'[34]

Ironically Sarah had come to agree with her husband (now that he was safely dead) in his disdain of clerics. Having impatiently sat through one highly political High Church and anti-Whig sermon, she exasperatedly exclaimed in her diary 'All our Dissentions are owing to the Vileness of persons in the Sacred Ministry...The Pretences made by the priesthood from Time to Time that the Church was in Danger is only a Trick to make the Laiety passionate for that of which they themselves have been Negligent.'[35] The clergy had 'brought Matters to that pass that people are become almost Indifferent whither they have any Religion or not'.[36] Sacheverell himself was better fitted for 'a Bear-garden or Punch's Theatre' than a church. So disgusted was she by the politicization of the pulpit that she admitted being 'under a Temptation to Neglect going to Church Especially att this Time when too many preachers meddle with Matters beside their Function and Omit Teaching the Doctrines of Faith and Holy Life'.[37] She abandoned attending state-sponsored fasts or days of prayer, such as 5 November or 30 January (in commemoration of the regicide), for she found that 'Preachers so Rant' about non-spiritual matters on those days that they failed to edify.[38] When she did go to one, a 29 May celebration of the restoration of the Stuarts in 1660, she found, even in the queen's chapel, an ungodly scene. Rather than concentrating on their prayers, 'the Men Ogle and Cringe to the Ladys, For which they return Smiles and Drop Curtesies the whole Time of Divine Worship'.[39] Such behaviour was 'so unsuitable' that she resolved 'never to Appear there more' and later remarked that the day's service was merely 'a Heap of Hypocritical Lies'.[40] By December 1710 Sarah thought the 'High Church politicians' were acting a farce: pretending to be for religion, whilst really seeking riches and power.

Sarah believed that the 'uncivil' war that she discerned in politics had also infected social conversation. Even before the Sacheverell affair she had observed in 1701, in the bitter aftermath of Spencer's trial, that 'it is the business of most people to abuse one another. I cannot Converse a few hours, but when I come to reflect on what hath been said I am displeas'd with my Self or others'.[41] In 1705, when the occasional conformity disputes had reached a shrill height, she also was struck by the 'censoriousness and insincerity' of those she spoke to, nauseated by how kindly they treated each other face to face and 'how hardly they will use them behind their backs'.[42] But her anxiety about the state of conversation seems to have increased after the Sacheverell trial, since talk seemed only to disguise rampant hypocrisy. Thus in December 1710 she noted, 'If you find that Men Use obscure Corrupt Speech, be Assur'd 'tis to Deceive and their Intentions are Deprav'd. Speech is the Image of the Mind. If a man Mince and Disguise it, 'tis a Sign of a Hypocrite and of litle worth. Such have been most Speech's from the Throne, and ye Late Addresses to It.'[43] Early in 1711, reflecting on the rise of Lord Treasurer Harley, who she thought was a consummate dissembler, 'an exquisite juggler', a master of 'artifice and dissimulation' with a 'great character for hypocrisy', she wrote that 'Dissimulation Consists in a Vain Shew of What wee are Not; and Infinite litle Crafts, and Acts of Deceit, which Men practise upon one another in their Ordinary Conversation and Intercourse, which Is Gross Iniquity.'[44] Dissimulation now passed for political wisdom, she lamented. Indeed, she filled page after page with reflections on hypocrisy and lying.

She therefore liked (and copied extracts from) *The Spectator*, which aimed to curb the rage of (High Church) partisanship and foster a more polite world of moderate, moral, and beneficial conversation. The ideal of politeness was one of rational exchange and debate, enlivened with wit, but without stooping to abuse. Yet the irony was that politeness could also lead to hypocrisy, since the truly polite person hid their feelings in order to be agreeable. Politeness, a term which became fashionable around the turn of the century, thus required its own deceptions. To be sure, it required moderate and rational conversation in which the interlocutors knew when to listen as well as when to talk; but, one guide suggested, the conversation also had to be 'pleasing' and as the chameleon 'changes its colour with every plant it approaches, so the wise man adapts himself to the several humours and inclinations of those he converses with'. Indeed, as the guide recognized, 'Politeness or good breeding, does not always inspire a man with humanity, justice, complaisance and gratitude, but yet it gives him the outside of those virtues and makes him in appearance what he should be in reality.'[45] Thus although politeness used dissimulation for good ends, it is possible to see how in the wrong hands it could be another code for rank hypocrisy. Politeness was to become one of the dominant codes of the eighteenth century; and its development was fostered not just by the conspicuous consumption of a consumer society but also by a reaction against political and religious zeal of the type exemplified by Sacheverell and the intemperate debate about his trial. But the price of moderation was the potential for merely presenting a veneer of acceptability.

The stress placed on hypocrisy both by Sacheverell and his critics suggests that anxieties about its prevalence had reached new levels. Recognition of its apparent pervasiveness in the later Stuart political culture, and the analysis offered by commentators then, may be especially valuable to an age that fears hypocrisy as a uniquely modern political disease. Political hypocrisy is as old as partisanship, and the two are connected. Lamenting the fate of a bishop who had been abused for not voting for Sacheverell's innocence, Sarah concluded that the party system itself fostered impressions of hypocrisy because it removed the scope for honest independent thinking: 'Tho' you may be Honest you Can't Seem So in Two Parties.'[46] Her remark highlights another paradox of partisan politics: although politicians seek the trust of the people, they do all they can to undermine the people's trust in their rivals by making the latter appear as hypocritical as possible, and thus the logic of partisan politics is to undermine the very commodity, trust, that all politicians need. Sacheverell's trial also suggests both that any public should be wary of those who make accusations of hypocrisy or who claim integrity, since they themselves may not be sincere, and that it can be very difficult to discern the true hypocrite (if that is not an oxymoron). Both Sacheverell and his enemies thought a conspiracy of hypocrites against the State and the Church was very real, but they disagreed about who the plotters were:

each accused the other. If, therefore, there were forms of hypocrisy that were dangerous, how could the public judge who was a hypocrite? Sarah Cowper's answer was that, since we cannot know the hearts of politicians, we have to evaluate their motives by their actions rather than their words. Her experience also suggests that trust, once broken, is very difficult to repair; but also, given how long anxieties about hypocrisy lasted, that the public can endure low expectations of political honesty, and hence that it recognizes the paradox in the game and even the part that it itself plays in it.

There may even be a creative side to hypocrisy. Hypocrisy rests on the notion of an outer self masking an inner one—the notion illustrated in this book's frontispiece. This two-faced man was not new of course; it is suggested in the classical figure of Janus, whose head looks simultaneously in different directions. But playing with the idea of an inner and outer self became a feature of later Stuart culture. Masquerades, in which the public disguised themselves in assemblies for dance, became very popular forms of entertainment; and the idea of doubleness was the key to a good deal of satire, a genre that flourished in the later Stuart period. Satire often relied on exposing the fraudulent outer self. For example, Charles Davenant's 'Tom Double' tracts, published in the first decade of the eighteenth century, created the character of a duplicitous modern Whig, whose inner self-seeking is exposed via a conversation with a confidant that is 'overheard' by the reader. Manley's satire of the Whigs similarly worked by revealing the secrets that they wanted to remain hidden. The hypocrite was often thought of as masked or cloaked or hidden behind a curtain (a visual code that can be found in many of the images of the period). Unmasking, uncloaking, pulling back the curtain were all ways in which 'truth' or the true self could be uncovered. And that act was often a dramatic, even theatrical one—on which many a play, plot, or image turned. Dror Wahrman has located the birth of the 'modern self' in the later eighteenth century and related it to a sudden revolution in the theatricality of outer selves; but we can find this masked self alive and embedded in political culture very much earlier.

The notion of a double self was important in the development of a sense of individual identity. The notion that there was a real inner self, to which you could be sincere or hypocritical, seems an important step towards a modern notion of an autonomous self. If the seventeenth-century Puritan self had merely been a selfless mirror of God, then the eighteenth-century enlightened self was aware of an inner duality, a voice that was something other than God or the Devil. This was what the philosophizing earl of Shaftesbury was trying to get at in a book published in 1710 called *Soliloquy*, a book that was loaned to Sarah Cowper but about which she said she could 'not comprehend the meaning of one page'. In it Shaftesbury advocated the need for everyone to talk to their own 'demon, genius, angel, guardian-spirit' in the form of an internal dialogue—or soliloquy, as he called it—a process which would allow any individual to 'discover a certain duplicity of soul, and divide ourselves into two partys', by which he meant two sides of our self that could then talk to one another. 'RECOGNISE YOUR SELF; which is as much to say, Divide your self, be two', Shaftesbury urged. This partition would allow the cultivation of the nobler, better self, rather than the baser self-interested self, through a process of internal dialogue. This was all the more necessary, he argued, because contemporary vices—ambition, avarice, corruption, lewdness, superstition, credulity, and bigotry—all 'put us on terms of greater distance and formality with our selves'. The mistake, Shaftesbury believed, was that 'our real and genuine SELF is sometimes suppos'd that ambitious one which is fond of power and glory'; whereas the real self was in fact the selfless, nobler self.[47] That real self was only knowable after a process of internal dialogue, though for Shaftesbury this rested on philosophical rather than spiritual introspection.

SACHEVERELL AND PRINT FEVER

The Cowpers caught the print fever with which Sacheverell had infected the country. In the autumn of 1710 William Cowper published a pamphlet in which he refuted the High Church Tory leader Henry St John, whose account of his party's triumph Cowper described as little more than 'a fable', a 'romance', or 'falshood'.[48] William defended the out-going Whigs and discerned 'a real conspiracy... of the Tories to enslave the Nation', disguised by their branding of all Whigs as 'Atheists and Republicans'. Cowper ended by urging the proper depiction of the contrast between the Whigs, who had the country's good at heart, and the 'black Hypocrisy' of the Tories, who sought to deliver the country into the hands of the Jacobites. Sarah Cowper, perhaps alluding to this spat, noted that 'A Paper Battle is on foot between Parties who Pelt at each other all the Dirt they Can Rake Up.'[49] That battle included *An Auction of State Pictures*, which was a High Church Tory attempt to expose the familiar story of the 'curious faces of hypocrisy' amongst the Low

Churchmen. The pamphlet had an illustrated frontispiece (Figure 5.5) that plays on the idea of verbal and visual portraits. Amongst the pictures under the hammer was one that could be sold 'to a Quaker'. Spencer was being satirized, for the hypocrite is described as being 'as *Stout* as his brother in any cause', and the charge was a familiar one: 'if you would know his full Character call him anything but what he would be call'd and you can hardly miscall him: for indeed he is almost any thing but what he would be thought to be'. The *Auction* thus continued what Manley had begun.

Figure 5.5 The frontispiece from a High Church tract satirizing the hypocrisy of the Low Churchmen, including Spencer Cowper. The image plays on the uncertainty of representations in portraits.

Figure 5.6 Sarah Cowper owned this visual summary of the case against Sacheverell.

Contemporaries were used to seeing text and image interacting and reinforcing one another. Sarah Cowper records that she enjoyed the cheapest form of print, ballads, which combined the two; and in the later Stuart period the genre of topical single-sheet prints, with an image at the top followed by an explanatory text, flourished, with far more published than ever before. The latter were much more expensive than ballads—often over a shilling rather than the few pence a short tract might cost—and so had a more restricted audience; but Sarah Cowper collected several and so did others. A volume in the British Library has a copy of Sacheverell's trial with thirty-four prints glued at appropriate places into it.[50] Although it is not possible to be precise about exactly when that was done, it is through these and other printed images that we can piece together a little of how the public might have reacted to the trial. The images nevertheless need some decoding, because they used a good deal of symbolism and allusion to make their points. They were 'speaking pictures' and according to one pamphlet (which perhaps overstates its case) they were 'the chief' tool used by opponents of Sacheverell.[51] The story they tell nevertheless relates closely to the duality and duplicity discussed in the last section.

The process of giving visual form to abstract ideas, concepts and values is clearly present in a print owned by Sarah Cowper which, like many others at the time, self-consciously proclaims itself an emblem in its title.[52] Emblems have a long history, for Renaissance art had made extensive use of symbolically significant objects or characters. Invented as a genre in Italy in the 1530s, and common in the seventeenth century, emblems often gave visual power to verbal stereotypes, proverbial expressions, and commonplace assumptions. They could also take certain objects or people and give them symbolic meaning; or give abstract ideas a visual form. The emblem was thus an ideal form through which to convey ideas in a simple, accessible form. The profusion of emblematic prints during the Sacheverell affair may in part have been influenced by the 1700 and 1709 English translations of a classic Italian work on emblems, Cesare Ripa's *Iconologia*, originally published in 1593, which offered 'moral emblems' of vices and virtues.[53] As the introduction to it made clear, images are 'the representatives of our notions', giving 'body to our thoughts, thereby to render them visible'.

Sarah Cowper's single sheet image and text encapsulates the Whig prosecution of Sacheverell that took over 300 pages of trial transcript (Fig. 5.6). It shows 'what one must expect if the High Church gets uppermost', and depicts a carriage of the type that Sacheverell rode in each day to Westminster Hall. In the image, as in life, he was mocked for choosing a coach with lots of glass, so that the adoring crowds could see him; but here the passenger is 'Perkin', the nickname for the Stuart Pretender, and Sacheverell is riding the lead horse, driving the High Church to Jacobitism (the subject of another printed image owned by Sarah Cowper). In many texts Sacheverell was described as a 'trumpeter' of sedition; and in the print he literally trumpets 'tantivy High Church' (tantivy means 'to ride at full tilt' but was also a nickname given, at the time of the Popish Plot, to High Church Tories). He rides a horse labelled 'passive obedience' and 'non-resistance', urged on by the Devil for a coachman. The cavalcade tramples on 'Moderation', 'Toleration', 'Liberty', and 'Property'—the watchwords of the Whigs—and dangling from the coach is the symbol of French slavery, the wooden shoe. The whole scene is surrounded by a picture frame, as though we should step back from the events and view them for what they are. The 'Explanation of the text' then drives the point home. It imagines a time when subjects were mere slaves to the will of tyrants and did anything they asked; a time when 'passive obedience' and 'non-resistance' prevailed. But, the verse relates, men at last used their reason and realized that whole kingdoms were not to be undone by the tyranny of one man who seemed to be sent from Hell; and so the whole nation rose in arms to assert their rights and nature's laws. The print thus requested the 'unprejudiced' viewer/reader to fear the French-like slavery into which the nation must descend if Sacheverell prevailed; and that fate could be avoided by resistance to tyranny. Here then was the Whig version of the trial, laid out with simplicity and power.

The point of this analysis, besides showing how loaded with meaning many visual symbols were in the period (they were 'iconographic', in the jargon) and stressing how text and image worked closely to reinforce each other, is nevertheless to juxtapose the print with another one that at first glance looks very similar (see Figure 5.7).

This Tory response copies the format of the print it refutes almost exactly but each element is reversed, for now the image is used to suggest that it was the Whigs who drove the nation towards anarchy, confusion, and the loss of religion and liberty. The Devil still drives, but Ben Hoadly rather than Sacheverell is at the front, on a horse labelled 'Moderation', followed by 'Presbytery' and 'Republican tyranny', strapped together by 'slavery', 'rebellion' and 'occasional conformity'. As this suggests, the print makes great play of Civil War memories: the horses trample Charles I and 'monarchy', the earl of Strafford (executed 1641) and 'loyalty', Archbishop Laud (executed 1645) and 'episcopacy' (Church government by bishops), as well as the 'liberty of the subject'. The Book of Common Prayer (the symbol of the Church of England's liturgy) and 'Magna Carta'

LIKE COACHMAN, LIKE CAUSE: OR, AN EMBLEM,

Of what we must expect, if Low-Church gets uppermost.

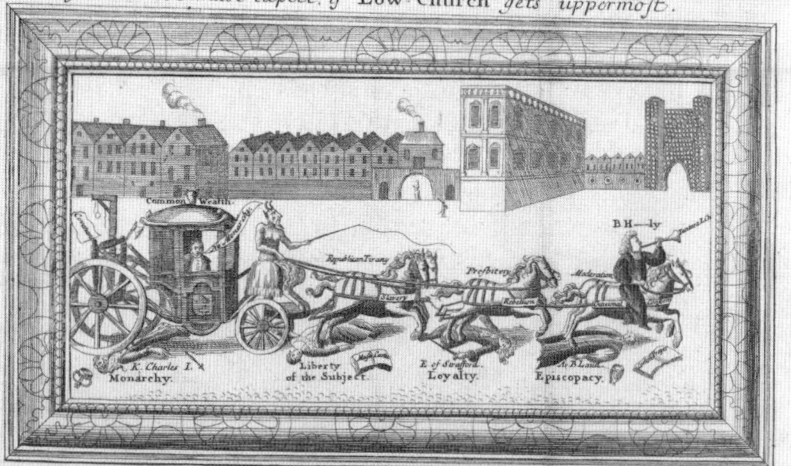

EXPLANATION.

In days of old when men had any awe
Of God, and paid Obedience to his Law,
Were more ambitious to be Good than Great,
They then Obey'd their King for CONSCIENCE SAKE,
As God's Annointed and as One whom He
Had by a Wise, a Just, and Good Decree
Seated with Power on the Regal Throne;
And therefore SUBJECT unto Him alone:
He did they knew by Jure Divino sway
The Royal Scepter, therefore did obey,
And their sincere Allegiance to him pay.
Nothing could then provoke them to rebell,
Because a Rebells Doom they knew too well.
Thus it continu'd 'till the World at last
Did after many years and ages past
Grow more Licentious, Wicked, and Profane,
And Men more Base and Turbulent became;
Scorning the poor Restraint of Government,
Inspite of Heaven they grew fully bent
To throw aside the Sneaking Servile Yoke,
Oppose their King and God himself provoke.
And thus RESISTANCE came at first in Vogue,
Rebells were Honest, Loyal Subjects Rogues.
The Devil highly did commend the Motion,
The which he back'd with this accursed Notion;
That Kings by Nature were no more than they,
Like them a Vessel made of Common Clay.
And thus at length in Arms whole Nations rose,
And did their King, and God himself oppose.
And so alass a Bloody Crew of Old
Of Great Brittania's Offspring, we are told,
Under the Saint-like Mask of Reformation
Did sadly ruin both the Church and Nation,
It's Grievances pretending to redress
When I durst say they thought of nothing less.
Religion Liberty was all the Cry,
And to secure the Laws, their King must die.
These Sons of Belial this infernal Crew
Both King and Subject did at length undo;
And Liberty it self a Victim fell
By those Accursed Instruments of Hell.
And then the silly Sotts when 'twas too late,
Bemoan'd their wretched and unhappy State,
And Gods assistance did again implore,
Whom they so basely had despis'd before;
Who did their Church and Monarchy restore.
But some there are alass, who not content
With any sort or kind of Government,
To Egypt back do cast a longing Eye,
Hope to be fool'd once more before they die.
Let such impartially but view this print,
And I am sure they'll say there's something in't
The Devil drives, the Patron of Rebellion
Is in the Coach, and H—ly rides Postillion.
The Steeds are fierce, and such become the Cause:
See under feet th' Crown, our Liberty, & Laws.
Behind the Covenant and Ropes you see,
To shew the Nation what their Doom must be,
Should Whigism once get the upper hand;
The good the wholesom Laws of this our Land,
Nay and the Church we seem so much to prize,
Must to those Rebels fall a Sacrafice:
And that same Liberty which now we boast
We may be sure will be for ever lost.
Let who will say there's nothing in this print,
I'll swear the Devil and OLD NOLL is in't.

Figure 5.7 A High Church response to the previous illustration.

(the symbol of law and liberty) lie cast down on the ground. The carriage is labelled 'commonwealth', in reference to the period without a king between 1649 and 1660, and, hanging behind it, is the 'covenant', the Solemn League and Covenant of 1643 which obliged those who took it to further the Reformation in England, a document which was seen by many as binding men to rebellion. Just as the print emulates but inverts the Whig version it attacks, so the 'Explanation' copies the form and subverts the message. It asserts that 'in days of old' men used to accept that God had anointed kings to rule by divine right ('jure divino') over them and that resistance was wrong; but men had grown 'licentious, wicked and profane' and scorned these restraints and rose in rebellion against their king under the 'mask of reformation'. At last these instruments of Hell undid both king and subjects; and though some repented and implored the return of the monarchy, others still harboured the good old cause of rebellion. The message was clear: 'should whiggism once get the upper hand' the Church and constitution were doomed. So rather than the Pretender in the coach, the Low Churchmen were driving 'old Noll', Oliver Cromwell. Fifty years after the restoration of the monarchy in 1660, the memory of the civil wars and commonwealth were still fresh enough to be used for polemical purposes, a vivid illustration of how the Revolution of 1688–9 was, for High Church Tories at least, uncomfortably like the mid-century revolution.

In these prints, as in many more, we can see that political argument had taken a visual turn. Polemical and satirical prints in dialogue in this way were relatively uncommon before the Sacheverell affair; the practice had first occurred in the 1640s, was reused during the Popish Plot and crisis of 1679–81, but it became routine during the height of partisan fervour in 1710–11. There were at least six tit-for-tat images, some including a third counter-response as well. Here, then, was innovation of a kind that was to have an enduring impact on the way in which political debate was, and still is, conducted. Visual satire was, of course, not in itself new; but the duality on which satire is based was undoubtedly boosted by the production of two conflicting images in dialogue with each other. Once we lay these two images side by side it is possible to see the 'double vision' caused by partisan politics. The same event—the trial of Sacheverell—was seen and interpreted in two completely different ways. Both saw liberty as being threatened by a devilish plot; but what the High Churchmen saw as the destruction of Church and State, leading to the tyranny of a commonwealth, the Low Churchmen saw as the destruction of hard-won rights and values, leading to the slavery of a Stuart restoration.

In these prints a few individuals—Sacheverell and Hoadly princi-pally, supported by a gallery of others, such as the Low Church Bishop Burnet—are made to represent others; they became emblems of the principles and parties they stood for. As a result, their personas were vigorously contested. Their characters, actions, and motives had all become contingent and relative to the partisan eye of the beholder. Thus whether Sacheverell and the others had been accurately or inaccurately treated was highly subjective and depended on partisan allegiance. They literally 'framed' their prints with explanations that taught the reader or viewer how to see what was in front of their eyes. Both sides were trying to 'unmask' the 'real' Sacheverell or the 'real' Hoadly.

Who, then, was the real Sacheverell? At one level, of course, it was obvious who Sacheverell was. He was the man staring out from many portraits, such as the mezzotint in Figure 5.8.

Figure 5.8 A portrait of Sacheverell using the new technique of mezzotint.

With his characteristic prominent eyes and parted wig he must have been instantly recognizable to large numbers who had never met him. Indeed, we might say that Sacheverell was one of the first non-royal persons to court a culture of celebrity and to acquire a visual fame, just as he was the first non-royal to go on a 'progress'. But Sacheverell was also an emblem for the Church—we know that his portrait was carried by Tories in several election campaigns. As a symbol his identity could also be inverted, to the extent that at times it seems as though there are two very different Sacheverells on view. Take for example, the single sheet woodcut in Figure 5.9. Here, as the accompanying text made

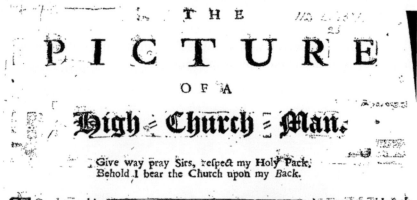

THE PICTURE OF A High-Church-Man.

Give way pray Sirs, respect my Holy Pack;
Behold I bear the Church upon my Back.

TO draw him to Perfection I here present him in his full Length, that the Publick, and such as are Lovers of Monsters, may not lose an Inch of him, tho' Black; (like a Lobster) be indeed his Natural, or Original Colour, yet to shew him truly, he shou'd be Printed in Crimson, or Bloody Colours; for he is Apostles, or Church Dragoons, that instead of wagimg War with the D----l, is always founding a Charge against his own Brethren; which

he manages with such High-Church Fury, and in moderate Zeal, that Woe ao the Poor Dissenter, or Moderate Church-Man, that comes within the reach of his Flaming Sword: Danger and the C----h, are two great Words with him, of which happy Doctrine he is so brimful, that he is a meer speaking Trumpet, and may with a favourable Winds, sometimes when he is deeply elevared on the Subject he heard as far as St. Germains; yet for all his Zeal, 'tis though

that if the Faggots were clapt to his A----e, he'd hardly die a Martyr for that Church he mtkes such a Noise of.

Figure 5.9 Sacheverell portrayed as a High Church Fury with a flaming sword.

clear, was Sacheverell the High Churchman depicted as a 'speaking trumpet' of 'fury and immoderate Zeal'. This was a very different Sacheverell to the one promoted by his admirers (and himself).

So too was the surprisingly harsh portrayal of Sacheverell found painted in a volume of Aesop's fables by its owner (Figure 5.10). This is one of three hostile caricatures, the only topical allusions in the book and ones that, as the crossing out suggests, someone at one time thought it better to erase.[54] In this image, Sacheverell is again,

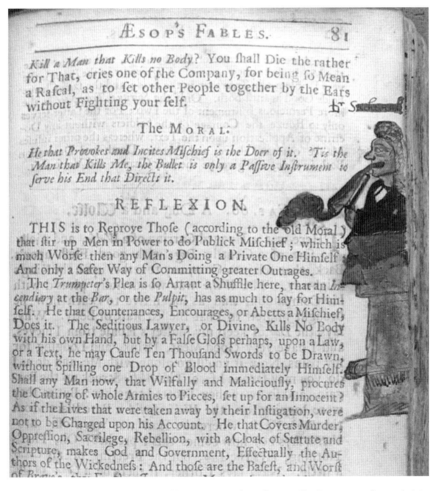

Kill a Man that *Kills no Body?* You fhall Die the rather for That, cries one of the Company, for being fo Mean a Rafcal, as to fet other People together by the Ears without Fighting your felf.

The M o r a l.

He that Provokes and Incites Mifchief is the Doer of it. 'Tis the Man that Kills Me, the Bullet is only a Paffive Inftrument to ferve his End that Directs it.

REFLEXION.

THIS is to Reprove Thofe (according to the old Moral) that ftir up Men in Power to do Publick Mifchief; which is much Worfe then any Man's Doing a Private One Himfelf: And only a Safer Way of Committing greater Outrages. The *Trumpeter's* Plea is fo Arrant a Shuffle here, that an *Incendiary* at the *Bar*, or the *Pulpit*, has as much to fay for Him-felf. He that Countenances, Encourages, or Abetts a Mifchief, Does it. The Seditious Lawyer, or Divine, Kills No Body with his own Hand, but by a Falfe Glofs perhaps, upon a Law, or a Text, he may Caufe Ten Thoufand Swords to be Drawn, without Spilling one Drop of Blood immediately Himfelf. Shall any Man now, that Wilfully and Malicioufly, procures the Cutting of whole Armies to Pieces, fet up for an Innocent? As if the Lives that were taken away by their Inftigation, were not to be Charged upon his Account. He that Covers Murder, Oppreffion, Sacrilege, Rebellion, with a Cloak of Statute and Scripture, makes God and Government, Effectually the Au-thors of the Wickednefs: And thofe are the Bafeft, and Worft

Figure 5.10 A hand-painted illustration of Sacheverell, depicting the pulpit's incendiary trumpeter mentioned in the text. Sacheverell was nicknamed 'the trumpeter' elsewhere in print. Sacheverell's name has been written above his head and subsequently inked over, though it is still legible.

literally, the 'trumpeter' of public mischief, and he is used to illustrate the moral 'He that provokes and incites mischief is the doer of it.' This anti-Sacheverellian caricature is all the more unexpected, since the edition of Aesop in which it appears is the translation by the Tory Roger L'Estrange, whose morals and reflections on Aesop's stories were politically charged and generally intended—as here—to denigrate Nonconformists, against whom L'Estrange kept up a constant barrage of writing. The owner of the book, an apothecary named Jeremiah Cliff, seems to have disliked Sacheverell so much that he could read against the grain of the reflections that L'Estrange had intended.

Reading against the grain also seems characteristic of the collector of prints who pasted sympathetic images into a copy of the official version of Sacheverell's trial. It is not entirely clear when the volume was bound, and it is possible that they were inserted later in the eighteenth century, but a number of the plates have what appears to be a contemporary handwritten page reference on them and the location of the images was deliberately subversive. For example, *A British Janus* (Figure 5.11), which depicts a Low Churchman as two-faced (half churchman, half tub-preaching-Dissenter), is deliberately placed opposite a prosecution speech that attacked Sacheverell, in order to undermine its force.[55] Thus in the speech, Sacheverell and his abettors were blamed for 'conspiring the ruin and destruction of the Church, when under the Disguise of a False Zeal they prostitute her sacred name, to carry on dark and deep designs, fatal both to Church and State'. But although the Whig prosecution was depicting Sacheverell as a dangerous fraud, the image instead depicts his *enemies* as the duplicitous ones, 'the true semblance of a hypocrite', as the text below it declared. The image thus refutes and undermines the character of Sacheverell being painted by the prosecution in the trial. So was Sacheverell the sincere upholder of the Church or a trumpeter of sedition? This question was raised in another set of prints (Figure 5.12 A and B), which explicitly asked to be read alongside the portrait of Sacheverell that graced the frontispiece of the printed version of the trial. The first, Whig, print, depicts the doctor being inspired by the Devil (the father of all lies) and by the pope. The suggestion is that he was in league with both. The second image, the Tory riposte, shows instead the High Churchman sending the Devil fleeing, and the papal hat, or tiara as it was known, is kicked away. In this print, Sacheverell is inspired by a figure representing a bishop of the Church of England. The Tory print was pasted into the copy of the trial,

Figure 5.11 A satire of a Low-Churchman, showing him to be hypocritically straddling both the established Church's pulpit on the left hand side and the tub-preaching of the Dissenters on the right.

opposite (and therefore bolstering) the transcript of Sacheverell's defence speech. Interestingly, a Tory tract was also published to attack this very Whig image and it spent many words trying to correct the image of Sacheverell as depicted by his enemies.[56] Indeed, the mass of biographical information spewed forth in the press about the doctor shows the paradox of making a particular man an emblem for the Church: he was (like the Cowpers) both an abstraction, and hence the object of attack and manipulation, but also, because of the intense attention he therefore received, an individual whose personality, vices, and virtues were known about in great detail. He was both cardboard cut-out and real man, but the personas were sometimes difficult to distinguish when he was the subject of polemic.

A

B

Figure 5.12 A and B At the top a satire of Sacheverell, showing the Devil and the pope whispering in his ear, and at the bottom a refutation of it, showing the doctor casting both away.

Figure 5.13 Detail of a response to the previous two illustrations, showing fame trumpeting Sacheverell, whose portrait is held aloft by two angels.

A third print in the sequence (Figure 5.13), which is again pasted into the trial volume, depicts Sacheverell (again via the ubiquitous portrait) held aloft by angels and his fame trumpeted. The accompanying text ridicules Whig attempts to tarnish Sacheverell's 'qualities'.

The Whig response to this is immortalized in a staircase mural at Hanbury Hall in Worcestershire, owned by a Whig MP Sir Thomas Vernon. In what could be seen as a direct rebuff of the eulogistic print portrait of the doctor, John Thornhill (who also decorated the new dome of St Paul's Cathedral in London) has Sacheverell and his sermon burnt by the torches of the Furies, who were put to flight by an allegorical Father Time (Figure 5.14)

These examples reinforce the sense of double vision noted earlier, of two ways of seeing the same person and of the 'doubleness' of that person. Partisanship heightened a sense of hypocrisy because two personas seemed to be clearly visible, dependent on the viewpoint of the beholder; and this duality made Sacheverell (just as it had Spencer or William Cowper) a contingent figure. His character and his motives could be seen very differently from different perspectives.

This sense of *relative truth* is rather important. It is tempting to equate the idea that truth is relative with the postmodernist movement of the late twentieth century; but it might also be applied to the pre-modern and even the modern world. The questioning of

Figure 5.14 The 'incendiary' Sacheverell is himself committed to the flames, in a mural at Hanbury Hall. The title of his sermon, *The Perils of False Brethren*, is just visible behind his portrait which is taken from one of the many print portraits published at the time.

traditional assumptions was often achieved by showing how things could be seen or done differently. By representing a given 'truth' from a different angle, it could become obvious that such 'truths' were not universal but rather shaped by custom or ignorance, prejudice, or superstition. Montaigne's relativism in the sixteenth century had led him to question the existence of any single truth. And relativism was a powerful tool in the Enlightenment onslaught. Voltaire, for example, used England to show France that French truths were not universally valid; Montesquieu did the same, and used Persia to critique French morals. For many in the Enlightenment—long before the relativity of post-modernism—truth was a relative value.

The torch being put to the portrait in the Hanbury Hall mural was an echo of Parliament's order to burn Sacheverell's sermon. But another printed image shows this event very differently (Figure 5.15). Playing on the idea of a book auction—a second-hand market was emerging as print became more profuse—the woodcut shows the state hangman, Jack Ketch, selling books in a perverse auction in which the highest bidder was able to consign his purchase to the flames. Although Ketch is offered just 2d for a collection of Daniel Defoe's *Review* ('full of disobedience to princes, teaching their people to rebel against government'), he is offered a whopping £500 by the Dissenters to throw Sacheverell's sermon ('its excellency has exceeded all that ever has been preached by High Church men') into the fire. Whereas the Hanbury Hall mural delighted in the burning of Sacheverell and his sermon, in this print the burning of Sacheverell's sermon is a lamentable outrage, the result of the malice of the Dissenters. Sacheverell is represented as the victim of a form of brutal censorship.

Figure 5.15 Sacheverell looks on from the coach as his sermon is burnt.

Perhaps in response, another print (Figure 5.16) takes the familiar portrait of Sacheverell and adds an approving padlock to his mouth, a reminder of the parliamentary ban on his preaching for three months. The image of a censored Sacheverell whose works had been cast into the flames is deeply ironic. For Sacheverell's High Church supporters burnt Benjamin Hoadly's works (and even an effigy of him), which suggest that, when it suited them, they were happy to do exactly what they condemned. More importantly, it had been the High Churchmen who had supported restrictions on the press for most of the pre-

Figure 5.16 The doctor with his mouth padlocked.

revolutionary period. And it was the High Churchmen who, after the loss in 1695 of government control over print prior to publication, lobbied for the restoration of some 'regulation' of a press that was seen as hostile to the Church. Sacheverell had wanted to thunder out 'anathemas', proscriptions, against his enemies, so he could hardly complain when one was issued against himself.

Moreover, in what is perhaps the greatest irony, Sacheverell's defence counsel had, during the trial, themselves invoked a decree, issued by the University of Oxford in 1683 which had ordered a whole cartload of Whiggish and Dissenting books onto a bonfire.[57] Since Oxford was a training ground for parsons, and hence a bastion of High Church Toryism, Sacheverell's defence had used the decree to support the case they were making about the long-running threats to the Church's doctrine. In 1683, in the wake of the alleged plot against the king's life, the university had castigated the right of resistance and the contractual nature of authority that had been put forward in print by a variety of authors, whose works they had condemned to the flames. Thus although Sacheverell was depicted after the judgment as a martyr to restrictions on his speech, he had, during his trial, sought support for his case from a High Church book-burning. So dangerous did the Whigs regard this move that, on the day he pronounced judgment against Sacheverell, Lord Chancellor Cowper also announced that the 1683 Oxford decree was to be burnt alongside the offending sermon. There was, of course, an apparent inconsistency here too: in burning the 1683 Oxford decree, Parliament seemed to be ordering a burning of a document which had itself ordered burnings. Parliament, like Sacheverell, seemed to be doing the very thing it condemned.

These ironies illustrate that the struggle for freedom of expression was laden with paradoxes and inconsistencies. It was not the case that the lapse of government control over the press in 1695 suddenly initiated an era in which speech was entirely free; Parliament continued to condemn, and even to burn, books. Even so, by the time of the Sacheverell crisis it was far more usual for print to be used to condemn print. Censure rather than censorship prevailed. That censure was made explicit in several of the Tory printed images produced in the Sacheverell affair, through the depiction of libraries of dangerous books that needed refuting. Thus a hostile satire against the Low Church figurehead, Benjamin Hoadly, shows his bookcase containing the works of John Locke, John Milton, Thomas Hobbes, Algernon Sidney, John Toland, James Harrington, and Bishop Burnet

(Figure 5.17). Apart perhaps from Burnet, whose work suggesting that the Revolution of 1688–9 had been a conquest was burnt by order of Parliament in 1693, all the other authors would find a place in any account of an English intellectual Enlightenment, for they argued for a contractual basis of authority.[58] In other words, important works of theory were censured in the simplest of visual satires in the cut and thrust of the Sacheverell controversy.

Figure 5.17 A detail of a satire depicting the Low Church Benjamin Hoadly with a bookcase of books. The titles were all Whig or republican tracts, indicating that Hoadly's ideas were dangerous.

Fifteen years after the lapse of the Licensing Act, there was thus still a good deal of ambiguity about the right to free speech and to print that speech. There was no clear triumph of liberal values. Freedom to print did not mean freedom to print sedition or libel; what constituted sedition or libel was still being defined. Censure had replaced censorship; but this, too, was liable to backfire, since the act of censuring could serve either ironically to promote the thing being condemned, by focusing attention on it that it might not otherwise have achieved, or to multiply the problem by provoking passionate defences of it. Yet the huge print debate surrounding the Sacheverell controversy suggests that Britain was moving from book-burning to a process in which print routinely countered print. Both Sacheverell and the Whigs had sought to repress those they saw as attacking their fundamental values; but both provoked a torrent of print, indicating that attempts merely to burn and ban were counterproductive. It was a lesson the incoming Tory government learned. Instead of reintroducing press censorship, in 1712 it acted in a more recognizably modern way and passed a tax on newspapers.

The Sacheverell furore prompted one of the largest floods of print that had ever rolled off English presses. More than a thousand items were published, ranging from single sheets to full-blown treatises. This was a larger number than for any other earlier single controversy and the output of the press now exceeded the totals achieved in the heady days of the Civil War. The scale and nature of the printed debate in 1710 confirms the importance of public opinion. The 'public' had acquired a place as judge or umpire of disputes between the parties. That role was enlarged by the frequent electioneering (there were elections on average every two and a half years between the succession crisis in Charles II's reign and the accession of the Hanoverians); by campaigns to get signatures or seals to petitions and addresses (of which those in 1710 were merely the latest in a series of nationwide appeals); and by the vying between the parties over a range of issues, from the conduct of the war and the nature of the economy to the issues of fundamental constitutional, religious, and political principle. It was not just the peers who were judging events such as Sacheverell's trial; a more informal court, that of public opinion, was now listening to and evaluating the evidence. Indeed, as the election of 1710 made clear, public opinion could be at odds with that of the government and exert such pressure that a government could fall.

The remarkable extensiveness of the printed debates nevertheless takes us back to the central concern of this chapter, the deceptions and dualities inherent in partisan politics. One of the disconcerting features of the war of words was that it could be highly deceptive and manipulative of a public that might not be capable of discerning the tricks of the propagandists. Advocates of press freedom had argued that print was an essential means to getting nearer to truth; but there were growing worries that the press could be used instead to manipulate and deceive, rather than properly to inform, the people. Sacheverell's defence team had themselves pointed to the pernicious effect of print in spreading blasphemy, heresy, irreligion, and sedition; but his admirers were as quick as any to rush into print to publicize and defend his views, and to use all the arts of the propagandist. Delarivier Manley's seductive mud-slinging against the Whigs was but one more example of how sophisticated and powerful the art of manipulation appeared to have become. Both sides were worried that the press, and the power of words, could be used to mislead the nation, to trick them into voting for a party that pretended to have its best interests at heart but which really pursued a hidden, and possibly sinister, agenda. The press was thus both the arena in which politics had to be fought; but also one which lent itself to lies, half-truths, and dissimulation on all sides. The liberation of the press had accompanied the development of party politics; and the incentive of partisans to lie and misrepresent their views in order to attract votes, denigrate their opponents, or deflect criticism was so high that they sought to use all the means, including the newly free press media, to achieve that. Print and politics had become inextricably linked.

The silver lining was that print had also to be hugely inventive if it was to win an audience. In the hands of Manley, Defoe, and Jonathan Swift, but also of much less well-known writers, a political and literary desire to persuade or even to deceive was accompanied by creativity, a liveliness of imagination and expression, and experiment with genre.

Although the verbal and visual satire of the period is sometimes difficult to appreciate because it was so closely tied to events and personalities of a distant era, the genre of satire thrived—indeed partly depended—on exposing the hidden deceptions of public life.

FANATICISM

Sacheverell might also have helped shift culture in another important way, by giving a further boost to the English idealization of moderation and sobriety of debate. For what seemed to be a conflict about religion and politics was also a profound discussion about how human beings should interact with one another. Ironically the vehemence with which partisans tore strips off one another—what some called the 'rage of party'—necessitated the condemnation of the extremes of partisan polemic. An ideal of polite and moderate rationality was developed to oppose it. Key to this debate, as it was to the Enlightenment more generally, was the notion of 'fanaticism'.

In the years immediately before Sacheverell's trial, England had already experienced a controversy about zeal, fanaticism, and the impostures that might lie behind it. In 1707 a small group of 'French Prophets' had arrived in England and acquired a small but enthusiastic following. The prophets claimed miraculous powers and to be messengers of God, even prophesying the resurrection of one of their followers. They predicted the destruction of London and other cities, claimed to be able to cure maladies, spoke in foreign languages, and shook with religious emotion just like the Quakers. They sparked an extensive print debate, with ninety hostile tracts published between 1707 and 1710 against them, many expressing revulsion at the enthusiasm they saw.[59] That debate influenced both the way in which Sacheverell's sermon was received, and the meaning of the terms 'fanatic' and 'zealot' that were levelled both at Sacheverell himself and by Sacheverell at the Dissenters. These terms had always been loaded; but they were now very highly charged and even more the object of ridicule.

So when Sacheverell, like many High Churchmen, had applied the term 'fanatics' to all Dissenters he was deliberately reopening an old sore. Not only could he utilize the condemnation of the French Prophets, but he could also invoke the association, forged in the 1640s and 1650s, between enthusiastic religious Dissent and disorder. Indeed, Sacheverell had explicitly linked religious fanaticism to rebellion and resistance. That association was made repeatedly by many others, as the image from a 1713 publication (by Manley's publisher John Morphew) shows (Figure 5.18). The title of the work, *The Whigs Unmask'd*, is significant, not only because it again plays on the idea of unmasking and unveiling the truth but also because it shows how the stereotype of the seditious fanatic was extended to encompass the entire Whig Party. A curtain has been pulled aside to let in the light; Britannia holds the shining doctor's portrait as an enlightening antidote to Whig sedition. High Church Tories saw the

Figure 5.18 The fanatics on the left hold a banner proclaiming 'No peace' and 'Rebelion'. Sacheverell, by contrast, reflects the light of obedience and non-resistance.

Whigs as fanatical conspirators plotting rebellion; and Sacheverell had unveiled and revealed their true identities.

Yet Sacheverell was in turn called a fanatic—even 'the Arch-Phanatick' by one critic.[60] A Low Church clergyman, William Bisset, published a best-selling character assassination of Sacheverell under the title *The Modern Fanatick*, and it proved so popular that he followed it up with two further parts, each using the term 'Fanatick' in the title. Bisset claimed, at the end of 1710, that he had 'not heard so much fanaticism in all my life, as within these last 12 months' from the High Churchmen, and that Sacheverell was a fanatical man of 'fierceness and rage' with a 'goggling wildness' in his eyes. Bisset also alleged that the rioters who had attacked the Dissenting Meeting Houses in London during the trial were the 'real Fanaticks'. In turn a visual satire of Bisset was published as *The Picture of a True Fanatick*. It shows him in his study, graced with a portrait of Hoadly and the arms of the mid-century commonwealth, inspired by the Devil. The charge of fanaticism was thus one bandied about on both sides. The High Churchmen saw the Dissenters as fanatics who had already once plunged England into civil war; the Low Churchmen thought that Sacheverell's intemperate zeal, rage, and bigotry, directed against the Dissenters, was its counterpart. And both sought to uncover, unveil, expose the other, convinced that hidden under an outer, insincere but plausible veneer there lay the true fanatic.

The hostility from both parties to the religious and political fanaticism that they perceived in the other fed into a wider cultural shift. Fanaticism, particularly when linked to prejudice and bigotry, was one of the chief bugbears of the Enlightenment, which instead championed reason, moderation, polite sociability, toleration, and impartiality of judgement. For the early Enlightenment, fanaticism or zeal was both a state of mind, a mental frenzy, and an intemperate way of arguing and behaving. Fanaticism was characterized by an overheated imagination, by a hatred of others that could overflow into rage or sinisterly boil within, and by a closing of the mind to the reasonable behaviour of others. It was allied to 'enthusiasm', a word that had little of its modern, positive connotation of excited interest and instead implied over-excited fervour. From the 1650s, when the Quakers and other sectarians became physically convulsed by their faith, 'enthusiasm' had increasingly meant, as one writer of the 1650s put it, 'an extraordinary, transcendant but natural fervency, or pregnancy of the soul, spirits or brain, producing some strange effects, apt to be mistaken for supernatural'.[61] Enthusiasm was condemned in both politics and religion.

The opposite of fanaticism or enthusiasm was moderation, both as an end in itself that could achieve harmony within the individual or the State and as a way of being, a calm, sociable, and considered mode of behaving with others. Moderation was sobriety, a willingness to listen to the arguments of others in a dispassionate way, a desire to examine a question impartially and rationally, a desire to place sociability above division or reason above passion, a tolerance of others' views even when disagreeing with them. The sheer excess of the Tory rage in 1710 provoked an ever greater idealization of moderation. Not surprisingly, lip-service to moderation was suspected by the High Churchmen as simply a veneer, another level of hypocrisy, covering a lukewarmness of attitude to the things that mattered, a cunning and dangerous indifference that could undermine the things it professed to want to protect. Sacheverell's attack on the 'false brethren' had itself been a shaft aimed at those who professed moderation and it prompted many more. Moderation was not needed, the doctor declared, when the Church and State were in danger. In such times, moderation was dangerous; zeal in defence of the Church and State, zeal against fanaticism, was the solution. Moderation, then, that most a-politically sounding of characteristics, was not a-political at all but a contested term.

SACHEVERELL'S LONGER-TERM LEGACY

The Sacheverell trial had an enduring legacy, not just in the idealization of moderate politeness or in shaping the policies of Robert Walpole when he became prime minister in 1720. In 1791 Edmund Burke, himself utterly immersed in the Whig culture that stemmed from Walpole's Whiggery, devoted most of a pamphlet to a detailed discussion of the Sacheverell trial. His *Appeal from the Old to the New Whigs* was written to attack the French Revolution and its principles, and to vindicate Burke from the critics of his *Reflections on the Revolution of France*, who had accused him of deserting Whig principles. These 'New Whigs', Burke said, were mistaken in seeing events in France as a repeat of the British Revolution exactly one hundred years earlier. Whereas the Revolution of 1688–9 had been entirely beneficial, Burke insisted, the French Revolution of 1789 was 'a positive evil', merely a 'wild attempt to methodise anarchy; to perpetuate and fix disorder'. The French revolutionaries were, he protested, intolerant, impious, tyrannous, cruel, and aggressive, the very opposite of what the British revolutionaries had been. And in order to show how his own ideology exactly mirrored those of the revolutionaries of 1688–9, and 'for the express purpose of stating the true grounds and principles of the [British] Revolution', Burke analysed and quoted liberally from the prosecution speeches against Sacheverell. Universal Whig principles were to be found there, or nowhere, Burke suggested. In other words, the prosecution case made at the trial of Henry Sacheverell was the best guide he could think of to the fundamental principles of the Whig Party that dominated so much of the eighteenth century, and hence also to the right way of thinking about the ordering of society.

Burke believed that the trial justified his own views. 'The foundations laid down by the Commons, on the trial of Doctor Sacheverell, in justifying the Revolution of 1688–9, are the very same laid down in Mr Burke's *Reflections*', he asserted (writing in the third person to impart more of an objective air). There was a right of resistance, Burke admitted, and that had been demonstrated at Sacheverell's trial; but that right, he insisted, could only be exercised as a last resort, when necessity required it. In any case, it owed nothing, he insisted, to the doctrine of natural rights so admired by French revolutionaries and their British sympathizers. Natural rights—rights derived from a state of nature, in which men had lived before entering into any civilization or government, and which inhered in them even in civil society—were, for him, dangerous abstractions. They had not been appealed to by the prosecutors of Sacheverell, he said. The 'rights of man', favoured by the French revolutionaries and Burke's own critics, were thus incompatible with civil society and were a betrayal of the principles set out by the Whigs in 1710.

Burke was both right and wrong in his analysis of the Sacheverell trial. He was wrong that natural rights played no part in it. The 1683 decree by the University of Oxford, invoked by Sacheverell's defence, had set out an ideology of rights and contractual power that the High Churchmen detested. The ideas that Oxford had condemned to the flames were: that civil authority was derived from the people; that there was a 'compact' or contract between rulers and ruled; that if rulers became tyrants they forfeited their right to rule; that self-defence was therefore a 'fundamental law of nature' that could override all others; and that the basis of civil authority was natural rights.[62] The debate about the right of resistance that Sacheverell raised could thus not be divorced from a larger debate about where legitimate authority came from and who held it. And the condemnation of the 1683 Oxford decree alongside Sacheverell's sermon in 1710 implicitly championed natural rights and the powers that they conferred on the people. Even so, Burke was right that the Whigs of 1710 did not argue for the routine exercise of power by the people: the contract between ruler(s) and ruled set up a legislative power which was the representative of the people. Only when that legislature was subverted, and hence representative consent was no longer possible, was resistance justified. Government by consent, the ideal pursued by the Whigs, was thus not direct *democratic* government, but *representative* government.

Burke's invocation of the Whig prosecution of 1710 nicely shows the long shadow that the trial of Henry Sacheverell cast over the eighteenth century. But it was also deeply ironic, for the Whiggish Burke has also been seen as the intellectual father of a conservatism later hailed by a modern Tory Party. His appeal to the traditions of the past, and the honour he paid to an 'ancient constitution', with its institutions of monarchy and aristocracy, together with the very limited role he allowed the people, do indeed suggest a conservative ideology. But the irony of Burke's position highlights that the Revolution of 1688–9 could itself be read in two very different ways. For Burke, the Revolution was the exception that proved the rule; the people only had an exceptional role in governance, at elections and, in rare cases of *extremis*, when the executive power trampled on the constitution. For others, who set up Revolution Societies in the late eighteenth century to mark the centenary of 1688–9, it was proof that the people should have a much more important role. This tension amongst the Whigs was apparent in 1710 as much as 1790 or 1791. And if 1688–9 could be seen in two different ways by Whigs it was also seen in two lights by Tories, either as a lamentable necessity to obtain a Protestant monarchy or as a betrayal of Protestantism and fatal weakening of the institutions of monarchy and Church. The rallying cry of 'Church and King' was still potent in 1791, when a mob shouting the slogan went on the rampage in Birmingham and attacked the house where revolution principles were being toasted by those luminaries of the Enlightenment, Joseph Priestley and Josiah Wedgewood.

6

DESPAIR AND DEMONISM

In 1712 Jane Wenham, the last woman in England convicted of witchcraft, was accused of the unusual crime of 'conversing familiarly with the Devil in the Shape of a Cat'. Wenham was tried in the same courtroom in which Spencer had been tried for the murder of Sarah Stout, and her diabolic crime took place in a village just over eight miles north of Hertford. Indeed, the Devil seemed to haunt Hertfordshire. Spencer Cowper had been alleged to have murdered Sarah Stout at 'the instigation of the Devil'; and Quakers like her were said by their enemies to be deluded by demons, to worship the Devil and to bewitch others. Sarah's suicide (giving Spencer the benefit of the doubt and assuming that she took her own life) was also ascribed to the temptation of the Devil. Was this apparent prevalence of the Devil a sign that the early English Enlightenment was still wedded to older ways of thinking? Or might we see, in the fact that Wenham was spared the capital punishment she deserved as a witch, a change in attitudes to Satan?

The Devil has appeared numerous times in preceding pages. Sacheverell memorably wanted to anathematize 'hypocrites and unbelievers, with all liars, that have their part in the lake which burns with fire and brimstone, with the Grand-father of Falsehood, the Devil'. And devils have adorned many of the images reproduced in this book—devils pointing to the ranks of fanatics; a devil puffing up the pride and lust of a male Quaker; the Devil leering at a female Quaker; a devil driving the coach of State, or whispering sedition in the ears of clerics. As these examples suggest, contemporaries still worried about the capacity of the Devil to seduce, tempt, corrupt, and insinuate evil. He could shape thoughts and plant ideas. He was able to 'rub our temples with his opium of poisonous suggestions', as one minister memorably put it in 1657.[1] Resisting him was all the more difficult because of the Devil's capacity for disguise: Satan could hide and cover himself, even (according to the Bible) in light as well as lies. The Quakers, the liars, the hypocrites, explored in earlier chapters, were thus devil-like.

Yet the images of the Devil reproduced in this book, used in the partisan and polemical battles we have been examining, are not particularly frightening. They are emblematic, metaphoric, sometimes even comic, rather than fearful in their own right. Even though the Devil could still be depicted as insinuating evil, he had become more of a stock character than a terrifying presence. It was not that evil or the idea of the Devil went away, but that during the later seventeenth century demonism—the power of the Devil—was challenged and reoriented in a variety of ways. There was an active debate in the second half of the seventeenth century about the nature of Hell, and especially about the eternity of Hell's fires, to the extent that one scholar, D. P. Walker, has referred to 'the decline of hell' in this period. A sermon by John Tillotson, a few months before he was made archbishop of Canterbury, caused something of a sensation in 1690 when he sought to soften the threat of Hell by suggesting that a benign God was not obliged to enforce a sentence of eternal damnation. The sermon was said by one High Church critic to have been carried round by atheists and deists who thought it 'set mankind free from the slavish notion of eternal torments'.[2] Rethinking God in the ways described earlier also necessitated rethinking the Devil, since the decline of a Calvinistic God (who saved only a few and destined the rest to Hell) necessarily reduced the size of the kingdom of darkness. Sarah Cowper thought that only 'dull and stupid spirits' thought of Hell as real. Rather, she observed tellingly, it arose 'out of a man's self'.[3] In this she was perhaps echoing Milton's Satan, who cries 'Which way I fly is Hell; my self am Hell.'[4]

At the same time diabolic responsibility for suicide and witchcraft was being reassessed. Suicide was, for most of the sixteenth century, seen as a crime against God, a sin inspired by the Devil that merited the forfeiture of all goods and a gruesome burial in the public highway, with a stake plunged through the body. But suicide, once thought of as the result of the Devil's temptation to despair, came to be seen more a matter of a disturbed mind, reflecting a sense of great human, rather than supernatural, agency and also a shift from soul to mind as the seat of disorder. The first half of the chapter explores these issues by returning to Sarah Stout's suicide (if that is, indeed, what it was). This occurred at a time of national debate about suicide, since many feared that it was on the rise at this time and sought explanations for this. Libertinism and atheism were again both blamed. The refusal of Sarah's mother to accept that her daughter could have committed such an act, because it violated Quaker beliefs, also throws into the spotlight an interesting debate about how far religious enthusiasm was responsible for suicidal melancholy. Sarah could stand as a classic example of a religious melancholic whose decision to end her life was taken in a moment of unsound mind brought on by the pressures of her faith. In this reading of events psychology rather than demonology offered a more convincing explanation of what induced her despair. This leads us to consider natural explanations of melancholia and of the religious enthusiasm that could cause it. Analysis of the Quakers and other religious 'fanatics' helped to disseminate ideas about 'animal spirits' as the mechanical means by which the soul, mind, and body interacted, and even by which 'inspiration' spread. Animal spirits were not incompatible with a belief in the Devil; but they tended to focus attention on natural rather than supernatural causes.

Suicide was one way in which beliefs about the Devil were refracted; another was witchcraft. Belief in witchcraft, the most dangerous form of which was thought to be a compact with the Devil, was similarly under scrutiny and the last conviction of a witch occurred in Hertford in 1712. A number of factors lay behind the trend of declining prosecutions and convictions. One was the scepticism of judges and lawyers, who increasingly demanded higher standards of legal proof. Explanations of unusual events by science, medicine, and reason could also be invoked instead of (or at least alongside) the supernatural and combined with a suspicion of religious enthusiasm, superstition, and, as we have seen, changing ideas about God and the Devil. Socio-economic factors also played a part: since allegations of witchcraft were often directed against the marginalized poor, better systems of poor relief and a levelling of population-growth reduced some of the underlying communal tension. The improvements in provision for the poor were in part a reflection of a growing State, one that was less reliant on supernatural notions of divinely appointed monarchy. The waning of the witchcraft craze was not limited to England. It is worth recalling that in 1711 in Puritan New England, the judgments against the twenty found guilty in Salem of witchcraft between 1692 and 1693 were reversed and the families of the victims compensated.[5]

So there were larger currents afoot across Europe and North America. The Hertford case becomes emblematic of these; but it also highlights the power of English anticlericalism and a lively debate about the roles of revelation and the supernatural. To the clergymen behind the trial, belief in demonic witchcraft was justified by Scripture and hence to deny it (and the spiritual world) was to question both the Bible and the power of the supernatural (including God) to intervene on earth. But critics of the prosecution sought physical and psychological explanations for the strange occurrences that were said to have occurred. As with the debate over suicide, natural causes were increasingly invoked. And critics also attacked a purely religious explanation. They refuted claims that the Bible talked of witches; and they suspected the clerical responsibility for Jane's prosecution was merely the culmination of a more metaphorical High Church witch-hunt initiated by Sacheverell and others. Whilst not explicitly denying the Devil, such critics minimized, even marginalized, his role.

Neither the shift in attitudes to suicide or witchcraft was the result purely of factors novel to the late seventeenth century. There had been a history of scepticism about witchcraft since the sixteenth century and attitudes about suicide were evolutionary rather than revolutionary. Nevertheless, the culture of the later seventeenth century encouraged and accelerated both trends in interesting ways. Both suicide and witchcraft had been thought of as manifestations of the Devil's capacity to intervene in the natural world and invade the minds and souls of individuals. But by the early eighteenth century such attitudes were increasingly being questioned. In a sense, the body was becoming perceived as less porous to evil spirits and more literally self-contained. And, in England at least, a partisan political culture was both reshaping ideas about the inspiration of malice and evil (blaming partisans as much as the Devil) and, as we shall see, influencing the reaction to allegations of witchcraft.

Indeed, partisanship was thought of as its own form of witchcraft. The people were often said to have been 'bewitched' by the parties. Indeed in 1726 Daniel Defoe argued that the Devil no longer needed the intermediaries of witches and goblins, for modern, partisan man had now become so sophisticated in his wickedness that he turned directly into a devil. In Defoe's eyes, Satan could now inhabit men even without their knowing it; humans were inhuman, playing 'devils to one another'. And he linked this development to the partisan culture we have been exploring. 'Anger, Envy, Revenge, Hatred, Wrath, Strife'—the extreme passions most associated with the rage of party—were signs that a man was 'possess'd, the Devil is in him'.[6] Partisanship had made Whigs and Tories the modern devils. The conviction that religion was being used as a veneer to cover sinister but essentially human self-interest and ambition (a conviction that, as we have seen, underpinned both sides of the partisan battles of the later Stuart period) seemed to suggest that corrupt human nature as much as the powers of the Devil was at work.

MELANCHOLIC DESPAIR AND SUICIDE

One important condition for understanding contemporary thinking about natural and supernatural forces was melancholy, which was thought to leave sufferers particularly vulnerable to despair, and hence to suicide and the temptations of the Devil. Melancholy was certainly a point at issue in Sarah Stout's trial, since Spencer Cowper sought to represent her as melancholic. Her family, of course, denied this, claiming that the afternoon before her death, she had happily joined the crowds who turned out to see the judges make their customary grand entry into Hertford for the assizes and was 'as Brisk and Airy... as Merry and Pleasant as any amongst them'. Since she had even invited a female friend to dinner the next day, they said, she could have had no intention to commit suicide. Her mother and brother protested that they had 'never observed her Melancholly, and all her intimate Companions do assert the same'. At the original coroner's inquest Spencer Cowper had seemed to confirm this, saying that 'he did not observe her any ways Melancholly'.[6] But at his trial, a different version emerged, closely related to Spencer's claim that she had been lovesick but also playing on the stereotype of the melancholic religious enthusiast.[7] Sarah had allegedly told one witness that 'her Melancholy had occasion'd an intermitting Feaver', and, when recommended a doctor, Sarah 'said her distemper lay in her Mind, and not in her Body, and she would take nothing, and the sooner it did kill her the better... She said nothing delighted her now, neither reading nor anything else.' Another witness used the same word, melancholy, to describe Sarah:

> I can say she always acknowledg'd her self extreamly Melancholy, and when I have asked her how she did, she has said pretty well in Health, but so much troubled with Melancholy she could not tell what to do with her self.

Sarah's maid had been forced to admit, under cross-examination by Spencer, that her mistress had been 'melancholy', though she put this down to the effects of illness—a 'great pain in her head'—rather than to any infatuation. Spencer produced two further local witnesses, explicitly to prove that Sarah was melancholic, and then called his own sister-in-law, Judith, to give evidence. The latter recounted a visit that Sarah had made to London in the spring of 1698. The two women had often been together and Judith claimed she was never an hour alone with Sarah without noticing 'something of her Melancholy'. On two occasions, Judith insisted, Sarah had talked of wishing she was dead:

> the last time I saw her, was at my Sisters Lodgings, and I sent for her to drink a dish of Tea with us, and she came in a great toss and melancholy; saith I, What is the matter you are always in this odd Humour? saith she, I can't help it, I shall never be otherwise; saith [Judith Cowper], for God's sake keep such Thoughts out of your Head as you have had, don't talk any more of throwing your self out of Window; saith she, I may thank God that ever I saw your Face, otherwise I had done it; but I can't promise I shall not do it.

This was not mere invention. In a letter that was produced neither at the trial nor subsequently, Spencer's wife Pennington wrote to Judith about Sarah: 'betwixt you & I she is got into a very ill way, so excessively melancholy that she is strangly alter'd & tells me she has no Joy of her Life! I have given her all ye advice I can (& some I can give, in that case, which comes from wofull experience) but to very little purpose.'[8] Perhaps the letter was never used in evidence because it suggested that Spencer's wife had needed to deal with her own melancholy, which might have opened up questions about the state of his marriage.

In stressing Sarah's melancholia, Spencer had been drawing on a stereotype, just as much as he had when implying Sarah's lustfulness, for melancholia was associated closely with excess emotion, and particularly with immoderate love and religious devotion. There is an interesting ballad literature on young women who killed themselves for love—Samuel Pepys collected it—but it is the link with religious devotion that Spencer perhaps especially wanted to exploit.[9] In 1621—though subsequently frequently revised before his death in 1640 and running to eight editions in the seventeenth century—Robert Burton, an academic cleric who himself suffered from melancholy, published an *Anatomy of Melancholy*. Burton saw melancholy as a 'disease of the soul', for which he was a 'spiritual physician'. His work nicely shows both that religion and science were not separated in the seventeenth century, and how musing on the soul led to an early form of pyschology. Burton's work explored the many different types of melancholy, but the two that most concerned him were love and, more controversially, religion. In his discussion of religious melancholy, Burton suggested that the Devil worked through politicians and priests, to induce superstition, fear, and ignorance. Religious melancholics displayed a love of their own sect but hatred of all others, obstinacy, peevishness, 'blind zeal', and belief in incredible things. Burton associated this with vehement anti-popery, and hence with those protestant sectarians who:

> out of too much zeale, in opposition to Antichrist and humane traditions, and those Romish ceremonies and superstitions, will quite demolish all... will admit of no ceremonies at all, no fasting dayes, no crosse in Baptisme, kneeling at Communion, no Church musicke, &c. no Bishops Courts, and Church government, rayle at all our Church discipline, and will not hold their tongues... No interpretations of Scriptures, no comments of Fathers, no Councells, but such as their owne phantasticall spirits dictate, by which spirit misled many times they broach as prodigious paradoxes as Papists themselves. Some of them turne Prophets, and have secret revelations... some of them are so farre gone with their private Enthusiasmes, and revelations, that they are quite madde, out of their wits.[10]

Burton thought such religious melancholy, inspired by the Devil or by 'rigid ministers' who made their flocks fearful, induced despair, and warned that this could lead to suicide. Burton was writing before the Quaker movement had arisen, but his analysis had obvious relevance. Dissenters themselves recognized the problem. In Bunyan's *Pilgrim's Progress* (1678) the pilgrims Christian and Hopeful became bogged down in the Slough of Despond, impeded by the Giant Despair who tempted them to commit suicide.

Melancholy was thus associated with enthusiastic religion, with the Devil, delusion, despair, and suicide. Dissenters and particularly sects such as the Quakers seemed to be perfect examples of the disease. *A Sad Caveat to Quakers* (1657) recounted how William Pool, a Quaker apprentice from Worcester, was found drowned in a river shortly after 'the prince of darkness had appeared to him in the shape of some godly personage, and this credulous young man was apt to believe that it was Christ'. Misled by 'the temptation and impulsion of the devil', the youth had taken his own life.

The Quakers were particularly vulnerable to accusations of being possessed because of their unconventional ideas about the Devil. Protestants of all kinds saw an inward battle with Satan; doubts and temptations, which were seen as the Devil's tools, were part of that struggle. Unlike most Protestants, however, the Quakers believed in the perfectibility of man, and hence in the possibility of man's triumph over the Devil. In a purified state, the Quaker would be filled with inner light that displaced Satan, a doctrine that placed the sect at odds with most of Protestantism. This conviction was one of the points of contest between Henry Stout and the independent minister in Hertford, William Haworth. Stout thought the Devil far less powerful than Christ, who could fill the true believer and give him 'the Armour of Light against all the fiery Darts of the Wicked'.[11] To the Quakers' critics, however, the Devil had not been banished at all; rather the Quakers were possessed by Satan himself or, as Haworth put it, they had transformed Satan into their angel of light. Haworth insisted that Satan was 'not yet bound up in hell' and that the Hertford Quakers were 'in the snare of the Devil', possessed by the 'Satanical Spirit' of lying.[12] Quakerism was thus, as the title of one 1692 tract put it, 'a grand delusion', its members mistaking the Devil for God; they were literally bewitched.[13] Thus in 1707 another pamphlet accused them of being 'Sorcerers' who used 'witchcraft' to convert and 'bewitch' their followers.[14] Mary Stout attacked Haworth for saying that the female Quaker preachers were 'witches'.[15] It followed from this that Quakers were particularly vulnerable to satanic temptations—both to demonic lust but also to demonic despair and thoughts of suicide. Moreover, whereas Protestants both within and outside of the Church of England could defend and protect themselves against the Devil with prayer and worship, the Quakers' rejection of these, in their conventional form, meant that, in the eyes of their enemies, they lacked the shield available to others. So the Quakers could be depicted as possessed by the Devil and as lacking the defences available to Protestants to help them withstand his temptations.

As was perhaps inevitable, the association between suicide, demonic despair, and Dissent also became caught up in partisan rivalries. In 1682, during the High Church Tory persecution of Dissenters, John Child, a Baptist minister, published a call for Nonconformists to return to the national Church; but his apostasy induced such guilt that he killed himself two years later. His death was seen by churchmen as further proof of the link between Dissent and despair; but it was also used by the Dissenters as proof that the Devil had persuaded Child to abandon his faith. The most political case of suicide was nevertheless that of the earl of Essex in 1683. Essex, a leader of the first Whigs, had been arrested for plotting an insurrection and assassination of the duke of York and imprisoned in the Tower. He was

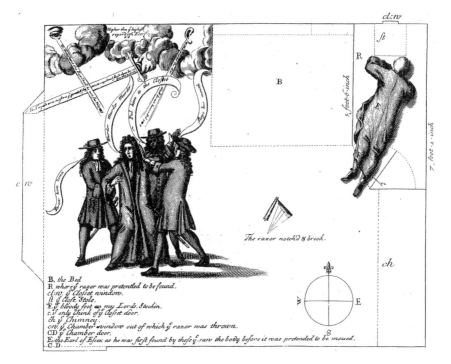

Figure 6.1 The suicide of the earl of Essex represented as murder. The author of the tract from which this is taken, Laurence Braddon, dedicated himself to proving that the coroner's verdict of suicide was not justified by the evidence.

found dead, with his throat slit. For the Tories, Essex was thus guilty of rebellion against God as well as against his king; but, in an interesting reversal of the Sarah Stout affair, the Whigs tried to prove that Essex's 'suicide' had been murder. A pamphlet campaign, which blamed the future James II for authorizing the murder, picked over the forensic evidence. John Locke, the Whig philosopher who had been trained as a doctor, wrote a manuscript supporting the conspiracy theory. Indeed, suspicion that he had a hand in the published version of the earl's 'Barbarous Murder' seems to have helped to trigger Locke's flight into exile in Holland.[16] In one 1689 publication a frontispiece carefully set out how the murder must have taken place.[17] The post-revolution attempts to vindicate Essex were halted only when his widow intervened to say that she did not suspect foul play.

If the Dissenting or Whiggish melancholic was a danger to himself, the deist was thought to be an even greater one because he offered a rationalized justification for suicide: that man was in charge of his own destiny and that suicide was not always wrong and could even be honourable. The most notorious deist who asserted this was Charles Blount, who Sir William Cowper knew well, since they both belonged to the vehemently Whig Green Ribbon Club and shared a desire to bar James duke of York from succeeding to the throne. Indeed it is possible that it was Blount who gave Cowper the deist tracts by James Boevey. Blount killed himself in 1693 and his High Church critics argued for an intrinsic link between deism and despair.

Blount had written some important Whiggish and virulently anti-Catholic pieces; but it was his deism and anticlericalism for which he was most remembered. In 1679 he published *The Last Sayings* of Thomas Hobbes, reproducing extracts from the latter's *Leviathan*, which many took to be religiously sceptical as well as politically dangerous because of its displacement of the authority of the Church. He quoted Hobbes again in a 1683 attack on miracles, *Miracles, No Violations of the Laws of Nature*, which also drew heavily on the work of Benedict Spinoza, a Dutch radical who was at the centre of the radical Enlightenment.[18] Indeed, Blount's work was the first English translation of the Dutch deist. In the same year Blount published another deist work, this one influenced by Lord Herbert of Cherbury, whose five principles of religion—that God exists; God ought to be worshipped; that the heart of religion is found in virtue joined with piety; that evils must and can be expiated by means of repentance; and that people face reward or punishment after this life—were shared by Boevey. But it was Blount's *Oracles of Reason*, published just before his death in 1693 that perhaps sealed his reputation as a freethinker, since it contained further attacks on miracles and priestcraft, and championed nature, reason, and liberty of judgement. The *Oracles of Reason* was, it will be recalled, quoted at Sacheverell's trial as proof that irreligion was afoot. Blount's publication included work by his friend (and would-be biographer of Delarivier Manley) Charles Gildon and it was Gildon who wrote a biography of Blount as a preface to the latter's *Miscellaneous Works*, published in 1695.[19] The biography caused a sensation, because in it Gildon explained and defended Blount's suicide.

Blount had fallen in love with the sister of his dead wife, but the Church had refused him permission to marry her. Having tried in vain to persuade her to marry him without clerical approval (arguing that Leviticus merely barred a man from sexually enjoying a wife's sister if he did not marry her), Blount attempted suicide, dying a month later of his injuries. Gildon suggested that Blount held the view that there was no *absolute* law against suicide but rather that there were 'various limitations and exceptions', for otherwise there 'wou'd be no room left for Honour, Virtue or indeed for Honesty, no regard to public good'. There were, he insisted, times when all these factors demanded self-killing. Blount, according to Gildon, went even further, arguing that each individual had the right to judge when these conditions prevailed and hence 'Every man is...Judge or rather disposer of himself.' Indeed, Gildon quoted a line from a Dryden play, *The Conquest of Granada* (1670), in which the independent and swashbuckling hero Almanzor tells the last Moorish king of Granada 'I my Self am King of Me.' Blount also invoked classical precedents for honourable suicide, such as Cato, Brutus, and Cassius. Here, then, was a radical, non-Christian notion that the individual, rather than God, was the 'disposer of himself'. It was no wonder, then, that in 1699 the High Church cleric and polemicist Charles Leslie argued that deists advocated suicide as a matter of principle, or that another essayist said that suicide was being looked on as 'a thing indifferent, that may be good or bad according to the circumstances with which it is attended', rather than a breach of an absolute divine injunction against self-killing.[20] At the end of 1699 another clergyman, John Adams, similarly condemned the 'free thinking Gentlemen' who claimed the 'liberty of following their own reason' and for treating life 'as a dull Business, not worth a Man's care'. He, too, castigated the new 'principle' that justified suicide on the grounds that 'I and no other am to be Judge in this Case; therefore if Life by the want of any Good, in which I place my Happiness, becomes an Evil, and Death seems good to me, I do but follow Nature in killing my self.'[21]

As one historian of suicide puts it, the period from the 1680s to about 1720 may be termed the 'libertine era of suicide. Protagonists arose to assert their right to do the deed with spirit and with consciences intellectually justified by philosophical libertinism.'[22] Another suicide in 1700 seemed to confirm this trend. In 1700 Thomas Creech, an Oxford don (and absentee rector of Welwyn in Hertfordshire) who had translated the works of Lucretius, hung himself. Lucretius was a Roman poet who argued that the world was governed by natural processes, the regular motions of atoms, rather than any divine will and that death was merely a ceasing to exist which should not be a fearful event. Lucretius had thus argued in favour of suicide and he, and the philosopher Epicurus who he followed, became highly fashionable in the later seventeenth century. Although it seems unlikely that Creech took his own life in order to exemplify Lucretian philosophy (he too seems to have been unlucky in love), it did not help that he allegedly died with a copy of a tract justifying suicide to hand. This was *Biathanatos*, which had been written by the poet John Donne at the beginning of the seventeenth century to deny that suicide was always sinful. Although not published until 1646, Donne's relativist position—suicide was neither good nor bad in itself but dependent on circumstances—caused shock and it is significant that it was again republished in 1700, when such ideas were gathering support.

It is true that Gildon published a retraction in 1705 of his own support for suicide, but by then Joseph Addison, one of the most influential writers of his day, had already written a play, not performed until 1713, about Cato, the Roman who had famously taken his own life and who was also taken to exemplify republican virtue in his resistance to Julius Caesar. Addison had given Cato many lines in which he discussed the Stoic philosophy of fortitude and the Platonic (but pagan) idea of the immortality of the soul, and Cato had expressed indifference about whether he died, before killing himself in the final scene. By the end of the eighteenth century there were no fewer than twenty-six English editions of the play, a further dissemination of ideas about virtuous suicide in a non-Christian context.

A publication of 1704 also sought to drive home the connection between atheism and despair. *The Judgment of God Upon Atheism and Infidelity* (1704) told the story of one George Edwards, who, partly as a result of his reading, 'believed nothing of a future state; but look'd upon Religion as the Device of Men'. Edwards was led into disbelief in the 1690s when he concluded that there was no evidence that anyone believed in the Scriptures and became distrustful of all those who pretended to be religious. On the one hand he thought the Dissenters were 'Knavish, so Hypocritical and Malicious, Implaccable and Uncharitable, Factious and Worldly', and on the other that Churchmen were 'Intemperate and Prophane, so Sensual, Debauched and Covetous'. Edwards set out his atheistic belief system in a remarkable document that he gave to his parish priest, John Smith. In it, Edwards repeated many of the ideas familiar to us from Boevey's work, but without his belief in a deity. Edwards thought that 'many take up their Belief of God and the Creation, as part of their Education and Notion, more than any Conviction of their Minds and Consciences'; that most belief was superficial and insincere; and that many people acted well because of their good nature even if they were not religious. Edwards thought that God was just a delusion— 'the Fancy of most Mens Brain'—and that the mechanical world needed no God to explain it. It was 'eternal and of Matter, existing without any more Power than Matter and Motion'. In death men merely went to 'their Mother the Earth and there end'; he made no mention of the Devil.

Having read the document the vicar rightly concluded that Edwards believed in 'no GOD, no Supreme or Spiritual Being, no Providence, no Angels, no Spirits, no Resurrection or Judgment, nor any Life after this'. But the cleric found this a miserable, absurd, and irrational set of views, not least because the world must have had a beginning and therefore needed a creator. Edwards failed to reply to his vicar's entreaties and, lacking a moral compass, descended into a libertine lifestyle of 'lewd and vicious Courses' in the company of 'base Woman' (even on Sunday mornings when the rest of his household was at church). He contracted a venereal disease and, drinking heavily, he became 'like a Mad Man'. Fearing that he showed signs of despair, the vicar wrote a letter urging Edwards to trust God and not to let Satan 'hurry you to Desparation', though this clearly failed, for Edwards blew his brains out, having rigged up an ingenious contraption that fired three guns at his head simultaneously. The message of the tract recounting his end was clear. Atheism led to despair as surely as religious enthusiasm, and hence to suicide. Smith observed that there had been many others in Edwards's position: 'besides the famous Ch[arles] Bl[ount] several other persons of Atheistical Principles' had 'been given up to Madness and Folly, even to lay violent Hands upon themselves'. Indeed, it seemed to many that the later seventeenth century saw an increase in the suicide rate. Thus in 1705 the diarist John Evelyn thought it 'never was known that so many made themselves away as of these late years among us, among both men of quality and others'.[23] Statistics published in the contemporary *Bills of Mortality*, which collected data on deaths in London, certainly seemed to bear this out—though increased reporting in periodicals no doubt helped to raise the impression of more suicides. Was the Devil winning?

As Smith's remark that atheistical suicides had been left to 'the instigation of the Devil and their own desperate Passions' suggests, Churchmen still impressed on their audiences a link between suicide, religious unorthodoxy, and the Devil. But in blaming the growth of atheism, they were also acknowledging that attitudes were changing. Indeed, suicide would become one of the moral touchstones for Enlightenment thinkers. It was an issue that at once expressed a breach with orthodox Christianity and the growing allowance of man's control over his own body. In 1732 the Italian, Alberto Radicati, published (in London where he was living) a *Philosophical Dissertation upon Death* that argued that suicide was never culpable. He, like Donne, was a relativist: 'the conscience which people make of things called morally good and morally bad is not real', he said, not universal but local and particular.[24] Indeed, moving away from the seventeenth-century notion that men were God's property and that He controlled the world, it became difficult to see suicide as wrong. In this view all events are not God's but authored by his creatures.

It is certainly true that old ways of thinking about suicide continued after 1700 (it was not until 1823 that the humiliation of a suicide's burial at a crossroads was finally abandoned). Nevertheless there does appear to have been a shift of attitude, in part the result of medical advances and in part the result of a cultural shift. As Michael MacDonald and Terence Murphy have suggested, from the second half of the seventeenth century suicide was gradually secularized and decriminalized. 'Attitudes to suicide changed profoundly in the century and a half following the English Revolution', they write. 'Judicial and ecclesiastical severity gave way to official leniency and public sympathy for most people who killed themselves.' What had been a religious crime increasingly came to be viewed as one associated with temporary insanity. One indication of this was the decline in convictions for 'felo de se' (self murder), with all its attendant stigma and loss of goods, in favour of a verdict of 'non compos mentis' (unsound mind). The latter had been returned on Sarah Stout; and by the mid eighteenth century it was the norm. In one particular instance we can even see this shift from 'felo de se' to 'non compos mentis' occurring. In 1686 Dorcas Pinkney, who was noted to have been 'much dejected with Melancholy' before her suicide, was originally convicted of a 'felo de se'; but the verdict was set aside because she was found to have been 'Distracted'.[25]

This trend had become sufficiently noticeable by 1700 for it to be lamented by clergyman John Adams. There was, he sighed, 'a General Supposition that every one who kills himself is non Compos, and that nobody wou'd do such an Action unless he were Distracted'. His interesting work reflected another shift, for in meeting his critics he felt compelled to move away from a debate based on scripture to one rooted in 'the Principles of Natural Reason only'. Adams's justification for arguing on his enemies' territory was simple: 'they who undertake to defend the Lawfulness of Self-Murther (of which there are many in this Age), proceed chiefly upon Natural Principles, and will not hearken to any Thing from Revelation till these are answered'. The clerical Adams therefore constructed a critique of suicide with virtually no reference to Scripture. He opposed suicide on the grounds that it was an offence against man's creator, who he did call God, though by that term he meant the deist non-scriptural God who was a supreme being. Men were, he insisted, still the property of God, not of themselves, even if that God was not the God of the Bible; they had a 'Right of Use, but not a Right of absolute Propriety'.[26] Adams's argument also put a good deal of stress on nature's law of self-preservation and on the obligation to the community in which one lived. Adams was acknowledging that the debate had to be argued on his opponents' terms, in which the Christian God was displaced by God as the Creator, the laws of nature, and the laws of civil society. And in that schema, the Devil played very little part.

ANIMAL SPIRITS

It was also the case that there was a medicalization of melancholy, even if its precise physiological and psychological causes were still unclear. One of the foremost anatomists and founders of neurology Thomas Willis (Professor of Natural Philosophy at Oxford and Fellow of the Royal College of Physicians as well as the Royal Society), excluded the Devil from physical interference with the brain. In works published in the 1660s and early 1670s, he preferred natural causes and thereby offered an explanation for diseases which had 'usually by Ignorant People, been ascribed to Witch-craft and possessions of the Devil'.[27] Willis's advance was to focus on the brain, which he anatomized (with Christopher Wren providing the drawings to

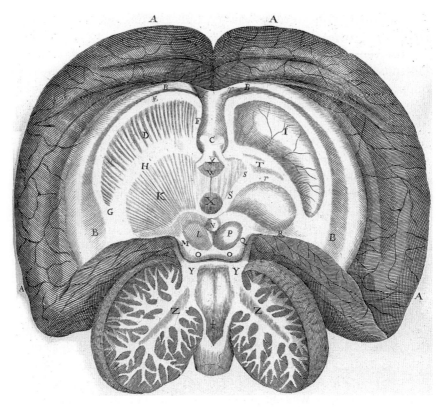

Figure 6.2 'A new anatomy of the Humane Brain' by Dr Thomas Willis, from his *Practice of Physick*. Willis was the first to seat melancholia in the brain.

illustrate his work). It was in the brain, Willis argued, that 'nervous juyce' or 'animal spirits' were generated; these animated the rest of the body as they moved through it. And melancholy, he suggested, depended on the state of the brain-generated animal spirits, for sometimes these flooded and even spilled out of the body ('as in joy, eagerness and boldness'), but at other times (such as sorrow, fear, and worry) they contracted 'so as not to be coextensive with our body'. Melancholy was thus a physical contraction of the brain-generated animal spirits, and could be cured by stimulating the spirits through 'pleasant talk, or jesting, Singing, Musick, Pictures, Dancing, Hunting, Fishing, and other pleasant Exercises'. Willis's friends were mostly High Churchmen and his theory was compatible with an attack on Dissenting claims to divine inspiration; evens so, his analysis offered a corporeal rather than a religious explanation for melancholy.[28]

Earlier we saw how science was applied forensically to try to help determine cause of death. It was also applied to try to explain religious delusion; natural causes were sought for what had previously been ascribed to the supernatural. This quest involved an interesting medicalization of the human condition, an attempt to examine how the body, soul, brain, and mind interacted. A fascination with melancholic fanaticism thus spurred the pursuit of a rather important science. It was in this period that neurology was born and strides were made in recognizing the brain as the key organ through which mind and body were connected. The soul, the conscience, the mind, and the imagination were gradually being rearranged in order of importance, to reflect a greater preoccupation with the mind. This was reflected in the investigations into the brain and the 'animal spirits' that connected it with the body, and in attempts to locate a physical organ for the soul.

The animal spirits invoked by Willis were an old, but revitalized, notion. The Greeks and Romans had talked about them; but in the later seventeenth century they acquired a new importance in order to explain how the body transmitted messages internally. The 'new science' advocated by the Royal Society rested on a mechanical and dynamic notion of rational forces acting on one another; so it seemed evident that there had to be some medium by which forces of the brain, imagination or soul could act on the body. From the second half of the seventeenth century, then, the study of animal spirits (or 'effluvia' and 'ether', as they were also sometimes called) would become essential to the modern understanding of electrochemical nerve impulses.

Quite what animal spirits were, though, was problematic: were they a fluid or an ethereal wind or 'vapour', and how did they work? Speculation about this was provoked by the convulsions (and to some the delusions or imaginations) of sectarians such as the Quakers. Was religious enthusiasm the result of physiological factors? Was there a difference between inspiration, religious frenzy, convulsions, or prophecy and mind-related disorders such as hysteria, madness, and melancholy?

Willis's science was helping to probe the question of where thoughts, and particularly melancholic or evil thoughts, came from. The Hertford High Churchman Ralph Battell had been sure that the answer was theological: 'the Devil is dayly and hourly suggesting evil motions to us', with God helping us to resist, creating an internal struggle of choice.[29] But a growing array of semi-medical, semi-religious explanations was complicating this conclusion. The Dissenting minister, Richard Baxter, who had worked for ten years as a doctor thus wrote *Preservatives against Melancholy and Overmuch Sorrow* in which he argued that religious melancholics ought to be seen as psychologically disturbed. Baxter retained his belief in the Devil and other spirits; but a medicalized notion of melancholy did call this into question or at least added another layer of explanation. We get a fascinating insight into this process through the account of George Keith, who had himself been a Quaker until, in 1700, he conformed to the Church of England and then puzzled why he had earlier been led astray.[30] His answer was a mixture of both old and newer ways of thinking.

The Quakers believed that if you emptied your mind of all thoughts, God could pierce through. But Keith argued that 'a false Light, or a false and evil Spirit may so get into a Man, and so fascinate and inveighle his affection, and so to speak bewitch and charm it', that the mind could be deluded. This, he believed, was what happened in Quakerism, which failed to distinguish between good and evil thoughts. Thus much was commonplace: the mind was permeable to external forces, good and bad. But Keith went on to suggest that evil thoughts were 'partly natural and partly diabolical'; that is to say, 'the efflux of a malitious Spirit' was both 'very Poisonous and Mortal' but also 'a degree of Witchcraft'. In this account, malicious ideas were communicable through the efflux or animal spirits; but Keith stressed the natural processes at work. Thus what the Quakers took to be the life of God circulating through their community was 'nothing other than the vigor and vivacity of the Animal Life and Spirits, invigorated and enlivened by the force of imagination, highly fortified and exalted'. The efflux, Keith proposed, was passed through the voice, through words, through sounds, through touch, and even through facial expression. Although conversions by such techniques led some 'to think there was some Art of Witchcraft or Diabolical Magick among the Quakers', Keith doubted if this was the case. He did not ascribe conversions to:

> any particular Demon or Devil, but as I have already said, a certain efflux or effluvium of Animal Volatile Spirits, transmitted from one to another, the which Volatile Spirits, being material and Corporeal Beings, are not Demons or Devils, but at most they are but Mediums or Organs and Instruments, by which Demons or Devils work upon Men's Bodies.

Keith thus did not deny supernatural forces; but he did think that natural explanations were key and invoked the work of a leading light of the Royal Society, Robert Boyle, who advocated a 'corpuscular philosophy' to explain all natural phenomena. 'With respect to these effluvia, I say, the Corpuscular Philosophy with some further improvements that may yet be made in it, seems best to resolve the Phenomena of all meer corporeal effects into corporeal causes.' The idea of enthusiastic religion as a physical contagion was nothing new—Hertford's curate of the 1630s, Thomas Edwards, when condemning the sects in 1646, had talked of their 'gangrene'—but animal spirits seemed to offer an explanation of how this process worked. Disordered animal spirits were an 'effluvium' that passed from one body to another; and even if the natural process was not fully understood it was a mechanical process that did not need to invoke the direct intervention of the Devil.

George Keith's ideas about the social contagion of enthusiasm appears to have been deeply influential on John Trenchard (who quoted him approvingly) and the third earl of Shaftesbury, both writers of enduring importance whose works were republished throughout the eighteenth century. Trenchard argued that 'everything in Nature is in constant motion, and perpetually emitting effluviums and minute particles of its substance, which operate upon and strike other bodies' so that the 'poisonous and melancholy vapours streaming from an enthusiast' caused 'distraction and raving' like 'the Bite of a mad dog'. For him, this was part of a larger argument about the history of superstition, which he associated with priestcraft (and hence he also associated enthusiasm with established religion). Deliriums and prophecies, he insisted, 'however strange at first sight, are easily to be accounted for by natural causes'. Failure to recognize this, he warned, resulted in superstition, 'the impostures of pretended prophets, the frauds of priests, and the dreams and vision of enthusiasts', together with 'most of the stories of conjurors and witches, spirits and apparitions, fairies and hobgoblins'.[31]

The third earl of Shaftesbury also analysed contagious religious panics in a *Letter concerning Enthusiasm* (1708) in which he argued that religious enthusiasm was infectious and suggested, like Keith, that it could even be communicated in a look. His remedy was bold. He thought that enthusiasm was curable with large doses of ridicule and good humour, which he thought far preferable to (and more effective than) persecution. Indeed, he thought that 'provided we treat Religion with good Manners, we can never use too much good

Humour, or examine it with too much freedom and familiarity'.[32] It was this witty freedom of thought, and his denial of miracles, that had landed Shaftesbury in hot water. The works of both Trenchard and Shaftesbury had been among the anticlerical horrors read out by Dr Sacheverell's defence as proof of an attack upon the Church.

Both Trenchard and Shaftesbury were writing in response to the delusions of the so-called French Prophets who had arrived in England in 1707 and had sparked an extensive print debate about why zeal seemed to be infectious amongst their followers, a debate that once again focused attention on animal spirits. As Hillel Schwartz puts it in his study of the Prophets, 'the physics and physiology of aether and animal spirits were developed in a consciously theological context'.[33] Animal spirits and effluvia were useful because they were compatible with a supernatural power, since they could be the medium through which the commands of God or the Devil were transmitted, and hence both prophets and critics could invoke them. But they also offered a more naturalistic, mechanistic explanation that fitted the emerging scientific and rational culture, and tended to make it easier to see enthusiasm as a bodily condition. Thus Benjamin Hoadly, the Low Church scourge of Henry Sacheverell, argued that 'Persons may have what you call Prophetical involuntary motions and agitations, by the force of nature, under the power of a distempered Mind; without the assistance of any superior Spirit, whether good or bad.'[34] Or as a physician put it, 'there is no Enthusiasm of any sort without a fever in the soul . . . seated chiefly in the animal spirits'.[35]

Other critics of the French Prophets insisted that they were simply impostors and that their claims to supernatural powers were invented. This was the view of Francis Hutchinson, a Suffolk clergyman, who concluded that the prophets were either frauds, mad, or diabolically possessed but not divinely inspired.[36] Demanding exacting standards of legal and scientific proof that cast the claims of the French Prophets into doubt, he believed the so-called miracles performed by them in France lacked any convincing evidence other than their own testimony; only public demonstrations could convince. He sought natural explanations for the miracles that John Lacy, one of the English leaders of the French Prophets, claimed. One of these, in which Lacy glided across the floor in a trance, Hutchinson ascribed merely to the strength possessed by those who are temporarily mad; another, Lacy's alleged curing of an actress's blindness, he thought a 'counterfeit'. Thus 'the great Bulk of their pretended Facts were Delusion, like Witches Feasts'. So if they failed the test of 'fact', the 'miracles' had their origin either in insincerity or in the complexity of the human soul: 'When its Strings are stretched too far, either by much Study, vehement Devotion, mystical Divinity or the supposed presence of an invisible Being, and its Tongue is let loose to speak its own Thoughts, it will surprise both itself and Hearers with its own Flights, Prayers, Prophesies or Exhortations.' For Hutchinson the soul was a finely tuned instrument; it needed devotion but excessive devotion made it play out of tune. Hutchinson wrote both about the French Prophets and, as we shall see shortly, also about witchcraft, because both were concerned with claims about supernatural powers and delusions. Hutchinson emerged as one of the most hailed sceptics about witchcraft but he wrote in the light of his earlier examination of the French Prophets. His conclusion that claims about supernatural intervention needed a high level of proof was common to both of his publications.

A POLITICAL WITCH-HUNT

Issues of proof and natural causes were also at the heart of debates over witchcraft, but the prosecution of Jane Wenham in 1712 also owed a good deal to the political and religious tensions aroused by the Sacheverell furore. Sacheverell, the Quakers and witchcraft were all bundled together in one High Church tract of 1710, which imagined a cleric's dream that was had at the witching hour, 'the usual time for Furies and Hobgoblings to dance the wild Morris, and old Hags and Night Mares ride a Hunting on Human Carcasses'. In this nightmare, old 'Oliverians' and Dissenters held sway, with 'a Female Quaker that was foaming and raving against Dr Sacheverell (who just then pas'd by) in such a violent manner, that she fell in a Fit' and began to shower names of abuse on the clerical dreamer: 'wicked Hireling, thou Priest of Baal, thou Lamb of the Whore of Babylon . . . thou Man of Sodom, thou Child of the Devil . . . Limb of Lucifer'.[37] In this inverted world of satanic and bewitched chaos, the world was ruled by Quakers, Dissenters and republicans. The association in the minds of their opponents between Quakers, the Devil and witchcraft was, as we have seen, a strong one, and in turn the Quakers called Churchmen 'witches, devils, antichrists'.[38] Certainly the High Churchmen made use of the language of witchcraft to demonize their enemies. Following the book of Samuel, which says 'rebellion is as the sin of witchcraft', High Churchmen repeatedly used the text polemically to attack Whig notions of resistance. Two visual satires of Ben Hoadly,

Sacheverell's Low Church nemesis who defended the right of resistance, therefore show him with the Devil.[39] Similarly, the belief that the Devil was 'the father of lies' also offered scope to satirists, so that Satan was depicted in two separate prints whispering lies either into the ear of Sacheverell or of his Low Church critic William Bisset.[40] Even so, there is a difference between polemical demonizing, aimed at delegitimizing an antagonist, and the truly demonic. The Devil was invoked in the partisan conflict because he was a good shorthand for everything that was bad, an emblem that still did conjure up an emotional response but not, perhaps, one of real fear and terror.

The polemical demonizing of 1710 nevertheless suggests that we should see Wenham's prosecution for witchcraft in the context of the Sacheverell affair and in particular the reanimation of High Church passions. His sermon, complained one tract, had unleashed a torrent of demonic intolerance and every pulpit '(as infected from Hell) Rings aloud with Diabolical Oaths, Execrable Cursings and damnable Language'.[41] The impeachment had unleashed a flood of High Church sentiment, a desire to reassert the power of the Church of England's ministry and to defend the Church against the danger posed by Dissenters and Low Churchmen who had been depicted as in league with the Devil. That conspiracy was what Sacheverell had sought to expose: he preached that the Puritans used a cloak of piety 'to amuse the witch and cover the devil and consecrate all infidelity, injustice, pride, lust, avarice and ambition, and the most execrable vices of Hell with the holy title of Conscience; which, in sad truth, is nothing but the visor-mask of cousenage, knavery and hypocrisy'.[42] Perhaps emboldened by such rhetoric, which blurred witchcraft and Dissent, the key protagonists in the prosecution were High Churchmen, including Sir Henry Chauncy, the hammer of the Hertfordshire Quakers. It is not surprising, then, to find that witchcraft became another of those terms contested by the parties. The High Churchmen prosecuted Jane Wenham for witchcraft; but according to one Low Church critic they also exercised their own form of witchcraft, for, he alleged, there was 'a kind of Witchcraft in priestcraft' and 'Witchcraft in Bigotry and Superstition'.[43] The Whig bishop, White Kennett, agreed and drove the point home in a sermon in 1715, entitled *The Witchcraft of the Present Rebellion*. Kennett alleged that the Jacobite rebellion was the result of 'political witchcraft' by the High Churchmen in Anne's reign. Witchcraft, he said, was, like the rebellion, the result of 'Impudent Pretence and Delusion only; a perfect Cheat and Imposition upon the credulous Part of Mankind'. And, with a particular swipe at the Wenham trial he noted that witchcraft prosecutions 'did begin to revive amidst the late Party-Zeal' which, if it had not been checked by the judges, 'GOD knows how far those Feats of Popery might have grown upon us'.

Certainly there were political and religious tensions in Hertfordshire that influenced the prosecution. Jane Wenham's parish, Walkern, lay very near the estate of the Cowper's rival, Charles Caesar, the Tory who had supplanted him as MP for Hertford. Caesar's brother-in-law, Ralph Freman, was MP for the county and an ardent High Churchman. Freman headed the Royston Club, which helped to ensure that Hertfordshire remained Tory for the first decades of the eighteenth century. The clergymen in and around Walkern were High Churchmen, linked to the Hertford Tories. Francis Bragge, who was present throughout and wrote a good deal about the case, was Chauncy's grandson. Although he did not himself enter holy orders until June 1712, a few months after the Wenham affair, Bragge was the son of the vicar of Hitchin, also called Francis. As a young would-be cleric with a name to make, Francis Bragge junior clearly saw the prosecution as a means of fostering 'a due Reverence and Respect to Prayers in general, and those of our Holy Church in particular' and hence of upholding spiritual belief in what he called 'this Age of . . . Infidelity'.[44] It may be significant that his father had published an extensive account of biblical miracles, divine acts which, he asserted, were 'not only out of the usual course of Nature, but far above the Powers of it' and that they inclined men both to embrace divine doctrine and 'to overthrow the kingdom of the Devil'. The supernatural, the Bragges believed, was thus an aid to belief, proof of Christ's divine mission.[45]

We know less about the views of the two other clergymen involved but they seem to be of a similar stripe. The wife of Godfrey Gardiner, vicar of Walkern and a fellow of King's College in Cambridge, was described as 'a fierce Bigot' and 'Zealot' who was the 'prime Undertaker in this Affair'.[46] The other, Mr Strutt, was vicar of Ardeley, Chauncy's parish, and was later accused of putting words into Wenham's mouth by 'ensnaring' and 'leading' questions, in order to induce a 'confession', so it is safe to assume that parson and High Church squire saw eye to eye.[47] Another cleric, one of the queen's chaplains Edmund Chishull, preached a High Church assize sermon immediately before the Wenham trial on the theme of *Modesty and Moderation, or the True Relative Duty of the Tolerated and Establish'd Parties in any Society of Men*. In it he demanded greater modesty from the Dissenters and said that it was impossible for Churchmen to be moderate when the Church was under attack. Sounding remarkably like Sacheverell's attack on false brethren (it would seem that this was a quite deliberate attempt to link Wenham's trial to Sacheverell's cause), Chishull alleged that when the Church was in danger, calls for moderation were 'the cry of some false or some unwary Friends within, answering to the call of those without'.[48] Although he also called for moderation from the Churchmen, this was only because he celebrated the High Church triumph of the passage of the Occasional Conformity Act in 1711, which barred Dissenters from holding local political office. Chishull's sermon thus ensured that the trial would be seen through the High Church lens.

Jane Wenham, however, did not come within the influence of the High Churchmen. Indeed she was accused of having joined the Hertfordshire Dissenters. After the trial, Bragge junior alleged that Jane had claimed 'she was prosecuted out of Spite, only because she went to the Dissenting Meetings' and that she drew charitable donations from those who now saw her as 'a precious Saint'.[49] Perhaps she was simply irreligious, for her parish priest declared 'that he never before heard that she used to go to any Place of Divine Worship and that he never took her to be of any Religion at all'.[50] But whether Dissenter or simply one of those who failed to engage with established religion, Wenham was, to the High Churchmen, ripe material for the Devil and the prosecution of her witchcraft was a means to bolster faith in the laity and the role of the clergy. Certainly there was sufficient heterodoxy in the area for them to be worried about, not just the Independents and Quakers discussed earlier, but also, less than ten miles away, in the person of Stephen Nye, rector of Little Hormead. Nye was the writer of important Socinian works in the late 1680s and 1690s—Socinianism being a simplified and anti-trinitarian version of Christianity (for which Nye coined the term 'Unitarian', which is still in use). Although Nye disliked party labels, his religious views were very close to those of John Locke and a strong belief in freedom of conscience placed him squarely outside the ranks of the High Churchmen, who used 'Socinian' as a term of abuse against anyone they suspected of falling short of full conformity with Church doctrine and ceremony. Even closer to home, a Dissenting Meeting was licensed at Walkern in 1699—a new threat to the established Church there.

Sarah Cowper, for one, was certainly convinced that the prosecution of Jane was another instance of High Church power-lust. She recorded in her diary—plagiarizing a pamphlet, *A Full Confutation of Witchcraft*, that appeared soon after the trial—that Wenham had been:

prosecuted by A Brace of High-Flying Parsons. Witchcraft Is Priest Craft. If They Cou'd Once fix this Belief in the Minds of the People that they were Endu'd with a Special Power of Dispossessing Persons by vertue of their Sacerdotal Office; how wou'd these Surmises Attract the Devotion of the Simple to Them, besides weighty Offerings. Some Such design must be att the Bottom of this Delusion. As this wou'd Not only Enrich them, So likewise it wou'd Raise their persons into greater Esteem; what Honours wou'd be thought too great for Such a Wonder Working Priest.[51]

Cowper's words reinforce Ian Bostridge's conclusion that although witchcraft theory retained its credibility beyond 1700 'the final crisis of the rage of party in England was a key moment in the dissolution of that credibility'.[52] Witchcraft trials did not end purely because of the Wenham case; but it represented a turning point, a high-water mark for a resurgent and ultimately defeated vision of a powerful Church State.

A caveat nevertheless has to be entered about the importance of the High Church tide for witchcraft trials, for a case from 1701–2, about a reputed witch called Sarah Morduck, does not fit this pattern, even though it does fit a history, shared by the 1712 case, about increasing judicial scepticism towards witchcraft. The judge, Sir John Holt (the man who had imprisoned Spencer Cowper on suspicion of murder) is the perfect example of how legal opinion had turned against witchcraft, since he was responsible for a series of judgments hostile to witchcraft prosecution. The Morduck case is worth examining in a little detail for the purpose of comparison with the Wenham trial. While both prosecutions attracted popular support and judicial hostility, the Morduck case shows how some Dissenters retained their belief in witchcraft and did not follow the more sceptical stance of other Whigs. Even so, it is perhaps important that the trial took place before the High Church furore in Anne's reign, and indeed at a time when Whig and Tory rivalries were temporarily at a low ebb.

The case concerned Richard Hathaway, a blacksmith's apprentice from Southwark, who had fallen ill with a complaint that baffled the medical profession.[53] Unable to find the cause, one of the hospital orderlies:

told him he must lye under some evil Tongue...so he came home again, and his Master and Mistress were acquainted with it, and they consider[ed] what Person it should be that should have any evil design against him. And at last they recollect that his Master had taken a

Room over the Head of Sarah Morduck, and she had gone to the shop often, and given them very ill Words, and she should be even with him one time or other; and therefore they concluded this Woman was the Person.

Hathaway thus became convinced that he had been bewitched and made ill by Sarah Morduck. He also made other claims that sounded incredible, including that he only recovered from his bewitched fits when he scratched out some of her blood. But Hathaway was a cheat. When an experiment was made, without Hathaway's knowledge, and another woman was substituted for Sarah Morduck, he still flew at her, drew blood and claimed to recover. His claims to be able to live without food were also disproved by a surgeon, who showed that he was secretly fed by a maid through a hole in the wall. Undeterred by the evidence stacking against him, Hathaway prosecuted Morduck for witchcraft; and the crowd was evidently on his side, since after her acquittal Morduck was attacked in the streets and was in danger of being 'torn in pieces'. It was at this point that Whig Dissenters intervened, not to rescue her, but to back her persecution as a reputed witch.

Morduck had sought protection from a magistrate, Sir Thomas Lane, who had been one of the character witnesses for Spencer Cowper at his trial.[54] At the time Morduck sought help, Lane was with Sir Owen Buckingham, another Whig Dissenting leader in London, and his son-in-law, David Hamilton. Hamilton was an eminent Whig doctor, one of the new breed of men-midwives and he would later become physician and confidant of Queen Anne—his diary recounting their meetings and the queen's thoughts was among the Cowper papers, presumably because William Cowper's wife was one of the queen's attendants and shared his moderate Whig views. Clearly suspicious that Hathaway might be pulling tricks, but not dismissing the possibility that he might really be bewitched, Hamilton offered to lock him up for a fortnight to test his claim to be able to fast indefinitely. The test nevertheless proved rather inconclusive, since the woman assigned to watch him was not continuously present. But if Hamilton had doubts, his father-in-law Lane did not and even encouraged the popular hostility towards Morduck, rather than trying to stop it. He refused to reprimand one of those caught assaulting her and even declared 'there was cause enough for it'. Lane had also allowed Morduck to be stripped (presumably to search her body for the Devil's mark) and permitted Hathaway to scratch her in order to witness, at first hand, his apparent recovery when he drew blood. Encouraged now by the authority of a magistrate, the crowd turned on the parish priest, Mr Martin, who had been trying to defuse the situation, and refused to attend church if Morduck was present. Worse still, the mob attacked Morduck in her home, 'pulled out her teeth, tore her Face, Hair and Cloaths, threw her on the ground, stampt upon her Belly, and threw her into the Street', a beating so severe that she had to remain in bed for a fortnight.

When matters came before Sir John Holt in 1702, in what was Morduck's second trial for witchcraft, Lane was severely reprimanded and in summing up the evidence against Morduck, Holt's scepticism about witches became all too evident. He had clearly found Lane's experimental scratching intolerable ('what rule they have for it either in Philosophy or Witchcraft I cannot tell', he remarked) and found Hamilton's experimental starvation equally absurd. He wondered whether the jury could believe it was in the power of 'all the Witches in the World, or all the Devils in Hell, to enable a man to fast beyond the usual time that Nature will allow; they cannot invert the order of Nature'. Hathaway must be a cheat. Thus directed, the jury found Hathaway to be an impostor and the following day he was successfully prosecuted for assault on Morduck, and for the riot against her. Holt had thus not only secured the defeat of the witchcraft prosecution but also exposed the prosecutors as frauds and thugs. The case is a clear sign of the judicial disapproval that was key to the end of witchcraft prosecutions, but it also exposes the degree of continuing popular and even magisterial support for witchcraft belief; and it reveals tensions within the Whig camp, with Lane and Holt taking very different stances despite their common political allegiance. Might William Cowper's harbouring of Jane Wenham be in some sense an atonement for the inhumane treatment meted out to another reputed witch by Lane, the Cowper family's friend? The Morduck case is also an interesting reversal of the Wenham trial, where the prosecution was pushed on by High Church clerics. In the Morduck case, the parish priest had been a voice of reason against the witchcraft hysteria of the mob; and it was the Dissenting Lane who appears to have backed the prosecution. Witchcraft cases seldom fit any one neat pattern. Moreover the failure of the medical profession in the Morduck case, both in encouraging ideas of witchcraft in the first place and then, through Hamilton, of exercising reason and restraint are further warnings that there is no simple story to be told about witchcraft being displaced by science.

Ten years later, however, the religious climate in England had changed. A decade of cries about the 'Church in danger', a clamour begun by the occasional conformity controversy and then made more shrill by the debate over Sacheverell, had both made the clergy paranoid about the state of religion and emboldened them to act in its defence. Indeed our knowledge of Jane Wenham's alleged witch-craft comes largely from the hostile pen of the young cleric, Francis Bragge, who began his 'full and impartial account' with a quote from Exodus, 'Thou Shalt not suffer a Witch to live.' Bragge's narrative, which forms the basis for the account that follows, set out the case against her.[55]

Jane, in this telling, was the stereotypical witch: female, old, and poor, unbridled by her husband, with a sharp tongue, and a long history of bad relations with her neighbours who thought they had materially suffered at her hands. A *Guide to Grand Jurymen about the Trial of Witches* (1627) summarized seventeenth-century assumptions when trying to account for why there were 'commonly more women than men' witches:

> 1. Satan's setting upon these rather than on men, since his unhappy onset and prevailing with Eve. 2. Their more credulous nature and apt to be misled and deceived. 3. For that they are commonly more impatient, and more superstitious, and being displeased, more malicious, and so more apt to bitter cursing, and farre more revengeful, according to their power, than men, and so herein more fit instruments of the Divell. 4. They are more tongue-ripe, and lesse able to hide what they know from others, and therefore in this respect are more ready to bee teachers of Witchcraft to others, and to leave it to children, servants and to some others, than men. 5. And lastly, because, where they think they can command, they are more proud in their rule, and more busie in setting suche on worke whom they may command, than men. And therefore the Divell laboureth most to make them witches.[56]

According to Bragge, Jane 'had been reputed a Witch for above 20 Years'. Twelve years previously, in 1700, she had been blamed for the death of a baby after she had stroked it, apparently in revenge for attempts to help her husband disown her. The baby's father had been asked by Jane's husband 'to speak to the Town-Crier at Hertford to cry down his Wife, lest any Person should trust her to his Dammage', since Jane's thieving was costing him dear, both financially and in terms of his reputation. Moreover, in 1703 another baby had died after being stroked by Jane, and on that occasion the child's body had also been 'so distorted that the Toes were turned back behind the Heel'. When asked later why she had not prosecuted Jane, the mother replied that 'she was a poor woman and the Child had no friends able to bear the Charges of such a prosecution'; but with the 'opportunity presenting itself' in 1712 'she laid hold of it to give her Evidence'. The 1712 prosecution thus brought to the surface long-standing suspicions about, and resentment of, Jane's behaviour.

As the first of these incidents suggests, Jane was reputedly a thief as well as a witch, perhaps forced into crime by the failure of her marriage. Her second husband (the first died in 1696) seems to have been estranged from her: certainly he refused to support her at her trial. Jane was said to have pursued 'a continued Course of Idleness and Thievery'. Shortly before Christmas 1711 she was caught stealing turnips from Thomas Adams's field 'and upon his Threatening her she threw them down' and 'begg'd Pardon, saying, she had no Victuals all that Day, and had no Money to buy any'. Adams thought nothing further of it until, symbolically enough on Christmas morning, he found 'one of his best sheep had died without any Signs of Illness', and more sheep wasted away. He suspected Jane's malice. Other animals died in unexplained ways and matters were brought to a head in February 1712 when a farmer, John Chapman, sought to blame her for the mysterious death of his livestock. Chapman had 'long entertain'd a Suspicion that the strange Deaths of many of his and the Neighbours Horses and Cattle were occasion'd by the Witchcrafts of this Woman, and thought that he himself had suffer'd by them to the value of £200'. When his servant Matthew Gilston began to behave oddly after an encounter with Jane, Chapman voiced his suspicions that Jane had bewitched him. Gilston had refused Jane some straw and in retaliation she was alleged to have possessed him, making him run a 'fool's errand' away from the barn in which he had been working, headlong into the local river. When Chapman next met Jane, 'in heat of Anger' he called her 'a Witch and Bitch'. 'Bitch' perhaps referred to Jane's additional reputation as 'a Whore' who frequently swore and cursed. But it may also have reflected the fact that Jane had earlier spurned Chapman's advances. Sarah Cowper, William's daughter, later recorded that:

I saw Jane two months before her Death, she then retain'd a modest, good look with a clean Complexion, & was intirely unlike what Witches have been always represented to be; I have heard many people say that at the time of her Trial she was a handsome Woman; & Jane herself always said that the Principal Evidence against her was a Person to whom she had denied Favours in her youth, and who always bore a spite to her for that Reason. I am apt to believe Jane did provoke him, for she had not the sweetest of Tempers. She had a peevish Virtue, & I suppose not only denied the Inamorato but expos'd him.[57]

In any case, insults such as 'witch', 'bitch', and 'whore' were deeply resented in early modern England and court records show many women going to court to refute such allegations and to preserve their reputations. So 'after the Scolding-bout was over' Jane thought 'that she would make him pay for his Words' and on 9 February 1712 applied to Sir Henry Chauncy for a warrant against him, 'expecting not only to get something out of him, but to deter other people from calling her so any more'. But rather than award her damages Chauncy asked the parish vicar, Godfrey Gardiner, to mediate in the dispute. Gardiner 'advis'd them to live more peaceably together' and ordered Chapman to pay her a shilling, but would allow Jane no further satisfaction. At this 'her anger was greatly kindled against' Gardiner and she 'went away in a great Heat, saying, If she could not have Justice here, she would have it elsewhere'. Her revenge was said to have been wreaked on Anne Thorn, an adolescent serving girl of between sixteen and seventeen years old, who worked in the Gardiner household and who had, according to Bragge, 'seen but little of the world, having never been far from home'. Mrs Gardiner later described her maid as of 'an extraordinary good character for her Sobriety, Diligence, and good Temper, by which she had gain'd the Love of all the Neighbourhood'. But the excitable role of young women in witchcraft allegations is again well known—the witchcraft prosecutions at Salem in 1692 had been triggered by the accusations of girls very similar to Anne. And as we shall see, the witchcraft expert Francis Hutchinson suggested that Anne's behaviour was in part the result of a state of heightened sexuality.

The manner in which Jane was said to have bewitched Anne was initially to propel her to perform a superhuman feat. Despite having dislocated her knee, Anne was impelled to run inexplicably fast (one estimate was over eight miles an hour) to a nearby village to collect sticks, climbing over a five-barred gate as she did so. Anne then ran back home 'and sat down in the Kitchen stript to her shirt-sleeves, howling and wringing her Hands'. She was discovered there by Mrs Gardiner and it was the vicar's wife who first suspected witchcraft. Once the suggestion had been made, Anne must have eagerly repeated it, for the following day Jane 'asked her why she told such Stories of her, as if she had Bewitched her? Anne Thorn answered, she had said nothing but what was true and she was the Cause of all her Disorder; to this Jane Wenham reply'd, if you tell any more such Stories of me it shall be worse for you than it has been yet, and shov'd her with her Hand'.

Anne's body seemed to be further bewitched the following day. She was struck speechless 'with strange Tremblings and Convulsions of Body'; and then repeated her sprint, this time leaping 'nimbly as a Greyhound' over the gate and running until 'her legs fail'd her'. Back home she collapsed into the first of a series of speechless fits. The day after, Anne (despite dislocating her knee again) insisted on another run. She 'flew up with such Strength that Two or Three Men could not hold her, tho' just before her Eyes were turned and sunk in her Head, and her Teeth set, so that she seemed to be giving up the Ghost'. Arthur Chauncy, son of High Church magistrate Sir Henry, 'perswaded Mistress Gardiner to let her go and he with Two or Three more Men, would follow her'. It was just as well they did, for when Anne got outside and 'saw the Way clear, she started, and ran directly to the River at the lower End of the Close. Arthur Chauncy caught her 'just as her Feet were in the Mire, and she was going to plunge herself into the Water', an act of attempted suicide. Chauncy and the others led her back towards the house but she 'cried out she must go back again' and they 'brought her to the River again' but would not let her in. She later recalled that 'she was violently tempted to drown herself'. In this case and somewhat in contrast to those considered earlier, suicide, it was being suggested, *was* the result of the temptation of demonic forces. For the High Church narrator Bragge and his High Church colleagues, the Devil was a palpable force.

Just as Hathaway had claimed that his fits were only cured by drawing the blood of Sarah Morduck, so Anne Thorn told Jane Wenham:

I must have your blood, or I shall never be well. She scratched Jane Wenham in the Forehead with such Fury and Eagerness, that the Noise of her Nails seemed to all that were present as if she scratching against a Wainscoat, yet no Blood followed; Jane Wenham holding her head still, and saying, Scratch harder Nan and fetch Blood of me if you can; yet still no Blood came, altho' her Forehead was sadly mangled and torn by the Girl's Nails.

Instead of showing sympathy with Jane, 'the Company began to expostulate with Jane Wenham, telling her, she was a wicked Wretch to abuse a poor young innocent Creature at that Rate'.

Jane protested her innocence 'and offered to be tried, by searching her Body, to see whether she had any Teats or by throwing her into the Water'. A Devil's mark in the form of a teat was commonly held to be a sign of a witch and custom had it that a witch floated in the water, whereas an innocent woman would sink. Jane was thus trying to clear her name by passing the traditional tests of witchcraft. Searching for the Devil's mark was indeed invoked by the magistrate, Sir Henry Chauncy, who was as ready to persecute a witch as he had been earlier to persecute the Quakers (and indeed the two were probably linked in his mind, since both were perversions of true religion). He ordered that Jane's body be searched, 'directing them to enquire diligently whether she had any Teats, or other extraordinary and unusual Marks about her, by which the Devil in any Shape might suck her Body'. But even he balked at a water test, which he thought was 'illegal and Unjustifiable'. Instead it was a scriptural test that seemed to expose Jane as a witch. 'One of the company', presumably one of the clerics:

> desired to let him hear her say the Lord's Prayer; she made several Attempts to do it, but could not, always missing Two or Three Sentences. Mrs Gardiner bad her try whether she could say it after her, and repeated it Sentence by Sentence slowly to her; but neither could she do this, to the amazement of all the By-standers.

The Lord's Prayer was one that every Protestant and godly person should know; an inability to say it suggested that some evil force was preventing her from speaking Christ's words. Anne, on the other hand, found Christ's words calming. Indeed, they were found to be the only remedy for her fits. As soon as vicar Gardiner 'repeated Three or Four Sentences of the Lord's-Prayer, she fell down on her knees and rehearsed the Prayers as well as anyone'.

Jane's inability to say the Lord's Prayer began to loom large with the clerics as proof of her witchcraft. She was unable to repeat the sentence 'Lead us not into Temptation but deliver us from Evil' to Robert Strutt, minister of Chauncy's parish of Ardeley, who had also come to interrogate her. Instead, she got confused and in one attempt to get it right mistakenly said 'Lead us into Temptation and Evil'. Jane 'try'd to excuse herself by alledging she was much disturb'd in her head by the Hurry she was in, saying, she wanted Rest', and it was later said that her confusion with the prayer was only 'her vulgar dialect', since she habitually used a double negative and said 'Lead us not into no temptation.'[58] But Strutt tried her once more the following morning and it was clear that this was Jane's breaking point. Asked by the vicar if she thought she could say the Lord's Prayer, she answered 'she believed she could, for she had try'd several Times in the Night'; but again each time she made 'the same Blunders as before'. When Strutt asked her if she 'had any Hand in bewitching' Anne she 'at first gave no positive Answer; but upon Mr Strutt's telling her, that if she was Guilty of such a vile Fact, it would be the best Thing she could do, both for the Salvation of her own Soul and the Good of others, to confess; then she began to relent a little' and, in front of witnesses she confessed she was a witch. Jane now admitted that 'she had a Hand in bewitching Anne Thorn' and that she had done it because 'the Girl had once vexed her'. When quizzed further, she admitted she had been a witch:

> for above Sixteen Years; and that it was before her first Husband died, who came to a very Miserable End, and was supposed to have been bewitched by her. Then they asked her what it was that induced her to enter into this Familiarity with the Devil? She said it was a Malicious and Wicked Mind; for when any of her Neighbours vexed her she used horrid Curses and Imprecations, on which the Devil took Advantage over her.

During the confession Jane had admitted that she used to take the shape of a familiar—the animal that was said to accompany a witch. Perhaps making use of this revelation, Anne's fits now took a new twist:

> she said she saw Things like Cats appear to her, telling her she must go; she said also, that always before a Fit she saw a Cat, which would not only appear to her, but speak, and tell her several Things, tempting her to go out of Doors. It was also taken Notice of, that a dismal Noise of Cats was at that Time and several Times after, heard about the House, sometimes their Cry resembling that of Young Children, at other Times they made a Hellish Noise, to which nothing can be resembled.

Several witnesses later confirmed that they had seen packs of cats that ran to Jane's house when confronted. Anne's fits also grew worse and even prayers now failed to revive her. 'She was cold as a Dead Corpse, her Jaws were fallen, her Nose pinched, her Pulse gone, and several that applied their Mouths to hers, affirmed there was not the least

Breath coming from her.' Everyone supposed her 'really dead, she lying without any Motion or Heat or other symptom of Life'. Yet, as they always did when they ran out of ideas, the household again summoned Jane Wenham, even though it was now late at night. 'As soon as she came into the Room the Maid started up and flew at her with amazing strength and Fierceness, saying, as before, Are you come again to Torment me? I'll have your Blood and tear you to pieces; which she would have done if she had not been kept down by main Force of Three or Four Men, who could hardly hold her.'

Here, then, according to the narrator of the events Francis Bragge, was 'convincing proof...that it was neither any Natural Distemper that produced these wonderful Effects, not yet any Trick or Cheat put upon the many Spectators'. Jane was sent to jail in Hertford, though she refused to say any more to her captors, fearing, as well she might, that they 'lay in wait for her Life, and would hang her from her own Mouth'. Once she had gone there was one last hunt for clues. The events of recent days 'brought to Mind several Old Stories of Witches' and it was remembered 'that strange Things have been found in the Pillow of the Witch. This put their Curiosity upon searching the Maid's Pillow', which Mrs Gardiner had herself newly stuffed. 'This was accordingly done, and there was found in the Down a great many Cakes of small Feathers, so closely joined together, that an ordinary Force could not pull them asunder.' Bragge, who had seen the object, said it was 'fastned together with a sort of viscous matter which would stretch Seven or Eight Inches in a fine Thread before it broke'. The cake of feathers was 'some Devilish Enchantment'. Bragge wanted to produce it in court 'but was over-ruled by others, who not without Reason supposing this to be the Charm, would have it all burnt, in hopes the Effects of it might cease. And it is remarkable that after the burning these Feathers the Maid was better and had no more Fits' until the trial itself. When the case did come to court, however, the judge chastised the prosecution for having burnt the evidence and said, with jocular irony, that 'he wish'd he could see an Enchanted Feather'.

The trial, at the Hertford assizes on 4 March, caused a local sensation. It was the topic of much rumour and those prosecuting 'found great Difficulties at the very first, most People who had seen nothing of it themselves, nor heard anything but imperfect Stories, and flying Reports, being very inclinable to believe nothing at all of it'. One talking point was the terms in which the indictment was drawn by the clerk who maintained that, since Anne was still alive,

Jane would not be charged with a felony. He therefore, and to the 'great surprise' of the prosecutors, indicted her only 'for conversing familiarly with the Devil in the Shape of a Cat'. There was not even a mention of Anne Thorn, even though she was the star witness. It is quite possible that the clerk, perhaps under the direction of the judge, sought to make the charge itself so ridiculous that the case would fail. The clerk had apparently only focused on the written testimony made by Anne on 26 February, that 'as she was lying in Bed, she saw a Cat sitting in the Window, which spoke to her'. In court two witnesses also claimed to have seen 'a Cat with a Face like Jane Wenham' and that cats had several times swarmed around her bed.[59]

But, although she did not figure as the victim in the charge against Jane, Anne made herself the centre of attention in court. She fell into a fit 'occasioned by the Sight of Jane Wenham' and had to be 'recovered' by a prayer, so that she was well enough to give evidence. The judge, Sir John Powell (who had also presided over the trial of Beau Fielding for bigamy, discussed earlier), was suspicious. He said 'that he never heard that in any Witches Trial before the Person afflicted fell into a Fit in Court; but for the Satisfaction of the Jury' he allowed Jane to be brought near Anne and to speak to her, 'upon which the Girl flew at her with great Fury as usual'. But when it was proposed 'that she might be pray'd for in Court' the judge 'was unwilling, saying, she will come to herself by and by'. When this failed to happen Edmund Chishull, who had preached the High Church opening assize sermon, 'offer'd and was permitted to pray'. Immediately, according to Bragge, 'the Colour came into the Maid's Cheeks' and she began to repeat the Lord's Prayer with the minister. 'It was extreamly well taken by all true Lovers of the Church that Mr Chishull should offer his Assistance at this time, when its Prayers were ridicul'd by too many that were present.' Indeed there were many that made 'a mighty Jest of the Maid's Recovery out of her Fits by Prayer'.

Despite Jane's protestation that 'she was a Clear Woman', the jury took just two hours to bring in their verdict, 'that the Prisoner was Guilty upon the Evidence'. It had been clear throughout the trial, however, that Justice Powell had no time for the witchcraft allegation. According to Daniel Defoe, Powell had asked Jane if she could fly; when she said she could, he replied 'So you may, if you will, then, I have no law against it'; and that on seeing the court full of fine ladies Powell said 'they must not look out for witches amongst the old women, but amongst the young'.[60] Certainly Powell had a keen sense of humour: Jonathan Swift described him as 'the merriest old gentleman I ever saw' who 'chuckled till he cried'.[61] Although his wit was wasted on Bragge, who resented what he called Powell's 'incredulity', Powell's sceptical stance nevertheless proved important. As William Cowper's daughter, Sarah, recorded in her diary:[62]

> The Judge who try'd her endeavour'd to make the Accusation appear ridiculous by playing on the Evidence with a great deal of Drollery; but the Jury was so senseless as to bring her in Guilty, & the Judge was forced to pass sentence of Condemnation on her to be burn'd;[63] however, He with my Father and [one of the Cowper's neighbours] Collonel Plummer represented the Case to Queen Anne, who by their persuasion pardon'd her.

Despite her conviction, then, Jane was reprieved, in part through William Cowper's intercession with Queen Anne. Indeed, between them, Cowper and Plummer ensured that Wenham remained protected. Plummer 'plac'd her in a little House near his own', and Lord Cowper and his wife also sheltered her. After Cowper and Plummer's death, Sarah Cowper and her brother continued to support Jane.

Although Wenham's conviction in 1712 was the last, it was to be another twenty-four years before the law on witchcraft was changed. The first statute against witchcraft had been passed in 1542 (though repealed five years later) and outlawed sorcery used to damage or find goods, or to 'provoke any persone to unlawfull love'. A new Act had passed in 1551 but the most important piece of legislation was the 1563 Act, introducing the death penalty for causing death by witchcraft and for conjuring evil spirits. Another Act in 1603–4 had increased the penalties for second convictions relating to intent to cause death or injury. Only in 1736 was the legislation repealed, replaced with a law against *pretending* to use any form of witchcraft. The last person to be prosecuted for this was in 1944 and the law was replaced in 1951 by the Fraudulent Mediums Act. These legislative changes punctuate a story of shifting attitudes and beliefs in which political and religious partisanship had, in 1712 at least, played a significant part.

THE DEBATE OVER THE IMPOSSIBILITY OF WITCHCRAFT

The Wenham case had shown many similarities with other witchcraft trials. Jane was in many ways the stereotypical witch (though perhaps better-looking than most, if Sarah Cowper's comments are accurate) in conflict with her neighbours and in league with the Devil. She changed shape, adopting the disguise of her familiar; she used charms; and customary means of identifying a witch seemed to confirm her guilt. Her chief victim presented symptoms that could not be explained by medical science, and had indeed at times displayed supernatural strength; she had also been tempted to commit suicide. She sought the blood of the witch, and was plagued by crooked pins, features that recurred in other witchcraft trials. Admittedly the degree of clerical involvement was unusual: the victim was a servant of a minister, and two other vicars had become involved, all convinced that they were confronting a witch. Yet, perhaps because of this, the case provoked a printed pamphlet debate that was unusually virulent and extensive. Indeed, the courtroom now extended to a wider public tribunal, the court of public opinion. Although 'thousands of people' had flocked to see Jane in gaol and 'so Vast a Number of People' packed into the courtroom that the crowd surpassed all 'in the Memory of Man',[64] the printed debate created an even more extensive, national, 'public'. What had been a local affair assumed a significance out of proportion to the events themselves.

Bragge's account of the trial was 'read with such Pleasure, that in a Month's Time it had a Fourth edition'.[65] Indeed, Bragge had something of a publishing sensation on his hands, further evidence of the power of the press and the public's appetite for the sensational. Besides his *Full and Impartial Account*, and a single-sheet summary of the trial, there were eight other print interventions, three of which were by Bragge himself. His publisher, Edmund Curll, who would become notorious as one of the most unscrupulous men in the business, had published High Church tracts during the Sacheverell affair; and clearly both he and Bragge were intent on making money from the controversy, even if this meant deliberately stoking the other side of the debate. Curll thus probably entered into a partnership with the Whig, Dissenting publisher John Baker, who is best known for publishing Defoe's works and whose paper, the *Protestant Post-Boy*, advertised his publications about the Wenham trial. Baker published three anti-Bragge tracts, so that between them he and Curll were pushing both sides of the argument in order to make lucrative sales.[66] We know that Curll paid Bragge the large sum of 3 guineas for the first 1,000 copies of his *Account*, with a further guinea for its reprinting;[67] and Bragge's final work, *The Witch of Walkerne*, was a shameless compilation of his earlier tracts. Not without reason, he was said to have an 'insatiable itch after scribling'.[68] The run of pamphlets from 1712 is worth listing, since it provides an excellent example of the extensiveness of print controversies and of public consumption of them:

1. Bragge, *A Full and Impartial Account* (at least four editions by mid May 1712)

2. *An Account of the Tryal, Examination and Condemnation of Jane Wenham*

3. *The Impossibility of Witchcraft* (three editions, the third of which had an appendix vindicating the author; the contents had already been published in serial form in the *Protestant Post-Boy*, issues 92–6, in April 1712; the tract plagiarized John Wagstaffe's *The Question of Witchcraft Debated* (1669))

4. Bragge, *Witchcraft Further Display'd* (printed by Curll)

5. *The Impossibilty of Witchcraft Further Demonstrated* (advertised in the *Protestant Post-Boy*, 31 May–7 June 1712)

6. *The Case of the Hertfordshire Witchcraft Consider'd*

7. *The Belief of Witchcraft vindicated* (advertised *Evening Post*, no. 433, 17 May 1712)

8. *A Full Confutation of Witchcraft* (advertised as being printed that day, *Post-Boy*, no. 2649, 1 May 1712)

9. Bragge, *A Defence of the Proceedings* (advertised as having been published the previous week, *Evening Post*, no. 439, 31 May 1712)

10. Bragge, *The Witch of Walkerne*.

The numerous prints were capitalizing on a debate in the press about the existence of witches that had been rumbling in the months prior to the Wenham case. The Whig writer Joseph Addison had recognized the persistence of witchcraft belief and instead of refuting it head on, attempted a more subtle, witty, moderate but Whiggish subversion of it in *The Spectator* in July 1711.[69] Professing to stand 'neuter' on the issue, he believed that whilst 'in general...there is, and has been, such a thing as witchcraft' he could 'at the same time can give no credit to any particular instance of it'. There followed a fictional account of how Sir Roger, Addison's fictional archetypal Tory squire who was used in the paper to gently mock the Tory mindset, had to be restrained from having an old woman bound over at the county sessions for witchcraft. And the paper ends on a warning note; complaining of the widespread belief in witches in rural England Addison noted that:

> When an old woman begins to doat, and grow chargeable to the Parish, she is generally turned into a Witch and fills the whole Country with extravagant Fancies, imaginary Distempers, and terrifying Dreams. In the meantime, the poor Wretch that is the innocent Occasion of so many Evils begins to be frightened at her self, and sometimes confesses secret Commerces and Familiarities that her Imagination forms in a delirious old Age. This frequently cuts off Charity from the greatest Objects of Compassion, and inspires People with a malevolence towards those poor decrepid Parts of our Species, in whom Human Nature is defaced by Infirmity and Dotage.

The implication was that belief in witchcraft was another prejudice that the urbane, polite, and charitable world surrendered. Yet a few months later this stance was questioned by Daniel Defoe who tackled the question 'whether there is any such thing as a Witch' in his periodical *The Review*, which was now courting Tory opinion for Defoe's patron, Prime Minister Robert Harley.[70] Defoe found legal support and scriptural testimony for witchcraft; and his depiction of a witch was highly traditional. Witches, he said, had 'a familiar or Personal Converse with the Devil, with whom they have enter'd into Hellish Compacts, Covenants and Combinations for the Hurt and Delusion of themselves and their Fellow-Creatures'. He was later to change his mind but at this time thought there 'can be no more Debate of the Matter' necessary to prove their existence.

The ten tracts devoted to the Wenham case have to be seen in the context of a wider printed controversy that had taken a decidedly political turn; but their success lay in clearly mapping out the two sides of the argument. On one side stood Bragge and the upholders of belief in witchcraft. For them, the Wenham case was indisputable, so that those who scoffed at witchcraft or failed to be convinced must be 'sceptics and freethinkers' who had 'beforehand resolved to believe nothing at all of it, let the Proof be what it would'.[71] As one tract hostile to witch-mongering put it, the High Churchmen made the least doubt about witchcraft 'a Badge of Infidelity; and not to be Superstitious passes for a dull Neutrality in Religion, if not Atheism'.[72] Certainly Bragge attacked the 'atheists' who denied all spirits—witchcraft for him was part of the spiritual world of Christianity, so denial of evil spirits led ineluctably to denial of all supernatural forces and hence ultimately of God. In this view, the defence of witchcraft was the defence of the Church and of religion; the similarities with Sacheverell are obvious. Part of Bragge's case was that witchcraft was scriptural. If one denied that the Bible contained instances of witchcraft and sorcery then people had 'better give up the Scriptures at once, as an intire Imposition'.

Bragge argued that the unnaturalness of what had occurred, far from making witchcraft impossible, required recognition that some non-human power was involved: 'the seeming Impossibility of the thing, proves it to be done by Witchcraft'.[73] Alternatively, as another tract, not by Bragge, suggested, witches might work with the course of nature—so natural explanations alone were not proof against the work of the Devil. Rather, God does not empower the Devil to perform 'what is above or contrary to the stated Course of Nature'.[74]

It is clear that Bragge was also drawing on ('ransacking' according to one critic) earlier clerical, legal, and scientific support for witchcraft (see Figure 6.3). His *Witchcraft Further Display'd* (1712) included reprints of two witch trials from the early 1660s, presided over by Lord Chief Justice Matthew Hale, that bore marked similarities with the Wenham case (victims vomiting pins, violent reactions to the touch of a reputed witch, a desire to draw the witch's blood, the witch tempting victims to suicide) and which had resulted in conviction. In one of these, tried in Suffolk in 1664, the prosecution had been backed by the testimony of Dr Thomas Browne, the same eminent physician whose work had been invoked during the trial of Spencer Cowper. Browne had been author in 1646 of an important work that surveyed advances in knowledge and listed 'a calendar of falsehoods and popular errors'. Yet, in relation to the two women accused, Browne had been 'clearly of Opinion that they were bewitch'd' and that whilst the fits of the victims might be 'natural' they were 'rais'd to a great degree, by the Subtilty of the Devil'.[75] Judge Hale was also an experimenter with the new science, yet he had allowed the conviction to stand. In other words, Restoration science, Bragge showed, was not at all incompatible with accepting witchcraft, particularly as many of its early practitioners were strong advocates of the Church of England. Browne had agreed that denying witches meant denying spirits and hence led to atheism.

Bragge had even earlier enlisted the evidence of a medic to support his claims. He reported how an anonymous 'very Ingenious Gentleman and able physician happened to be present' when Anne Thorn was experiencing her fits and had examined her, 'his Curiosity bringing him a little out of his way to enquire into the Truth of the Story of this Witch, which he had heard several Ways told'. During one of her deathly seizures he held a burnt feather under her nose 'and tho the Stink was so great' that those in the room were not able to bear it, 'yet the Maid received that strong Stream into her Nose without being the least affected with it'. He also saw her 'recovered by Prayer' and though he was a 'profess'd Unbeliever of Things of this Nature', as a physician he could find 'no Natural Disease' that could explain her condition which 'must be either Counterfeit or Preternatural'.

Bragge also quoted Joseph Glanvill, a Restoration cleric who had sought to combine his membership of the Royal Society with witchcraft belief, which he saw as underpinning rather than undermining religious faith. Another fellow of the Royal Society, the physician John Beaumont, who was deeply pious, also sought in 1705 to support the existence of spirits and witchcraft.[76] Indeed there were twenty-five tracts written in support of witchcraft published between 1660 and 1718, and these were said to be 'in Tradesmen's Shops and Farmer's Houses, and are read with great Eagerness, and are continually levening the Minds of the Youth, who delight in such subjects'.[77] One of these may have had a direct bearing on the Wenham case. In 1665 William Drage, a doctor from Hitchin (Bragge's father's parish), published *Daimonomageia a small treatise of sicknesses and diseases from witchcraft, and supernatural causes... being useful to others besides physicians, in that it confutes atheistical, sadducistical, and sceptical principles and imaginations.* The book related several local cases of 'diseases proceeding from witchcraft'. One of these involved a Dissenter, Mary Hall of Little Gaddesdon, who spoke as though she was a cat, ran 'fast and violently', and was tempted to suicide. Indeed, Drage observed that symptoms of possession included being able to leap five or six yards, speak in strange tongues, and have strength greater than 'four or five men', all of which featured in the Wenham case. The work ended with the observation, with which Bragge surely concurred, that 'whatsoever cannot be solved by the ordinary force and usual course of any Natural Causes, is thereby proved Supernatural and Spiritual'.[78]

Although the pro-witchcraft pamphlets were more numerous, the responses that they provoked on the other side of the argument set out a clear refutation of Bragge's position and asserted both the 'impossibility of witchcraft' and that 'witchcraft is priestcraft'. As the use of the word 'priestcraft' suggests, the self-serving and power-crazed role

Figure 6.3 The frontispiece to Nathanial Crouch's 1688 work, *The King-dom of Darkness*, which aimed to counter the 'Atheists of the Age' who scoffed at witchcraft.

of the clergy in the prosecution came in for a good deal of criticism. Witchcraft was said to be based on 'the Jugling Delusions of Confederated Impostors' and 'Zealots'; and its prosecutors were condemned as 'Ambitious, Covetous and Malicious Men' who indulged in human sacrifice.[79] Their 'pretended Exorcisms'—the prayers said to revive Anne Thorn—were 'meer Spiritual Juggles and the very Spirit of Priest-craft', asserted one tract, which argued that 'nothing but Self-Interest could induce them to propagate such Delusions'.[80] Indeed, it asked, if the clergy succeeded in reanimating the Catholic doctrine of exorcism, 'how expos'd and open should we lie to all the Inroads of Popish Superstition?' Another pamphlet thought the whole case rested on 'superstition' and 'Heathenish

Fables, afterwards improv'd by Papal impostors'.[81] Superstition was, of course, the key allegation that Protestants had made against the Catholic Church; now it was being seen as a tool of priestcraft. James Boevey's deist tracts had chronicled at length how organized religion had originated in the clergy's self-interested manipulation of superstitions and fears; and John Trenchard's 1709 *Natural History of Superstition*, discussed earlier in the chapter, had done something very similar. Their theme of clerical imposture and fraud was also key to the refutation of Bragge's argument that witchcraft had scriptural authority. Two tracts thus argued that the translations of the Hebrew words meaning 'impostures' or 'counterfeit miracles' as 'witchcraft' were inaccurate. Thus 'there is no such Thing as a Witch in Scripture'.[82]

The attack on clerical power and superstition was combined in the 1712 anti-witchcraft tracts with a stress on irrationality. Witchcraft belief was, *The Impossibility of Witchcraft* asserted, harboured 'only in Weak and Cowardly Understandings and Tempers'. Indeed, rather than relying on reason, witch-mongering was said to pander to the base emotion of fear, which was used by priests and politicians to manipulate the people. The tract also took the clergy to task for their 'impiety' in overvaluing the Devil. Believers in witchcraft had created a God of evil rather than good, for God would not allow a Devil, at the command of a witch, to gratify her evil desires. Witches, and a powerful Devil, thus did violence to the notion of an all-powerful but benign God, a view that rejected the idea that the Devil was in some way authorized by God to do evil. The denial of witchcraft was thus another sign of the shift in attitudes to God that we have seen throughout this book. Similarly, whilst the existence of spirits was not denied by those hostile to witchcraft beliefs, the spirit world was perceived as lacking corporeality: it was impossible for an evil spirit to make a contract with a human, as Wenham was alleged to have done with the Devil. And spirits were thought of as less capable of intervening directly in human bodies; the permeability of the soul and mind that had been characteristic of Puritanism was being challenged.

The tracts critical of the witchcraft prosecution also stressed that natural rather than supernatural factors had been overlooked. The clergymen were said to have given in to the 'crude Notions of Nurses and Old Women about things which might easily be solv'd by natural Causes' and they ought to be 'a little more conversant with the History of Diseases and enquire more narrowly into the Physical Causes of things'.[83] Thus *A Full Confutation*, which claimed to be written by 'a Physician in Hertfordshire to his Friend in London', offered physical explanations for the strange events and also reflected the demand for a higher standard of proof than had been the case for much of the seventeenth century. Anne Thorn's behaviour was ascribed in more than one tract to an epileptic fit, hysteria, or to mania raised to a pitch by the 'impetuous Motion of the animal spirits and rapid motion of the Blood'.[84] Even so, it was admitted that the state of scientific knowledge meant that a complete natural explanation could not yet be offered. 'The Truth is, want of Knowledge in the Art of Physick makes Men attribute mere Natural Distempers to Spirits; Nay, Physicians themselves, who have shewn Excellency of Skill in Anatomy and Chymistry' had added little to the techniques of diagnosis, so 'we are still in the Dark as the Abstruser Distempers of Human Bodies, especially such as arise from Melancholy; which are of so many sorts, and have such wonderful Effects, that whosoever should rightly Describe them, and make them plainly Manifest, would Discover to us an unknown World full of unheard of prodigious Monsters'.[85] To argue, as Bragge did, that 'every thing that is not to be accounted for, must of necessity be done by Witchcraft' was absurd because it made 'Human Wisdom the Measure of Natural Powers'. The answer was thus not superstitiously to accept witchcraft but to advance man's knowledge of the natural world.[86] Similarly, Jane's confession was explained away rationally: the self-delusion of some old women who believe themselves witches was understandable, it was said, when one 'considers the strange Effects of Melancholy, especially if heightened by Poverty, or want of Good Diet, by Ignorance, Solitariness and Old Age'.[87] Jane was merely a 'poor, stupid ignorant Wretch, that had been harrass'd out of her Senses, threatened by all the Parish, brow-beaten by the Justice, loaded with hard-mouth'd Depositions, closeted by Priests, and told the Advantage of confessing'.[88] It was not surprising she had stumbled when reciting the Lord's prayer.

The debate had raised key Enlightenment issues: the over-weening power of the clergy, superstition, irrationality, credulity and credibility, the nature of God and the Devil, and the role of science. It is true that scepticism about witchcraft was not itself new. From Reginald Scott's landmark work of 1584 onwards there had been many attacks. Scott's book was reprinted in 1665 and John Webster's 1677 pamphlet *The Displaying of Supposed Witchcraft* was an important Restoration refutation of Glanvill's attempt to buttress witchcraft belief. Webster thought that the supposed effects of witchcraft could be explained by natural causes, stressing the importance of melancholy, with which this chapter began. Webster observed that most men drowned in the ignorance and error of prevailing opinion; and he also asserted that witchcraft belief advanced 'superstition and popery'. The 1712 debates had not added anything particularly new to the debate; but they had focused on a case that gripped the public imagination, polarized national opinion, and politicized it.

VINDICATING JANE WENHAM

The book that is generally taken to have been the decisive, if not quite final, refutation of witchcraft belief was Francis Hutchinson's *An Historical Essay concerning Witchcraft*, published in 1718 and revised in 1720. This reviewed and refuted as many cases of witchcraft as Hutchinson could find. He discredited witchcraft, however, not because of anticlericalism or religious scepticism. He was himself a Whig cleric. Rather, he found witchcraft to be popish superstition (and hence irreligious) as well as irrational and to fall short of the standards of legal proof that had come to be expected. He also explicitly related the decline of witchcraft belief to the work of the Royal Society and the rise of the new science—though, as we have seen, the correlation was by no means a straightforward one. In the chapter in his *Historical Essay* on Wenham, Hutchinson noted that he had taken a particular interest in the case and had himself visited Jane, finding her, contrary to Bragge's smears, to be 'a pious sober woman' who was able to repeat the Lord's prayer 'with an undissembled devotion', though he confirmed that she made 'little errors of expression, as those that cannot read are subject to'.[89]

Hutchinson's preoccupation with witchcraft and its delusions was firmly rooted in the earlier controversies we have been exploring. As early as 1706 he had planned an attack on witch beliefs, but had been dissuaded by Hans Sloane, one of the Whig doctors who had given evidence in the Spencer Cowper trial. In April 1712, prompted by the Wenham affair, Hutchinson again wrote to Sloane for advice, since he was anxious once more to publish, wishing to show how witchcraft trials produced 'great trouble & disturbance . . . not only to the poor old Creatures, but to all timerous Persons, & the whole Neighbourhoods where they are'.[90]

It has usually been argued that Hutchinson nevertheless deferred publication, on Sloane's recommendation, until 1718. Yet it seems highly likely that one of the tracts in the 1712 exchange, *The Case of the Hertfordshire Witchcraft Considered*, was in fact by Hutchinson, although it was published anonymously. In his letter to Sloane, Hutchinson had said that he wished to show his work to Judge Powell, and asked Sloane to intercede to ask Powell if he could dedicate the work to him. *The Case* was dedicated to Powell. Its preface ends with the author's statement that 'it has been my fortune to be placed but a very few Miles distant from the Parish where these things were transacted', which had allowed him to investigate some material circumstances; and we know that Hutchinson had indeed visited Wenham. In his 1712 letter to Sloane, Hutchinson had wondered how judges would suppress such 'mischief' if a refutation was not made; and the preface to *The Case* similarly wondered 'where the Mischief will end, if this Humour be once indulged'. Moreover the wording and argument of the tract are fully at one with Hutchinson's printed views, both in his 1708 tract on the French Prophets and the 1718 *Historical Essay*. The first page of *The Case* refers to the 'credulous and unthinking Multitude', mirroring his remark about the 'credulous Multitude' at the start of the *Historical Essay*; and the latter begins with an imaginary dialogue in which a juror in the Wenham case seeks the advice of a cleric, echoing the structure of *The Case* which states that its intention is to be useful to jurors.[91] Moreover, the main section in the *Historical Essay* about Wenham becomes an unusually vitriolic diatribe against Bragge, who was also the target of *The Case*. And both texts, idiosyncratically, spell wizard with a double 'z'.[92]

Assuming, then, that Hutchinson did indeed write *The Case*, or at least had a hand in it, we have confirmation of the importance of the Hertfordshire trial for the man who wrote the classic refutation of witchcraft and new reason to re-examine his tract. In *The Case*, Hutchinson ridiculed the evidence put forward by Bragge; and urged natural and rational explanations for what had seemed supernatural. And his investigations had also uncovered some interesting new evidence about the girl at the heart of the case against Wenham. Hutchinson notes that the 'pretty maid' Anne Thorn had married James Burville, the witness who testified that he had been present when Ann thought she had heard cats talking.[93] In other words, she might have been deluded not by magic of the Devil but by the magic of love. Moreover, she was pregnant at the time she made her allegations, suggesting that her strange experiences were the result of either bodily or mental swings induced by her condition, or that Anne (a maid in a vicarage) was trying to deflect attention from her own scandalous and immoral behaviour. Certainly she ran away with her bridegroom very soon afterwards. As Hutchinson put it baldly in his *Historical Essay*, Anne Thorn was 'an idle Hussy, with child at the time, and was well as soon as her Sweetheart came and married her'.[94] Sarah Stout's passion, unfulfilled, had led her to melancholy and suicide; Anne Thorn's melancholy was dispelled by the marriage Sarah had craved.

Hutchinson's vindication of Jane Wenham was nevertheless not enough to dispel the controversy that surrounded her even to the grave. An entry in the diary of William Cowper's daughter is a salutary reminder of how Jane remained something of a popular outcast but also how the Cowper family, emblematic of the new Whig order established after Walpole's consolidation of power, sought to shape unenlightened popular beliefs and keep them in check. In December 1729 Sarah Cowper (named after her diary-keeping and long-suffering grandmother) noted in her journal that 'Mr Squire the Curate of Hertingfordbury gave me notice of the Death of Jane Wenham, a poor woman become famous thro the folly of her neighbours, being the last Woman in England (or at least in this part of it) that was try'd & condemn'd for Witchcraft.' Jane's death prompted Sarah to recall how:

> My Father & Mother always protected this poor Woman, & since their Death our Family has continued that Protection; my Br[other] paid 40s per Ann[um] for her House Rent; & the rest bestow'd their Charity on her occasionally. About two years ago, she fell into a decay which made her apprehend she shou'd die soon & she almost starv'd herself to save something to bury her decently, which I observing, promis'd to take that Charge upon myself, & on her earnest desire that her Character might be justified if possible from ye aspersion thrown upon it, I engaged if it cou'd be done without Riot, that a Sermon shou'd be preached something applicable to her misfortunes. With these promises this poor Creature was more pleas'd than with any thing I cou'd do to make her remains of Life Comfortable.[95]

Sarah was not the only one who expected a riot, for the curate, trying to prepare for the funeral, found that 'the poor People made abundance of difficulties of doing anything about her, even tho Dead'. The curate was nervous about his sermon. As he told Sarah Cowper:

I thought an Argumentative discourse to prove there was no such thing as that Communication with Evil Spirits which constitutes Witchcraft, & to enter into the merits of particular cases, wou'd only appear ridiculous to a great man, & occasion mirth & Laughter, instead of answering the solemnity of the Occasion. My endeavours were to remove an uncharitable Spirit of Vilifying Innocent people, & to shew the great aggravation of doing so when they are dead, & in their Graves; & I made a practical Discourse, concerning the Nature and Duty of a good Life & the blessed Consequences & Reward that attend good People after Death. Our Church was prodigiously crowded, the fullest that ever I saw it on any Occasion, & there was the utmost decency during the whole service; no Whispers, no Noise or disturbance, no tendency in the least to mirth and Laughter. I beg pardon for this Excursion, but I thought you wou'd desire to be satisfied in it.[96]

The sense of relief that it had passed off without an incident is palpable. And it is significant that the curate felt it necessary to steer his sermon on to safe, even platitudinous, ground. This was one rare moment when the divisions that have permeated this book were disguised rather than confronted.

Even though the curate was careful not to provoke his humble audience at Jane's funeral because they retained superstitions about her, it is worth stressing that Wenham's prosecution had been encouraged by the locality's educated elite, its clergy and magistrate. The case cautions against a neat elite–popular divide in attitudes to witchcraft and the supernatural. The elite did not simply abandon such beliefs while the superstitious populous clung to them, though it is true that judicial attitudes were critical. Rather, the witchcraft debate is another example of contested change. The Wenham case, together with the debates about suicide and melancholy, suggest that change was afoot, particularly in religious, political, and scientific culture, but that these shifts were also disputed. The arguments were divisive, widespread and ideological. The Wenham trial has to be seen in the context of the High Church enthusiasm that followed Sacheverell's trial and of a conviction that belief in the supernatural needed bolstering in order to support belief in God and the Church of England. Similarly the attack on witchcraft has to be seen as part of a politicized campaign against 'priestcraft' and reflected a demand for higher scientific and evidential standards of proof. Here, then, was another strand of a contested Enlightenment that operated at the very local level.

CONCLUSION: AN EXCEPTIONAL STORY?

The Cowpers and their locality of Hertford witnessed turbulent and changing times. Spencer Cowper's trial for the murder of the Quaker Sarah Stout not only revealed a mass of tensions that had split the town politically and religiously but also created new frictions between the one-time allies of the Quakers and the Whigs. The wider social and cultural shifts of the later seventeenth century were also reflected in other family crises. The diary of Spencer's rather strait-laced mother, Sarah, revealed tensions in her marriage to a man temperamentally and religiously at odds with her, and who kept her 'enslaved'. William Cowper's bigamous marriage also revealed an unorthodox view of morality and an unrestrained lust. These family affairs were publicly aired in the politicized scandal-mongering of Delarivier Manley and the Cowpers were precisely the sort of 'false brethren' that Henry Sacheverell had in mind when he thundered out his sermon on 5 November 1709. The involvement of both brothers in Sacheverell's prosecution was very fitting, since they personified the Low Church attack on the doctor. The High Church sentiment that the trial nevertheless unleashed provides the essential context for the prosecution of Jane Wenham in 1712, and helps to explain why the Cowpers not only intervened to save her from the death penalty but also protected even into her grave.

The Cowpers were, of course, a rather unusual family, not only because they were so dysfunctional but also because their actions and views can be reconstructed so fully. Their unusually complete family papers and the attention that they received in the burgeoning print culture allow us to reveal their secrets, reconstruct their attitudes and view them as others saw them. But although in some ways idiosyncratic, the Cowpers were also representative of larger cultural shifts; religious, political, sexual, moral, literary, economic, and scientific changes which shaped the lives of many others at the time, albeit in less dramatic ways. If their story has read like fiction at times, elements of it were an everyday reality across the land. Similarly, although Hertford was one of the most factious towns in Britain, the tensions and quarrels that divided it were all too apparent elsewhere. Such contests were not simply the preserve of an elite few; rather, they riddled the nation and cut across social hierarchies.

The Cowpers and their town have thus allowed us to explore the extreme bitterness of the dispute between political parties and religious groupings and also to show how political and religious changes had a wider cultural impact. Indeed, by studying one family in context it has been possible to demonstrate the interconnectedness of themes that are normally considered separately. Thus by examining the 'micro' it is possible to see how strands of the 'macro' history of the period intertwine and are deeply related. Thus the Whig assault on the political doctrine of patriarchalism opened space for a debate about the tyranny of husbands over wives. Public science and religion shared common debates over proof and certainty, delusion and deceit, which also permeated the fictional and political writing of the time. Morality came under pressure from the freedoms ushered in by religious toleration and from the questioning of accepted beliefs, as the scriptural source of conventional mores was challenged or even in some cases overthrown. Ideas about the relationship between God, man, and the Devil seemed to be in flux, affecting how suicide and witchcraft were viewed, and the latter was also influenced by the contest between the religious factions. Printed political and religious debates also cultivated ideals of reason, of moderation, of politeness that had much wider cultural force; and controversialists evolved increasingly sophisticated literary and visual techniques of persuading or misleading an increasingly powerful public. The restraints on the individual seemed to be being loosened by religious change at the same time as political partisanship and an emerging modern economy seemed to prioritize self- or partisan interest, creating worries about community and the public good. In other words we have been exploring something like a set of shifting world views, a process of interrelated and contested Enlightenment.

The term Enlightenment is useful because it breaches the artificial separation of the seventeenth and eighteenth centuries that plagues a good deal of the secondary literature and because, as an expansive term, it captures that essential intertwining of those different strands. The Enlightenment, at least in the ways that it has been approached in the last twenty years or so, fuses the social, political, cultural, literary, and economic as well as the intellectual. Yet the idea that England had an Enlightenment at all might puzzle some. It is more usual to talk about a European, French, or even a Scottish Enlightenment and to minimize the contribution from south of the border, though an important work by Roy Porter in 2000 did seek to emphasize the British contribution across the eighteenth century. My argument has not been one about whether English or Scottish philosophers contributed more. Instead, I wanted to stress that this early English Enlightenment raised many of the questions that would be central to the better-known European Enlightenment; that those questions arose out of everyday conflicts that produced quite sophisticated and extensive debates; and that they did so as much in the seventeenth as the eighteenth centuries. England's experience of two seventeenth-century revolutions forced it to work through questions of religious toleration, press censorship, the right of resistance, the separation of Church and State, a non-Christian God, wealth creation, the preference for reason over zeal and superstition, the grounds of morality, and scientific solutions over supernatural explanations. Whilst there were seldom neat divides along all these issues, we have seen how Whig/Dissenting/Low Church and Tory/High Church cultures differed markedly and how partisanship infused the different positions with polemical vigour. The Enlightenment was a contest between competing notions, a sort of cultural civil war, and we can find this occurring at the local and familial level.

Historians now often talk of 'enlightenments', rather than 'the Enlightenment', because they stress the ways in which the responses to issues varied according to space and time. The question arises, then, how far England's experience of this ferment at this time was unique. The answer is that the issues explored in this book were also being considered in other European countries at this time, particularly in France and Holland and America, but that the English context necessarily shaped and conditioned its experience. The Flemish historian Paul Hazard long ago identified the period 1680–1715 as one of a European crisis of the mind. He pointed to the religious challenges posed by Pierre Bayle, Jean le Clerc, Nicolas Malebranche, Spinoza, and others at precisely this time. They were engaged in similar problems about scriptural and secular authority, ideas about Heaven and Hell, about a materialist science and nature. The similarities across Northern Europe are sometimes remarkably striking. An appeal to reason as the key and sometimes sole guide to truth, a scepticism about Christian revelation, a confidence in man and science, and an anxiety about the inability to agree on accepted truths were shared across national boundaries. And of course England was influenced by Continental debates as well as helping to shape them. For example, the Dutch Balthasar Bekker's work *De Betooverte Wereld*, which sought to undermine belief in the Devil and his agents, first appeared in 1691; by 1695 it had been translated into English as *The World Bewitch'd*, published by Richard Baldwin, a steadfastly Whiggish bookseller. The successful invasion of England by the Dutch William in 1688 and his English coronation only served to underline how much Holland and England in particular had in common.

Yet in France the persistence of Louis XIV's authoritarian and Catholic monarchy necessarily created differences with England. To be sure, both England and France experienced serious unrest in the mid seventeenth century, both attacked fanaticism and disorder, and for a while in the second half of the century both nations appeared to be running on parallel tracks towards increasing the power of the monarch. But France did not experience a second revolution as Britain did in 1688–9. Political parties, liberty of worship, freedom of the press, and an ideology justifying resistance did not flourish across the Channel.[1] Britain's political revolution, which had in part been intended precisely to avert the closer reconciliation of England and France, was not exported to Paris. France did not experience the vigorous popular politics that accompanied frequent elections, and religious pluralism was officially proscribed after the revocation of the Edict of Nantes (which had granted some measure of toleration) in 1685. The revolution principles that were at stake in the Sacheverell trial were thus rather alien to the French. Whereas the Protestant Bayle fled France in 1700 never to return, John Locke, who had fled England in 1683, sailed back on the same ship as William of Orange and flourished, gaining office and preferment. In other words, the different trajectories of the two states produced different political and religious cultures, and these in turn necessarily shaped the wider cultural shifts taking place in both countries in different ways. England thus faced, and debated at length, issues that would become central French concerns later in the eighteenth century. It was because of English precocity that Voltaire's *Lettres Philosophiques ou lettres Anglais* (1734), published first in England a year earlier as *Letters Concerning the English Nation*, sought to popularize an English Enlightenment to a French audience. If we associate the Enlightenment with France in the eighteenth century, then we have to recognize that one of its leading spokesmen self-consciously looked back to England in the late seventeenth and early eighteenth century for much of his inspiration and critique. England's cultural revolution, refined in the crucible of small market towns such as Hertford as well as in the grand capital city, was exported abroad and helped to shape the European and American mind, though of course these also experienced the Enlightenment in their own different contexts and as a result of a variety of different influences.

As we have seen, this early English Enlightenment was a surprising one. Although the Enlightenment could be characterized by a stress on reason and moderation or by an attack on fanaticism and prejudice, in England these values were forged in the heat of intolerant, zealous, and immoderate partisan conflict. The story of the English Enlightenment cannot be told without fully understanding the two sides of that contest. Indeed, the High Churchmen, evidently in the long term on the 'losing side' of the argument, have (I hope) proved as interesting as the radicals to whom most attention is usually paid. The moral and intellectual panic that the High Churchmen experienced is deeply revealing, as all moral reform movements are, of a culture undergoing the bewildering uncertainties of change. Aware that the fundamentals of their faith were being challenged, the High Churchmen put up a strong fight that required their opponents to refine, but also to adapt, their arguments. Arguably, the resistance and endurance of the High Church Tories (well beyond our endpoint of 1712) forced Whig radicalism into accommodations and compromises that it might otherwise not have entertained, a dialectic process that is best exemplified by the moderate and compromising Whiggery of Robert Walpole in the 1720s and 1730s. An awareness that the Enlightenment has always involved a process of vigorous and at times bad-tempered debate might also be consoling. Many today see the Enlightenment as under attack from a world that has lost confidence in the power of reason to resolve all problems, in the march of progress and in a set of universally held civilized values. The story of the Cowpers suggests that these notions were contested from the start.

GLOSSARY OF TERMS

Anabaptist	See Baptist.
Arbitrary power	Acting outside the law; usually associated with the tyranny of kings or with popery (see below), as in the phrase 'popery and arbitrary government' which rested on the notion that Catholic states (most notably Louis XIV's France) were ones in which monarchs placed their own will above the law.
Atheist	Someone who did not believe in God; but also a term of abuse for those who lived loose lives as though there was no God or held unorthodox beliefs.
Baptist	A Protestant who believed that infant baptism should be replaced by adult baptism, since it required active consent. The Baptists were split theologically over the issue of free will. They were Dissenters and advocated freedom of worship outside the national Church.
Calvinist	A follower of John Calvin, the sixteenth-century Reformation theologian who stressed original sin and salvation through the grace of Christ. His theology stressed that it lay in God's mercy whether to save or damn, and hence a notion that some were predestined to be saved while the majority were predestined to damnation.
Catholics	See papists.
Censorship	See licensing.
Church of England	The Church of England was created by the Reformation in the sixteenth century and was a Protestant national institution that until the 1640s enjoyed a monopoly of legal religious worship. From 1646 it lost that status; but regained it in 1660. The Church of England was governed by bishops, had ministers or curates in every parish church, and regulated worship through a Book of Common Prayer. The 39 Articles set out its theological position. The phrase 'the Church of England as by law established' referred to the provisions enacted in the early 1660s which included an act requiring conformity to the national Church and penalties for failing to do so (see below, penal laws).
Commonwealth	See republic.
Comprehension	The revision of the forms of worship and/or theology of the Church of England to accommodate Dissenters (see Dissent).
Conformity	Adherence to the forms of worship and theological position of the Church of England.

Congregationalist	See Independent.
Conscience	The point of interaction between God and the self, informing individuals how to act a godly life.
Conventicle	A religious meeting of Dissenters (see below).
Corporation Act 1661	Required those who held office in towns and other corporations to show that they adhered to the Church of England.
Conventicles Act 1664	Revised in 1670, imposing penalties on Dissenters (see above).
Country Party/values	Prior to the Revolution of 1688–9 the Country Party consisted of those who opposed the Court Party constructed by the earl of Danby for Charles II in the 1670s. After the imprisonment of Danby in 1679 many in the Country Party became known as Whigs. But after 1689 the fact that Whigs were given Court offices blurred these distinctions. Some who saw themselves as 'patriots' and adherents of country values saw Court Whigs as having sold out and Country values (particularly a suspicion of the power of the State and public-spiritedness) were increasingly claimed by the evolving Tory Party (see below).
Court Whig/Tory	See Whig/Tory.
Debauchery	Loose living.
Declaration of Indulgence	A decree issued by Charles II (in 1672) and by James II (in 1687 and 1688) suspending the prosecution of laws against Dissenters and Catholics (see also penal laws; Dissenters; papists).
Dissent/er	The collective term for Protestants who, after 1660, were unable to comply with the forms of worship and theology of the Church of England. There were nevertheless considerable differences between the Dissenting groups. See also Nonconformity and fanatic.
Fanatic	Term of abuse for a Dissenter or religious enthusiast, though the term also carried overtones of political radicalism.
Freedom of worship	See liberty of conscience.
Friends	Members of the Quaker movement (see below).
Freethinker	Someone who explored spiritual 'truth' with a complete freedom of inquiry.
High Church	A position within the Church of England that championed the power of the Church and which resented toleration of Dissenters. The High Churchmen also opposed changes of worship and theology to accommodate (or 'comprehend') Dissenters. Often linked politically to the Tories (see below) though not all Tories were High Church.
Independent	A Protestant who believed in gathered communities of believers worshipping according to their own rites and theology, independent of the national Church of England.
Indictment	An accusation that someone has committed a criminal offence.

Irreligion	The absence of religious belief or practice.
Jacobite	A supporter of James II or the Stuart line after the Revolution of 1688–9.
Liberty of conscience	The freedom to follow spiritual truth according to the dictates of individual conscience.
Licensing	The system of regulating the press by requiring a licence from the state or Church prior to publication. Licensing lapsed temporarily in 1679 and permanently in 1695, though regulation of the press continued via laws of sedition and libel, and after 1712, via taxation.
Low Church	A position within the Church of England that, whilst supportive of the Church, disliked persecution of fellow Protestants and were thus relatively comfortable with toleration (see below) or even comprehension (see above). Many Low Church were Whigs though not all Whigs were Low Church.
Meeting	The term used by Quakers to describe their spiritual gatherings to listen to the 'inner light' of God, which replaced the church or chapel services used by other faiths. The term 'Meeting Houses' was also applied to Dissenting chapels more generally.
Nonconformity	See Dissent.
Occasional conformity	The practice whereby Dissenters took the sacrament according to the rites of the Church of England just once a year in order to qualify themselves, under the terms of the Test and Corporation Acts, for political office.
Papist	A pejorative term for a Catholic, so called because of a perceived allegiance to the pope above all other loyalties. See also 'Popery'.
Passive obedience	A principle of the Church of England, much beloved by Tories, that subjects should not resist their lawful monarch but had an obligation to obey even objectionable commands
Penal code/laws	The legislation enacted in the early 1660s which imposed penalties on those who were unable to conform to the Church of England. This was mainly directed against Protestant Dissenters and Quakers but also included provisions against Catholics.
Popery	A pejorative term for Catholicism but also often implying a political outlook linked to arbitrary forms of government (see arbitrary power).
Popish Plot	An alleged plot, revealed by Titus Oates in 1678, in which Catholics planned to kill the king and re-establish Catholicism in Britain.
Presbyterian	A Protestant Dissenter, from the largest of the sects, who differed from the Church of England over forms of Church

governance (disliking especially the power of a clerical hierarchy) and over some aspects of theology. By the early eighteenth century some Presbyterians were challenging orthodox belief in a trinity of God, Christ, and Spirit, and by the mid eighteenth century were known as Unitarians (a term coined in 1682).

Protestant — A follower of the reformed Churches that rejected Catholicism as a corrupt and superstitious form of religion. Dissenters were Protestant (sharing a reformed faith) though some High Churchmen equated Protestantism solely with the Church of England.

Press — A generic term covering all types of print which was produced in this period on hand-operated printing presses.

Quaker — A pejorative term for a sect that emerged in the 1650s, so called because of their 'quakings' when filled with religious fervour; they called themselves Friends.

Republic — A non-monarchical form of government also referred to as a commonwealth after 1649. After the Restoration, 'commonwealth' was often used pejoratively to describe those who were thought to want either the abolition of monarchy or a curtailment of monarchical powers and/or a return to the radical ideas of the mid-century revolution.

Restoration — The return of the monarchy in 1660, with Charles II's accession; but also a term used by historians to describe the reign of Charles II (1660–85).

Restoration crisis — See succession crisis below.

Restoration settlement — The settlement of constitution, religion, finance, and ideology achieved in the early years of Charles II's reign.

Revolution — Britain had two revolutions in the seventeenth century: (1) The revolution of 1641–60, when Britain experienced the outbreak of the Civil War, the temporary collapse of control over the press, an end to the Church of England's monopoly over religious worship and the emergence of Protestant sects, a republican form of government (1649–60), and social and political radicalism; (2) the Revolution of 1688–9, also known as the Glorious Revolution, involving William of Orange's invasion in November, the flight of James II, and the coronation of William and Mary in 1689. Although seemingly more of a palace coup than the mid-century revolution, the political, religious, and cultural consequences of the Glorious Revolution were far-reaching and more permanent than the earlier revolution, though they often built on its foundations.

Revolution principles — The ideology underpinning the achievements of the Glorious Revolution and its aftermath: constitutional restraints on arbitrary power, toleration for Protestant sects, a justification of the right of resistance against tyranny, an interventionist foreign policy against Catholic France and support for the fiscal innovations by which resources could be channelled into war.

Sect | A group of Protestant Dissenters, such as the Quakers, Baptists, Independents, and Presbyterians.

Succession crisis | The turmoil of 1678–81 sparked by the Popish Plot (see above) and the subsequent attempts to bar James duke of York from the succession to the throne because of his Catholicism. The crisis nevertheless was much broader than that, encompassing an attempt to unpick many aspects of the Restoration settlement (see above).

Test Acts | Passed in 1673 and 1678 aimed primarily at excluding Catholics from office-holding, but also barring Dissenters unless they conformed to the rites and worship of the Church of England at least once a year.

Toleration | Freedom of worship outside the Church of England, enacted in 1689 but previously attempted through declarations of indulgence (see above). Even after 1689 toleration remained controversial.

Tory | A pejorative term, derived from the name given to Irish thieves, applied from 1681 to a political party that stood initially for the combined power of monarch and Church, and was hostile to a return to anything like the mid-century republic and its values or ideas. The first Tories upheld the right of James duke of York to succeed to the throne, because to bar him might resurrect republican values. James's subsequent Catholic policies nevertheless forced some Tories to choose between monarch and Church. After the Revolution of 1688–9 many High Church Tories were hostile to revolution principles and some in the Jacobite wing of the party sought a restoration of the Stuarts. Court Tories were those prepared to accept governmental office. Post-revolution Tories were suspicious of the power of the State—unless it was exercised by a monarch, such as Anne, who favoured the Church.

Tory reaction | The period 1681–6 when the High Churchmen and Tories (see above) were dominant over their Whig rivals and purged them from local offices.

Whig | A pejorative term, derived from the name given to Scottish rebels, applied from 1681 to a political party that stood initially for barring the Catholic James duke of York from the throne, limiting the powers of monarchy and Church, hostility to popery and arbitrary government, and sympathy to Dissent. To enemies, this programme looked as though it was reviving the ideals of the mid-century revolution. After the Revolution of 1688–9 the Whigs moved from being a party of opposition to one of government; this produced a split between Court Whigs, who took office, and Country Whigs, who remained suspicious of the compromises involved in directing the government and State.

NOTES

Unless otherwise stated, all volumes are published in London.

INTRODUCTION

1. These examples are derived from Early English Books Online and often considerably pre-date those supplied in the Oxford English Dictionary. The Quaker Isaac Pennington's pamphlet *The Great and Sole Troubler of the Times* (1649) makes frequent use of the word self, including, on p. 24, the phrase 'Self-advancement, Self-interests, Self-ends, Self-designs'.

CHAPTER 1: THE TRIAL OF SPENCER COWPER

Details of the trial and medical experiments are taken from 'The Trial of Spencer Cowper, esq, Ellis Stephens, William Rogers and John Marson at Hertford Assizes, for the Murder of Mrs Sarah Stout, 1699' in T. B. Howell (ed.), *A Complete Collection of State Trials*, 21 vols. (1816), XIII, 1190–249; *An Account of the Full Tryal and Examination of Spencer Cowper Esq* (1699); P. D., *The Hertford Letter* (1699); *A Reply to the Hertford Letter* (1699); *An Answer to the Hertford Letter* (1699); *A Dialogue between a Quaker and his Neighbour in Hertford about the Murder of Mrs Sarah Stout* (1699); *Some Observations on the Tryal of Spencer Cowper* (1701).
The inquisition post mortem is at HALS, D/EP F96.
Manley's account of Spencer and Sarah is taken from *The New Atalantis* (1709). A good modern edition is edited by Ros Ballaster (1991). Secondary reading about Manley is listed under Chapter 4

1. They were alleged to have had two accomplices, Ellis Stephens and William Rogers.
2. Mrs Gurrey was later said to have exaggerated her evidence. Marson received only 50s. for work in the borough court, not £50: *A Reply to the Hertford Letter* (1699), 26.
3. William H. Cornog, 'Sir Samuel Garth: A Court physician of the 18th century', *Isis*, 29(1) (Jul. 1938), 29–42; C. C. Booth, 'Sir Samuel Garth, F.R.S.: The dispensary poet', *Notes and Records of the Royal Society of London*, 40(2) (May, 1986), 125–14; Thomas Brown, *Physick lies a-bleeding, or the Apothecary turned Doctor* (1697); *Reliquiae Hernianae*, ed. P. Bliss (1857), II, 267; Historical Manuscripts Commission, 7th report, 244b.
4. *The Post Man*, no. 634, 22 Jul. 1699.
5. The initials PD at the end of the work perhaps hint of a Dimsdale involvement.
6. This version of events was refuted in *Some Observations*, where it is alleged that no private conversation between Sarah and Spencer ever took place.
7. Their only child, Judith Madan, became a poet.
8. The grand jury could prosecute them for cohabiting illegally.

9. As *The Hertford Letter* (p. 24) put it, 'certainly his Wife would have observed something of it; and then she would not be importuning her every Month, by her Letters, to come to *London*, that she might injoy her sweet Company'.

10. He was perhaps the 'Nominal Quaker, her Quondam Admirer' who is alleged to have 'zealously' spread the report that Sarah had been pregnant. Henry Stout loaned money to a Henry Marson, a Friend who may have been his father; certainly John Marson admitted to being an 'acquaintance' of Spencer.

11. *An Answer to the Hertford Letter* (1699), 1.

12. *Hertford Letter*, 22; *Answer to the Hertford Letter*, 2.

13. HALS, DE/P (Panshanger MSS) F29, 133.

CHAPTER 2: PARTISAN FEUDS

The Hertford borough records are extensive at HALS, though the catalogue is a general one, so this chapter is more heavily annotated to provide references to specific documents. Some of the papers of the Cowper family, which are in the Panshanger collection at HALS, D/EP, are transcribed in John Lord Campbell, *The Lives of the Lord Chancellors*, 10 vols. (1857), V, 218–351. Sir John Chauncy's *The Historical Antiquities of Hertfordshire* (1700) gives a contemporary history of the town.

1. The chronology of events at the front of the book might be a useful reference point.

2. Cowper's advice is reproduced in *English Historical Documents 1714–83*, ed. D. B. Horn and Mary Ransome (1957), doc. 47, 194–6.

3. HALS BR, IX, 285.

4. John Lord Campbell, *The Lives of the Lord Chancellors*, 10 vols. (1857), V, 224.

5. *Smiths Protestant Intelligence*, no. 8, 21–4 Feb. 1681.

6. *Ibid.*

7. HALS BR, XXV, 91.

8. HALS BR, I, 76; XX, 557; HCR, I, 350.

9. HCR, VI, 358.

10. HALS BR, IX, 295, 297, 300–1.

11. Basil Henning (ed.), *The History of Parliament: The House of Commons 1660–1689*, 3 vols. (1983), II, 166.

12. HALS BR, XVII, 497, indictment 21 Jul. 1683.

13. There is a copy at HALS BR, I, 331. Cowper added the caveat that inhabitants could only vote if they did not receive alms.

14. HALS, DE/P F49, poem endorsed 'By W C' in the hand of Sarah Cowper.

15. Beverly Adams, 'The body in the water: Religious conflict in Hertford 1660–1702', PhD, University of London (2000) 88.

16. HALS BR, XXIII, 324.

17. HALS BR, XXXIII, 42.

18. Chauncy, *Historical Antiquities of Heretfordshire* (1700), Preface sig. B.

19. HALS D/ECy F20.

20. Chauncy, *Historical Antiquities*, Preface.

21. *Ibid.* 241–2.

22. HALS BR, I, 50.

23. Ralph Battell, *Vulgar Errors in Divinity Removed* (1683). The work also justifies music in services despite those who 'cry out' against 'the Organ, the lute or

the Harp' (p. 65). Battell justified the ceremonies and form of the Church of England's services and prayers, attacking those preachers who thought that saying whatever came into their minds 'is the only praying by the Spirit' (p. 119). See also Battell's *The Lawfulness and Expediency of Church-Musick* (1693).

24. Both father and son appear to have shared duties at the church and in the local school (see Adams, 'Body in the water', 185–6) but the sermon is clearly by Ralph junior, since his qualifications are listed on the title page.

25. Battell, *The Civil Magistrates Coercive Powers* (1684), 10–12, 15–18, 25. More in the same vein had come from Miles Barne, a royal chaplain, who preached the assize sermon in Hertford on 10 Jul. 1684, which was full of 'intemperate zeal' against the Dissenters (epistle dedicatory, Sig. A2v) though Barne preferred to call it 'unreserv'd affection for the KING and government' and 'a steadfast unfeigned adhesion to the Church of England in all Her Heights'. He asserted that 'so long as there is a Conventicle left in England, so long will there be a seminary of Schism and Sedition' (p. 9) and argued that the Dissenters derived their 'Rebellious Antimonarchical positions' from 'the Factious Calvin' (pp. 14–15). He wanted a 'constant, vigorous and resolute' persecution of them (p. 20).

26. Battell, *Vulgar Errors* (1683), epistle dedicatory, Sig. A3, 26, 38, 41, 43.

27. HALS BR, XXI, 2.

28. HALS BR, IX, 386; HALS, QSR 23/494, indictment, 21 Dec. 1696; *HCR*, I, 424–5.

29. HALS BR, XXIII, 149, 'The Humble Petition of Divers Inhabitants'.

30. HALS BR, I, 446–7.

31. *The Best choice for Religion and Government* (1697).

32. *The Trial and Determination of Truth In answer to the Best Choice for Religion and Government* (1697).

33. HALS, D/EP F 81, f.119, Pennington Cowper to Judith Cowper, 14 Jul. 1698.

34. *Post Man*, 23–6 Jul. 1698.

35. HALS BR, XV, 99–101.

36. HALS BR, I, 61.

37. HALS BR, XXXIII, 52.

38. HALS BR, XXV, 26.

39. Cornish Record Office, BO/23/72/23, P. Igne to Liskeard, 31 Jan. 1698. I owe this reference to the History of Parliament Trust archive.

40. Derek Hirst and Shaun Bowler, 'Voting in Hertford 1679–1721', *History and Computing* 1 (1989), 14–18.

41. Ashurst was the son of prominent Presbyterian and retained a sympathy for Dissent though he appears to have conformed to the Church of England. In 1687, perhaps for his possible support for James II (who knighted him), Sir William Cowper had privately called him 'a knave and an ill man', so there was some irony that he was now testifying on behalf of Cowper's son (HALS, DE/P F81, Sir William Cowper to his wife, 21 May 1687).

42. *Some Observations on the Tryal of Spencer Cowper* (1699).

CHAPTER 3: QUAKERS

The prosecution of Henry Stout and other Quakers in 1664 can be followed in William Smith's two tracts, *A True, Short, Impartial Relation containing the Substance of Proceedings at the Assize* (1664) and *A Second Relation from Hertford: containing the unjust Proceedings of some called Justices there* (1664).

The debate between William Haworth and the Hertford Quakers can be followed in the following tracts:

(a) William Haworth and William Dimsdale, *The Quaker Converted to Christianity* (1673; repr. 1690).

(b) John Crook (with comments by Mary Stout), *Rebellion Rebuked: in an Answer to a Scandalous Pamphlet, entitled The Quaker Converted* (1673).

(c) William Haworth, *The Quaker Converted to Christianity Re-established* (1674).

(d) Christopher Taylor, *A Faithful and true Witness to the light of Jesus Christ* (1675).

(e) John Crook, *The Counterfeit Convert Discovered, or William Haworth's book, entituled The Quaker converted to Christianity re-established refuted* (1676).

(f) Mary Stout and others, *The Testimony of the Hartford Quakers* (1676).

(g) William Haworth, *An Antidote against that Poysonous and Fundamental Error of the Quakers* (1676).

(h) [Hertford Quakers] *A Testimony for the Man Christ Jesus, repelling the poyson & fallacy of William Haworths pretended Antidote against the Quakers. From the people of [sic] Quakers at Hertford* (1676).

(i) William Haworth, *Animadversions upon...A Testimony* (1676).

(j) William Haworth, *Jesus of Nazareth not the Quakers Messiah...Or, a rejoynder to a book, entituled, The testimony of the Hartford Quakers for the man Christ Jesus vindicated* (1677).

(k) Henry Stout and others, *The Independent-agent* (1677).

(l) William Haworth, *An Answer to a sheet entitled The Independent Agent* (1678).

(m) Henry Stout and other friends, *The Malice of the Independent-agent again rebuked* (1678).

James Peterson, *The Pamphlet of the Lyar Discovered* (1678), a Quaker attack on tithes, responds to *The Voice of the Light*, 'a malicious sheet spread in and about Hartford', apparently written by one of the town's clerics.

The appeal case can be followed in *The Case of Mrs Mary Stout* (1700); *The case of Spencer Cowper* (1700); *Some Observations on the Tryal of Spencer Cowper* (1701).

1. George Fox, *Journal* (1694), 202, 223 (the pagination of this book is inconsistent and has three concurrent series of page numbers); George Whitehead, *Christian Progress* (1725), 93–4.
2. *These Several Papers were sent to the Parliament* (1659), 3, 7, 54–5.
3. Joseph Besse, *An Abstract of the Sufferings of the People call'd Quakers*, 3 vols. (1733–8), I, 28.
4. Violet Rowe, *The First Hertford Quakers* (1970), 27.
5. Adams, 'The body in the water', 64; Lionel Munby, *The Common People Are Not Nothing: Conflict in religion and politics in Hertfordshire 1575–1780* (University of Hertfordshire, 1995), 80.
6. Besse, *Abstract of the Sufferings*, I, 113–16.
7. William Smith, *A Second Relation from Hertford: containing the unjust Proceedings of some called Justices there* (1664).

8. HALS, NQ1 1A/1, Monthly and Quarterly Minutes of the Quakers. At the back of the volume are records of money paid out for William Cowper and money received from him, signed by Henry Stout.
9. HALS BR, IX, 278.
10. Adams, 'The body in the water', 106.
11. In some locations, such as York where the Quakers were more integrated into local society than in Hertford, 'sufferings' could be relatively mild—see David Scott, *Quakerism in York 1650–1720*, Borthwick Paper no. 80 (University of York, 1991). For a discussion of integration see Simon Dixon, 'Quaker communities in London 1667–c.1714', PhD, University of London (2005).
12. Hertford's cleric Ralph Battell jnr accused Calvinists of making 'God a Tyrant rather than a King' and instead stressed a God who was swift 'to forgive iniquity, transgression and sin and not to decree everlasting fire to it': Battell, *Vulgar Errors*, 17–18.
13. Joseph Smith, *Bibliotheca Anti-Quakeriana* (1873). See also <http://www.qhpress.org/cgi-bin/rmoore/antiq.html> for a bibliography of hostile tracts 1653–66.
14. William Haworth and William Dimsdale, *The Quaker Converted to Christianity* (1673), xii.
15. For the tracts in the controversy see the bibliography for this chapter. See also Beverly Adams, 'The "Durty Spirit" at Hertford: A falling out of Friends', *Journal of Ecclesiastical History*, 52(4) (2001), 647–74.
16. Haworth and Dimsdale, *Quaker Converted*, 21.
17. *Ibid.*, iii, xi–xii.
18. *Jesus of Nazareth not the Quakers Messiah* (1677), subtitle.
19. Haworth, *The Quaker Converted Re-established*, 131–2, 134, 136.
20. Mary Stout and others, *The Testimony of the Hartford Quakers* (1676), 40–55.
21. *The Malice of the Indpendent Agent again Rebuked* (1678), subtitle.
22. George Fox, *Iconoclastes: or a Hammer to Break Down all Invented Images, Image-Makers and Image-Worshippers* (1671), 4.
23. *The Quakers Art of Courtship* (1689), Preface, 3–4, 10.
24. The trial had lasted from 7 a.m. to 4 p.m.: *An Account of the Full Tryal and Examination of Spencer Cowper Esq* (1699), 2.
25. HALS, DE/P F96, 'Reasons Humbly offer'd against Mrs Stout's petition'.
26. HALS, DE/P F29, 11, 22 Sep. 1700.
27. Robert Raymond, *Reports of Cases Argued*, 2 vols. (1765), I, 555–7.
28. HALS, DE/P F29, 72, 17 Mar. 1701.
29. *Post Angel*, Mar. and Apr. 1701.
30. This is not entirely accurate, since John Stout did give evidence and the Quaker Affirmation Act of 1696 allowed Quakers to avoid swearing oaths. Perhaps Mary's religious sensibilities were nevertheless too great.
31. Spencer's fondness for money endured, for in the 1720s he even launched a legal claim on his dead brother's estate.
32. An account of elections in Hertford can be found in Eveline Cruickshanks, Stuart Handley, and David Hayton (eds.), *The History of Parliament: The House of Commons 1690–1715*, 5 vols. (Cambridge, 2002), II, 282–92.
33. Hirst and Bowler, 'Voting',16.
34. HALS BR, XXIII, 149.
35. HALS, DE/P F31, 20 Dec. 1705.

36. *HMC House of Lords*, ns, X, 35–6, 16 Apr. 1713. HALS BR, LXXV contains a good deal about the investigation into the misappropriation of land.
37. *A Compleat Collection of State-tryals, and Proceedings upon Impeachments for High Treason* (1719).
38. *A Critical Review of the State Trials* (1735), 717.
39. *Dunton's Whipping Post* (1706), 49–51.
40. Lothario was a character created by Nicholas Rowe's play *The Fair Penitent* (1703)—see Adams, 'The body in the water', 11.
41. *Lothario's Answer to Sarah the Quaker* (1729).

CHAPTER 4: MORAL PANIC AND MARITAL AFFAIRS

The diaries of Sarah Cowper are at HALS, DE/P F29–35. The other works by women quoted in this chapter are Mary Astell, *Some Reflections Upon Marriage* (1700); Judith Drake, *An Essay in Defence of the Female Sex* (1696); Mary Chudleigh, *The Female Advocate* (1700); Delarivier Manley's semi-fictionalized autobiography *The Adventures of Rivella* (1714). For Manley's *New Atalantis* see Chapter 1.

1. HALS, DE/P F29, 16, 13 Oct. 1700.
2. HALS, DE/P F30, 150.
3. HALS, DE/P F30, 131.
4. ODNB, Martin Clifford.
5. Annotation on p. 5 referring to the heretic 'Pelag[ius]' [Early English Books Online copy].
6. Clifford, *Treatise of Humane Reason* (1674), 2, 4–5, 9–11, 14, 28, 37, 66.
7. HALS, DE/P F29, 5, 29 Jan. 1701.
8. HALS, DE/P F29, 152, 6 Nov. 1701.
9. And in 1700 she was told that 'Mr Toland (lately a writer for the Socinian Tenets) had writ a poem, where in the person of Eloquence he declares, he will not Cease writing till he doth Extirpate Revelation (that is Christianity) and Monarchy, and Establish Deism, and a Commonwealth', HALS, DE/P F29, 14, 8 Oct. 1700.
10. John Toland, *Christianity not Mysterious* (1696), xxv, 107, 140–1, 147, 163.
11. HALS, DE/P F47, 5 vols. The following paragraphs draw from these. I intend to write about Boevey further elsewhere.
12. *Ibid.*, xxviii.
13. Michael Graham, *The Blasphemies of Thomas Aikenhead* (Edinburgh, 2008).
14. The ODNB entry on James Boevey suggests that all his extant manuscripts 'are dated 1665 or 1666' but one of the Hertfordshire manuscripts is dated 1692 and the others seem contemporaneous with it.
15. A copy of the manuscript vindication made its way to the library of future prime minister Robert Harley: William Oldys (ed.), *The Harleian Miscellany*, 10 vols. (1808–10), X, 183–7.
16. There is a discussion of this in Felix Raab, *The English Face of Machiavelli: A changing interpretation 1500–1700* (1964), App. 1.
17. Boevey's debt to Lord Herbert of Cherbury's *De Veritate* (1624) is evident in these five principles which closely follow Herbert's work. The latter was only available in Latin and French until 1937.
18. Charles Leslie, *A Short and Easie method with the Deists* (1696), 6.

19. *Ibid.*, 30.
20. D. Hayton, 'Moral reform and country politics', *P&P*, 128 (Aug. 1990), 48–91, quotation at p. 55.
21. *Reasons for Passing the Bill for the more Effectual Suppressing Vice & Immorality* (1699), 3, 13–14.
22. For a similar argument in relation to the American Revolution see Sarah Pearsall, *Atlantic Families: Lives and letters in the later eighteenth century* (Oxford, 2008).
23. Mandeville's poem 'The grumbling hive' (1705) became the basis for *The Fable of the Bees* (1714).
24. Lawrence Stone, *Broken Lives: Separation and divorce in England 1660–1857* (Oxford 1993), 27–8.
25. Cited by Adams, 'The body in the water', 136.
26. Friends House Library, London, ARB MSS 324/199a, 202, 205, 206, 208, 213, 217.
27. HALS, NQ1 1A, f.290.
28. Crook was a former member of John Bunyan's Bedford congregation and was recommended by Bunyan to Oliver Cromwell as a nominated member in 1653: Adams, 'The body in the water', 119; but he converted to Quakerism in 1654. He was described in 1669 by the established Church as a man of 'dangarous principles, a subtle fellowe and one who hath too much influence upon the people of that town': Lambeth Palace Library, Misc. Eccl. MS 639, f.216, cited Adams, 'The body in the water', 161.
29. John Crook, *Epistle to All that Profess the Light* (1678 and repr. 1696), 5, 14–17, 19, 24.
30. John Crook, *An Epistle to Friends for Union* (1698), 12.
31. *The Tryal of Spencer Cowper* (1699), 35.
32. Richard Vann, *The Social Development of English Quakerism 1655–1755* (Cambridge, MA, 1969), 137.
33. HALS, DE/P F30, 228, 8 Jun. 1704.
34. HALS, DE/P F29, 19, 25 Oct. 1700.
35. HALS, DE/P F29, 185, 31 Jan. 1702.
36. HALS, DE/P F31, 162, 16 Jan. 1706; F32, 298–9, 5 Nov. 1706.
37. HALS, DE/P F29, 44, 3 Jan. 1701.
38. HALS, DE/P F23, ff.2, 3, Sir William Cowper to Sarah, 26 Jul. and 31 Jul. 1702; F29, 249, 28 Jun. 1702; 252, 4 Aug. 1702.
39. HALS, DE/P F29, 55, 28 Jan. 1701.
40. HALS, DE/P F29, 13, 6 Oct. 1700.
41. HALS, DE/P F29, 16, 15 Oct. 1700.
42. HALS, DE/P F29, 8, 4 Sep. 1700; F29, 7, 30 Aug. 1700, cf. F30, 140, 14 Nov. 1703.
43. HALS, DE/P F29, 33, 8 Dec. 1700.
44. Somerset Record Office, DD/SR 4515, Mary Clarke to Edward Clarke, 14 Dec. 1698.
45. Subtitle of *Great Law of Subordination* (1724).
46. Julia Rudolph, *Revolution by Degrees: James Tyrrell and Whig political thought in the late seventeenth century* (Basingstoke, 2002), 39–46.
47. HALS, DE/P F29, 172, 30 Dec. 1701.
48. HALS, DE/P F29, 162, 2 Dec. 1701; F29, 13, 4 Oct. 1700.
49. HALS, DE/P F29, 243, 14 Jul. 1702.

50. HALS, DE/P F33, 27, 7 Feb. 1707.
51. Though she also noted ruefully that she still lacked 'peace and quiet of Mind': HALS, DE/P F33, 133, 27 Nov. 1707.
52. Sarah took notes on comments by Astell acknowledging the misery of an unhappy marriage and the inequality of the relationship; but interestingly she also copied those counselling fortitude and patience: HALS, DE/P F30, 190, which is an amalgam of Astell, *Reflections Upon Marriage*, 4–5, 32: see Ann Kugler, *Errant Plagiary: The life and writings of Lady Sarah Cowper 1644–1720* (2002), 53.
53. Judith Drake, *An Essay in Defence of the Female Sex* (1696), 22; Mary Wollstonecraft, *Vindication of the Rights of Women* (1792), ch. 9. Jamaica, the plantation to which Henry Stout had been sentenced in 1664, experienced a massive influx of black slaves in the later seventeenth and early eighteenth centuries: Trevor Burnard and Kenneth Morgan, 'The dynamics of the slave market and slave purchasing patterns in Jamaica, 1655–1788', *William and Mary Quarterly*, 58(1) (2001), 205–28.
54. Sprint later published this as *The Bride-Woman's Counsellor* (1709).
55. *The Female Advocate* (1700), 7, 13, 16, 22, 28.
56. Smith, 'English feminist writings', 730.
57. This paragraph draws on Hannah Smith, 'English feminist writings and Judith Drake's *An Essay in Defence of the Female Sex* (1696)', *Historical Journal*, 44 (2001), 727–47.
58. HALS, DE/P F58, f.2 Sarah to William Cowper, no date.
59. HALS, DE/P F81, f.62, William to Judith Cowper, 30 Apr. 1695.
60. HALS, DE/P F34, 10–12.
61. HALS, DE/P F29, 26, 22 Oct. 1700.
62. HALS, DE/P F30, 261, 13 Aug. 1704.
63. HALS, DE/P F234, 11–12, 2 Dec. 1729.
64. This paragraph is based on documents in HALS, DE/P F85.
65. She regretted that he gave 'any handle' to critics, though publicly she was loyal and said it merely revealed that people were envious of him: HALS, DE/P F30, 29.
66. *The Best Choice for Religion and Government* (1697), 22, 24.
67. *The Examiner*, 4 Jan. 1711. *The Examiner*, 1 Feb. 1711 noted that Cowper's successor as Lord Chancellor was 'wholly ignorant in the speculative as well as practical part of Polygamy...he is no free-thinker in religion, nor hath courage to be patron of an Atheistical book', the implication being that Cowper was guilty of all these.
68. British Library, Additional MS 61360, ff.174–81.
69. John Cairncross, *After Polygamy Was Made a Sin: The social history of Christian polygamy* (1974), 126.
70. William Lawrence, *Marriage by the Law of God Vindicated* (1680), 113.
71. John Turner, *Discourse on Fornication* (1698), 49, 55.
72. *Concubinage and Poligamy Disprov'd*, epistle dedicatory, B2, 19, 73, 78–9.
73. John Butler, *Explanatory Notes upon a Malicious Libel called Concubinage and Poligamy Disproved* (1698), Preface, A2 v3.
74. The following paragraph draws on Bernard Capp, 'Bigamous marriage in early modern England', *Historical Journal*, 52(3) (2009), 537–56.
75. John Spinke, *A letter, Truly Representing a Matrimonial case* (1711).

76. HALS, DE/P F211.
77. *The Female Tattler*, no. 1, 8 Jul. 1709; no. 3, 11–13 Jul. 1709.
78. John Oldmixon, *The Court of Atalantis* (1714), 179–81, where Charles Caesar becomes 'Caius'.
79. HALS, DE/P F31, 259, 14 Jul. 1706.
80. Delarivier Manley, *The Adventures of Rivella* (1714), 108–9.
81. Ruth Herman, *The Business of a Woman: The political writings of Delarivier Manley* (Newark, 2003), 74, quoting a letter from Sunderland to Sarah Churchill.

CHAPTER 5: FANATICS AND FALSE BRETHREN

Sacheverell's offending sermons were *The Communication of Sin* (1709) and *The Perils of False Brethren* (1709).

His trial can be followed in *The tryal of Dr. Henry Sacheverell, before the House of Peers, for high crimes and misdemeanors; upon an impeachment* (1710); *An Impartial Account of what pass'd most Remarkable in the last Session of Parliament* (1710); *A Compleat History of the Whole Proceedings of the Parliament... against Dr Henry Sacheverell* (1710); *High Church Display'd* (1711); Yale University, Beinecke library, Osborn mss box 21/22, 'Account of the Trial of Dr Sacheverell'.

Ann Clavering's account of the trial is in *The Clavering Correspondence of Sir James Clavering*, ed. H. T. Dickinson, Surtees Society, vol. 178 (1967).

The vast pamphlet literature that the trial provoked is catalogued in F. F. Madan, *A Critical Bibliography of Dr Henry Sacheverell*, ed. W. Speck (Lawrence, Kansas, 1978), which also contains very useful notes about the items.

Sir David Hamilton, the queen's physician, kept a diary that made its way into the Cowper family papers because Hamilton was at Court with William Cowper's wife Mary. It was published as *The Diary of Sir David Hamilton 1709–1714*, ed. Philip Roberts (Oxford, 1975).

1. *The Tryal of Dr. Henry Sacheverell* (1710), 150.
2. G. M. Trevelyan, *England under Queen Anne*, 3 vols. (1965), III, 55.
3. *Remarks and Collections of Thomas Hearne*, Oxford Historical Society, 8 vols. (1885–1907), II, 229, cited by Geoffrey Holmes, *The Trial of Doctor Sacheverell* (1972), 64.
4. The text was taken from St Paul's letter to the Corinthians.
5. *A Compleat History of the Whole Proceedings of the Parliament ... against Dr Henry Sacheverell* (1710), 5.
6. Quotations are from *The Tryal of Dr. Henry Sacheverell* unless otherwise stated.
7. The visual and material culture of the period is further explored in M. Knights, 'The materiality of visual print culture in the later Stuart period' in James Daybell and Peter Hinds (eds.), *Material Readings of Early Modern Culture, 1580–1720* (Routledge, 2010), ch. 5.
8. HALS, DE/P F33, 118, 27 Feb. 1710.
9. *The Clavering Correspondence of Sir James Clavering*, ed. H. T. Dickinson, Surtees Society vol. 178 (1967), 70.
10. *A Compleat History*, 111–16.

11. Yale University, Beinecke library, Osborn MSS box 21/22, 'Account of the trial of Dr Sacheverell'.
12. *A Compleat History*, 111–116.
13. Holmes, *Trial*, 161. What follows draws on Holmes, *Trial*, ch. 7 and 'The Sacheverell riots: The Church and the crowd in early eighteenth-century London', *Past and Present* (1976) and the sources cited there.
14. *HMC House of Lords*, VIII, 367.
15. The rioting influenced the queen's attitude to the impeachment, making her favour a mild punishment for fear of further disorder: *The Diary of Sir David Hamilton 1709–1714*, ed. Philip Roberts (Oxford, 1975), 6.
16. 'Account of the trial of Dr Sacheverell'.
17. *Clavering Correspondence*, 70–1.
18. *Ibid.*, 74.
19. HALS, DE/P F34, 234, 25 Oct. 1710.
20. HALS, DE/P F34, 249, 2 Dec. 1710.
21. John Morphew published a periodical, *A Collection of all the Addresses that have been Presented to her Majesty*, in order to reproduce the texts.
22. John Oldmixon, *The History of Addresses* (1709), 186, 350–3.
23. HALS, DE/P F34, 228, 10 Oct. 1710.
24. *Hamilton Diary*, 19.
25. HALS, DE/P F33, 119, 28 Feb. 1710.
26. HALS, DE/P F33, 119, 1 Mar. 1710.
27. HALS, DE/P F33, 120, 2 Mar. 1710.
28. HALS, DE/P F33, new pagination at end of volume, p. 14, undated transcription of poem.
29. HALS, DE/P F33, 122, 6 Mar. 1710.
30. HALS, DE/P F33, 128–9, 16 Mar. 1710.
31. HALS, DE/P F33, 151, 3 May 1710.
32. HALS, DE/P F33, 154, 11 May 1710.
33. HALS, DE/P F33, 190, 20 Jul. 1710.
34. HALS, DE/P F33, 148, 27 Apr. 1710.
35. HALS, DE/P F33, 212, 2 Sep. 1710.
36. HALS, DE/P F34, 107, 23 Mar. 1711.
37. HALS, DE/P F34, 130, 29 May 1711.
38. HALS, DE/P F33, 240, 7 Nov. 1710.
39. HALS, DE/P F33, 165, 1 Jun. 1710.
40. HALS, DE/P F34, 250, 29 May 1713.
41. HALS, DE/P F29, 49, 15 Jan. 1701.
42. HALS, DE/P F31, 65, 30 Apr. 1705.
43. HALS, DE/P F33, 256, 20 Dec. 1710.
44. HALS, DE/P F33, 323, 2 Jun. 1711.
45. *The English Theophrastus* (1708 edn), 110.
46. HALS, DE/P F33, 274, 3 Feb. 1711.
47. Shaftesbury, *Soliloquy* (1710), 17–18, 22, 123.
48. *The Letter to Isaac Bickerstaffe Esq. Occasion'd by the Letter to the Examiner* (1710).
49. HALS, DE/P F33, 214, 7 Sep. 1710.
50. BL, Sach. 445.
51. *The Picture of Malice* (1710), 10–11.

52. More such prints are available through the British Museum's publicly accessible, free website. See Further Reading for the URL.
53. It had been published in 1700 in Oxford and 1709 in London.
54. I am very grateful to Angela Jones of the V&A for drawing this to my attention.
55. BL, Sach. 445(8), placed between pp. 94 and 95 of *The Tryal*.
56. *The Picture of Malice*, 11–12 and *passim*.
57. *The Judgment and Decree of the University of Oxford* (1683).
58. Another print of 1711, *The Apparition* (BM Sat. 1569), also depicts Hoadly and a 'Low Church library' of seditious books.
59. Hillel Schwartz, *Knaves, Fools, Madmen, and that Subtile Effluvium: A study of the opposition to the French Prophets in England, 1706–1710*, University of Florida monographs, Social Sciences, no. 62 (1978), 40.
60. *The Ballance of the Sanctuary: or, Sacheverell Weigh'd, and found Light* [1710], 11.
61. Meric Casaubon, *A Treatise concerning Enthusiasm* (1655), 17.
62. The decree was reprinted in 1710 with a critical commentary in *University loyalty: or, the genuine explanation of the principles and practices of the English clergy, as established and directed by the decree...*

CHAPTER 6: DESPAIR AND DEMONISM

John Smith, *The Judgement of God upon Atheism and Infidelity* (1704) gives an account of the suicide of George Edwards.

The Wenham trial and controversy can be followed in Francis Bragge, *A Full and Impartial Account of the Discovery of Sorcery and Witchcraft* (1712); *An Account of the Tryal, Examination and Condemnation of Jane Wenham* (1712); *The Impossibility of Witchcraft* (1712); Bragge, *Witchcraft Further Display'd* (1712); *The Impossibilty of Witchcraft Further Demonstrated* (1712); *The Case of the Hertfordshire Witchcraft Consider'd* (1712); G. R. and A. M., *The Belief of Witchcraft vindicated* (1712); *A Full Confutation of Witchcraft* (1712); Bragge, *A Defence of the Proceedings* (1712); Bragge, *The Witch of Walkerne* (1712).

Francis Hutchinson, *An Historical Essay Concerning Witchcraft* (1718), provides commentary on the case and is reproduced in James Sharpe (ed.), *English Witchcraft 1560–1736*, 6 vols. (2003), VI. Edmund Chishull's Hertford assize sermon was printed as *Modesty and Moderation, or the True Relative Duty of the Tolerated and Establish'd Parties in any Society of Men* (1712).

1. Henry Symons, *The Lord Jesus his Commission* (1657), 39, cited in Nathan Johnstone, *The Devil and Demonism in Early Modern England* (Cambridge, 2006), 81.
2. George Hickes, *Some Discourses upon Dr Burnet and Dr Tillotson* (1695), 45, criticizing Tilltotson's sermon *On the Eternity of Hell Torments*, first published as *A sermon preach'd before the Queen at White-Hall, March 7, 1689/90* (1690).
3. HALS, D/EP F43, f.205.
4. *Paradise Lost* (1667), IV, 75.
5. It could be argued that the ministers of New England were as intent as the High Churchmen on shoring up the spiritual world.
6. Defoe, *The Political History of the Devil* (1726), 280, 389, 402.

6. *The Hertford Letter* (1699), 22–4.
7. The following quotations are from *The Tryal of Spencer Cowper* (1699), 6, 34–5
8. HALS, DE/P F81, Pennington Cowper to Judith Cowper, 14 Jul. 1698.
9. For the ballads see The 'English Broadside Ballad Archive' at <http://www.emc.english.ucsb.edu/ballad_project/>. In particular see Pepys 3.371, Pepys 3.326, and Pepys 3.304v.
10. Burton, *Anatomy of Melancholy* (1621), 756–7.
11. John Crook (and Mary Stout), *Rebellion Rebuked* (1673), 44.
12. Haworth, *Jesus of Nazareth* (1677), 45. In 1696 Charles Leslie warned about *The Snake in the Grass or SATAN transform'd into an Angel of Light*. As the title of one 1656 tract put it, *The Devil Turned Quaker*.
13. Edward Paye, *Antichrist in Spirit unmasked or Quakerism a Grand Delusion* (1692).
14. Francis Bugg, *Hidden Things brought to Light* (1707), xxxiii.
15. Mary Stout and others, *The Testimony of the Hartford Quakers* (1676), 45–6.
16. Richard Ashcraft, *Revolutionary Politics and Locke's Two Treatises of Government* (Princeton, 1986), 379–83.
17. Laurence Braddon, *Innocency and Truth Vindicated* (1689).
18. Spinoza's influence is discussed in Jonathan Israel, *The Radical Enlightenment* (Oxford, 2001).
19. Gildon, 'An Account of the life and death of the Author', prefixed to *The Miscellaneous Works of Charles Blount* (1695), unpaginated.
20. Charles Leslie, *A Short and Easie Method with the Deists*, expanded 2nd edn (1699), 45; *The Occasional Paper*, no. 1 (1697).
21. John Adams, *An Essay Concerning Self-Murther* (1699), 38, 78, 266.
22. S. E. Sprott, *Suicide: the English Debate from Donne to Hume* (La Salle, Illinois, 1961), 71.
23. *The Diary of John Evelyn*, ed. E. S. De Beer, 6 vols. (Oxford, 1955), V, 593
24. Alberto Radicati, *Philosophical Dissertation* (1732), 58–9.
25. Michael McDonald and Terence Murphy, *Sleepless Souls: Suicide in early modern England* (Oxford, 1990), 109, 125–6.
26. Adams, *An Essay Concerning Self-Murther* (1700), Introduction, 1–2, 10, 120–1.
27. David Harley, 'Mental illness, magical medicine and the Devil in Northern England 1650–1700' in Roger French and Andrew Wear (eds.), *The Medical Revolution of the Seventeenth Century* (Cambridge, 1989), 121.
28. Carl Zimmer, *Soul Made Flesh: The discovery of the brain and how it changed the world* (2004).
29. Battell, *Vulgar Errors*, 75.
30. George Keith, *The Magick of Quakerism* (1707).
31. John Trenchard, *The Natural History of Superstition* (1709), 8, 10, 12, 19–20.
32. Shaftesbury, *Letter concerning Enthusiasm* (1708), 49, 69.
33. Schwartz, *Knaves*, 34.
34. Benjamin Hoadly, *Brief Vindication of the Antient [sic] Prophets* (1708), 18.
35. [Francis Lee] *The History of Montanism* (1709), 345, cited by Schwartz, *Knaves*, 46.
36. Francis Hutchinson, *A Short View of the Pretended Spirit of Prophecy* (1708).
37. Isaac Bickerstaffe [pseudo.], *The Westminster Dream* (1710).
38. Francis Bugg, *Some Reasons Humbly Proposed* (1699), broadside.
39. BM Sat. 1534, *View Here the Pourtrait of a Factious Priest* (1710); BM Sat. 1569, *The Apparition* (1711). See also BM Sat. 1502, *The Schismatical Attack*.

40. See illustration 5.17. For Bisset see BM Sat. 1548, *The Picture of a True Fanatick* (1710).
41. *The Ballance of the Sanctuary* [1710], 14.
42. Henry Sacheverell, *Leicester assize sermon* (1706), 20.
43. Edmund Hickeringill, *Miscellaneous tracts, essays, satyrs, &c.* (1707), non-continuous pagination, p. 17 of *Priestcraft* and p. 6 of *The Survey of the Earth*.
44. Francis Bragge jnr, *Witchcraft Further Display'd* (1712).
45. Francis Bragge snr, *Practical Observations upon the miracles of our blessed Saviour*, 2 vols. (1702–6), Preface. The work was republished in 1710.
46. *A Full Confutation of Witchcraft* (1712), 20.
47. *Ibid.*, 23–4.
48. Edmund Chishull, *Modesty and Moderation, or the True Relative Duty of the Tolerated and Establish'd Parties in any Society of Men* (1712), 19.
49. *Witchcraft Further Display'd*, Introduction, unpaginated, last page.
50. *Ibid.*
51. HALS, DE/P F34, 123–4, 9 May 1712.
52. Ian Bostridge, *Witchcraft and its Transformations c.1650–1750* (Oxford, 1997), 132–6.
53. *The Tryal of Richard Hathaway* (1702).
54. Pennington and Judith Cowper were both at Lane's house in 1682: HALS, DE/P F81, letter to Judith Cowper, 2 Apr. 1682.
55. Francis Bragge, *A Full and Impartial Account* (1712).
56. Richard Bernard, *Guide to Grand Jurymen about the Trial of Witches* (1627), 92–3.
57. HALS, DE/P F234, 17, 13 Dec. 1729.
58. *Leisure Hour*, no. 144, 28 Sep. 1854. A cutting of this is in HALS D/EGr/39, Misc. papers about Walkern.
59. Another woman, Anne Street, also claimed to have been bewitched by Jane in the form of a cat that told her to kill herself. She, too, suffered fits and convulsions at roughly the same time as Anne Thorn.
60. Daniel Defoe, *A Tour through England and Wales: Divided into Circuits or Journies*, 2 vols. (1928), II, 157.
61. Quoted by Wallace Notestein, *A History of Witchcraft in England from 1558 to 1718* (1968), 328.
62. HALS, DE/P F234, 16–17, 13 Dec. 1729.
63. Sarah must have been confused, since the punishment for witchcraft was hanging not burning.
64. *An Account of the Tryal, Examination and Condemnation of Jane Wenham* (1712), broadside.
65. Francis Hutchinson, *An Historical Essay Concerning Witchcraft*, 130. The 4th edn was advertised as just published in *Evening Post*, Saturday, 17 May 1712, Issue 433.
66. Edward L. Ruhe discusses the apparent partnership of the Tory Curll with the Whig Baker and their joint promotion of the tracts on both sides of the Wenham case: 'Edmund Curll and his early associates' in John H. Middendorf (ed.), *English Writers of the Eighteenth Century*, (New York, 1971), 69–89.
67. BL, Add. MS 38728, f.33, 13 and 20 Mar. 1712.
68. *The Case of the Hertfordshire Witchcraft Consider'd* (1712), 86.
69. *Spectator*, no. 117, 14 Jul. 1711.
70. *Review*, 20 Oct. 1711.

71. Bragge, *Full and Impartial Account*, Preface.
72. *Full Confutation*, 4.
73. *Witchcraft Further Display'd*, 30.
74. *The Belief of Witchcraft Vindicated*, 23.
75. *Witchcraft Further Display'd*, 9.
76. John Beaumont, *An Historical, Physiological and Theological Treatise of Spirits, Apparitions, Witchcraft and other Magical Practices* (1705).
77. Hutchinson, *Historical Essay*, Dedication, xiv.
78. William Drage, *Daimonomageia* (1665), 32–42.
79. *Impossibility of Witchcraft* (1712), 26, 32.
80. *Full Confutation*, 5–6, 44.
81. *Impossibility of Witchcraft*, 2.
82. Ibid., 2–3, 6.
83. *A Full Confutation*, 42, 48.
84. Ibid., 12; *The Case of the Hertfordshire Witchcraft*, 47.
85. *Impossibility of Witchcraft*, 27.
86. *The Case of the Hertfordshire Witchcraft*, 36.
87. *Impossibility of Witchcraft*, 26–7.
88. *A Full Confutation*, 33.
89. Hutchinson, *Historical Essay*, 130–1.
90. BL, Sloane MS 4043, f.38, 3 Apr. 1712; Bostridge, *Witchcraft*, 143–4.
91. *The Case of the Hertfordshire Witchcraft*, Dedication, viii.
92. In the second edition of Hutchinson's *Historical Essay* (1720), 171, the reader is referred to a 'case' written by 'Mr Stebbing'. This has been taken to suggest that Henry Stebbing, the future High Church controversialist, was the author of the tract (Notestein, *Witchcraft*, 374–5). This seems unlikely for a number of reasons, not least that on p. 57 of *The Case of the Hertfordshire Witchcraft* the author says, 'I have known many even breathing out their last gasp, who have been revived again for several Days by a shrill and sudden screaming with the voice', a comment that the 25-year-old Henry Stebbing, whose whole adult life had been spent at Cambridge University, is very unlikely to have made. On the other hand, if Hutchinson was the author it is not clear why he did not openly admit authorship of the tract in the 1720 edition. Notestein, *Witchcraft*, 374 notes that the copy of *The Case* at Cornell University has a manuscript ascription to 'The Rector of Therfield in Hertfordshire or his Curate'. The rector at this time was Thomas Sherlock, who later became bishop of London in 1748.
93. Thomas Ireland also married Anne Street, another girl who thought she might have been bewitched, 'much to the ease both of [her] Body and Mind'.
94. Hutchinson, *Historical Essay*, 130.
95. HALS, DE/P F234, 17, 13 Dec. 1729.
96. Ibid., 18–19.

CONCLUSION

1. These conditions were more characteristic of parts of colonial America, however.

FURTHER READING

Unless otherwise stated, all volumes are published in London.

ONLINE RESOURCES

<http://www2.warwick.ac.uk/fac/arts/history/people/staff_index/mknight/research/devil> This website contains more images than are reproduced here, together with links to digitized primary or secondary sources.

<http://www.britishmuseum.org/research/search_the_collection_database.aspx> The British Museum collections database has a superb, searchable collection of printed images.

<http://www.bpi1700.org.uk/index.html> 'British Printed Images to 1700' contains thousands of prints and book illustrations for the seventeenth century.

<http://emc.english.ucsb.edu/ballad_project/> The 'English Broadside Ballad Archive' has many of the ballads collected by Samuel Pepys with searchable transcripts.

INTRODUCTION

Barry Coward, *The Stuart Age*, 3rd edn (2003).
Julian Hoppit, *A Land of Liberty? England 1689–1727* (2000).
John Jeffries Martin, *Myths of Renaissance Individualism* (2006).
Mark Knights, *Representation and Misrepresentation in Later Stuart Britain: Partisanship and political culture* (Oxford, 2005; paperback edn, 2006).
Steve Pincus, *1688: The first modern revolution* (New Haven, 2009).
Roy Porter (ed.), *Rewriting the Self: Histories from the Renaissance to the present* (1997).

CHAPTER 1: THE TRIAL OF SPENCER COWPER

Beverly Adams, 'The body in the water: Religious conflict in Hertford 1660–1702', University of London PhD (2000).
Kate Loveman, *Reading Fictions, 1660–1740: Deception in English literary and political culture* (Aldershot, 2008).
Vanessa McMahon, 'Reading the body: Dissection and the "murder" of Sarah Stout, Hertfordshire, 1699', *Social History of Medicine*, 19(1) (2006), 19–35.
Lionel Munby, *The Common People Are Not Nothing: Conflict in religion and politics in Hertfordshire 1575–1780* (University of Hertfordshire, 1995).
Julia Rudolph, 'Gender and the development of forensic science: A case study', *English Historical Review*, 503 (2008), 924–46.
Steven Shapin, *A Social History of Truth: Civility and science in seventeenth century England* (Chicago, 1994).

Barbara Shapiro, *A Culture of Fact: England, 1550–1720* (Ithaca, NY, 2000).

Larry Stewart, *The Rise of Public Science: Rhetoric, technology and natural philosophy in Newtonian Britain 1660–1750* (Cambridge, 1992).

Roger French and Andrew Wear (eds.), *The Medical Revolution in the Seventeenth Century* (Cambridge, 1989).

Oxford Dictionary of National Biography, entries for Spencer and William Cowper, Samuel Garth, Hans Sloane.

CHAPTER 2: PARTISAN FEUDS

Eveline Cruickshanks, Stuart Handley, and David Hayton (eds.), *The History of Parliament: The House of Commons 1690–1715*, 5 vols. (Cambridge, 2002).

Paul Halliday, *Dismembering the Body Politic: Partisan politics in England's towns 1650–1730* (Cambridge, 1998).

Tim Harris, *Politics under the Later Stuarts: Party conflict in a divided society 1660–1715* (1993).

——*Revolution: The great crisis of the British monarchy 1685–1720* (2006).

Basil Henning (ed.), *The History of Parliament: The House of Commons 1660–1689*, 3 vols. (1983).

Derek Hirst and Shaun Bowler, 'Voting in Hertford 1679–1721', *History and Computing*, 1 (1989), 14–18.

Ann Hughes, *Gangraena and the Struggle for the English Revolution* (Oxford, 2004).

John Miller, *Cities Divided: Politics and religion in English provincial towns, 1660–1722* (Oxford, 2007).

Lionel Munby, 'Politics and religion in Hertfordshire 1660–1740' in L. Munby (ed.), *East Anglian Studies* (1968).

CHAPTER 3: QUAKERS

Beverly Adams, 'The body in the water: Religious conflict in Hertford 1660–1702', University of London PhD (2000).

——'The "Durty Spirit" at Hertford: A falling out of friends', *Journal of Ecclesiastical History*, 52(4) (2001), 647–74.

——'The experience of defeat revisited: Suffering, identity and the politics of obedience among Hertford Quakers, 1655–1665' in Christopher Durston and Judith Maltby (eds.), *Religion in Revolutionary England* (2007).

J. Champion and L. McNulty, 'Making orthodoxy in late Restoration England: The trials of Edmund Hickeringill, 1662–1710' in M. Braddick and J. Walter (eds.), *Negotiating Power in Early Modern Society* (2001).

Adrian Davies, *The Quakers in English Society 1655–1725* (2000).

Catie Gill, *Women in the Seventeenth Century Quaker Community: A literary study of political identities 1650–1700* (2005).

Mark Goldie, 'The theory of religious intolerance in Restoration England' in O. P. Grell, J. I. Israel, and N. Tyacke (eds.), *From Persecution to Toleration: The Glorious Revolution and religion in England* (1991), 331–68.

Craig Horle, *Quakers and the English Legal System 1660–1688* (1988).

John Miller, 'A suffering people: English Quakers and their neighbours 1650–1700', *Past and Present*, 188 (2005), 71–103.

Harry Mount, 'Egbert van Heemskerck's *Quaker Meetings* Revisited', *Journal of the Warburg and Courtauld Institute*, 56 (1993), 209–28.

Kate Peters, *Print Culture and the Early Quakers* (2005).

Violet Rowe, *The First Hertford Quakers* (1970).

CHAPTER 4: MORAL PANIC AND MARITAL AFFAIRS

Ros Ballaster, *Seductive Forms: Women's amatory fiction from 1684 to 1740* (1992).

Shelley Burtt, 'The societies for the reformation of manners: Between John Locke and the Devil in Augustan England' in Roger Lund (ed), *The Margins of Orthodoxy* (1995).

Bernard Capp, 'Bigamous marriage in early modern England', *Historical Journal*, 52 (3) (2009), 537–56.

Justin Champion, *The Pillars of Priestcraft Shaken: The Church of England and its enemies, 1660–1730* (Cambridge, 1992).

——*Republican Learning: John Toland and the crisis of Christian culture, 1696–1722* (2003).

Faramerz Dabhoiwala, 'The pattern of sexual immorality in seventeenth- and eighteenth-century London' in Paul Griffiths and Mark Jenner (ed.), *Londinopolis* (2000), 86–106.

——'Sex and societies for moral reform, 1688–1800', *Journal of British Studies*, 46 (2) (2007), 290–319.

David Hayton, 'Moral reform and country politics', *Past & Present*, 128 (1990), 48–91.

Ruth Herman, *The Business of a Woman: The political writings of Delarivier Manley* (Newark, 2003).

Margaret Hunt, *The Middling Sort: Commerce, gender and the family in England 1680–1780* (Berkeley, 1996).

Jennine Hurl-Eamon, 'Policing male heterosexuality: The reformation of manners societies' campaign against the brothels in Westminster, 1690–1720', *Journal of Social History*, 37(4) (2004), 1017–35.

Ann Kugler, *Errant Plagiary: The life and writings of Lady Sarah Cowper 1644–1720* (2002).

David Lemmings and Claire Walker, *Moral Panics, the Media and the Law in Early Modern England* (2009).

Paula McDowell, *The Women of Grub Street: Press, politics and gender in the London literary marketplace, 1678–1730* (Oxford, 1998).

Michael McKeon, *The Secret History of Domesticity* (2005).

Craig Rose, 'Providence, Protestant union and godly reformation in the 1690s', *Transactions of the Royal Historical Society*, 6th ser., 3 (1993), 151–69.

Robert Shoemaker, 'Reforming the city: The reformation of manners campaign in London, 1690–1738' in L. Davison et al. (eds.), *Stilling the Grumbling Hive: The response to social and economic problems in England 1689–1750* (1992).

Hannah Smith, 'English feminist writings and Judith Drake's *An Essay in Defence of the Female Sex* (1696)', *Historical Journal*, 44 (2001), 727–47.

Lawrence Stone, *Broken Lives: Separation and divorce in England 1660–1857* (Oxford 1993).

Rachel Weil, *Political Passions: Gender, the family and political argument in England 1680–1714* (Manchester, 1999).

CHAPTER 5: FANATICS AND FALSE BRETHREN

G. V. Bennett, *The Tory Crisis in Church and State, 1688–1730: The career of Francis Atterbury, Bishop of Rochester* (Oxford, 1976).

J. Champion, *The Pillars of Priestcraft Shaken: The Church of England and its enemies, 1660–1730* (Cambridge, 1992).

——and L. McNulty, 'Making orthodoxy in late Restoration England: The trials of Edmund Hickeringill, 1662–1710' in M. Braddick and J. Walter, (eds.), *Negotiating Power in Early Modern Society* (2001).

Timothy Clayton, *The English Print 1688–1802* (New Haven, 1997).

George Every, *The High Church Party 1688–1718* (1956).

Claire H. L. George, 'Topical portrait print advertising in London newspapers and the Term Catalogues: 1660–1714', University of Durham PhD (2005). The thesis is available online at <http://www.newspaperadvertisements.wordpress.com/category/download-the-phd/><http://www.newspaperadvertisements.wordpress.com/category/download-the-phd/>.

Mark Goldie, 'The theory of religious intolerance in Restoration England' in O. P. Grell, J. I. Israel, and N. Tyacke (eds.), *From Persecution to Toleration: The Glorious Revolution and religion in England* (1991), 331–68.

Antony Griffiths, *The Print in Stuart Britain* (1998).

Michael Heyd, *Be Sober and Reasonable: The critique of enthusiasm in the seventeenth and early eighteenth centuries* (Leiden, 1995).

Geoffrey Holmes, *The Trial of Doctor Sacheverell* (1972).

——'The Sacheverell Riots: The Church and the crowd in early eighteenth-century London', *Past and Present* (1976).

Geoffrey Kemp et al. (eds.), *Censorship and the Press 1580–1720*, 4 vols., III: *1660–1695*, IV: *1695–1720* (2009).

Mark Knights, 'Occasional conformity and the representation of Dissent: Hypocrisy, sincerity, moderation and zeal' in Stephen Taylor and David Wykes (eds.), *Parliament and Dissent* (Edinburgh, 2005).

Joseph Monteyne, *The Printed Image in Early Modern London: Urban space, visual representation and social exchange* (Aldershot, 2007).

Eirwen Nicholson, 'English political prints and pictorial political argument c.1640–1832' University of Edinburgh PhD (1994).

John Redmond, *Reason, Ridicule and Religion: The Age of Enlightenment in England 1660–1750* (1976).

David Runciman, *Political Hypocrisy: The mask of power, from Hobbes to Orwell and Beyond* (Princeton, 2008).

Dror Wahrman, *The Making of the Modern Self: Identity and culture in eighteenth century England* (New Haven, 2004).

CHAPTER 6: DESPAIR AND DEMONISM

Philip Almond, *Heaven and Hell in Enlightenment England* (Cambridge 1994).

Ian Bostridge, *Witchcraft and its Transformations c.1650–1750* (Oxford, 1997).

Peter Elmer, 'Saints or sorcerers: Quakerism, demonology and the decline of witchcraft in seventeenth century England' in Jonathan Barry, Marianne Hester, and Gareth Roberts (eds.), *Witchcraft in Early Modern Europe: Studies in culture and belief* (Cambridge, 1998).

——'Towards a politics of witchcraft in early modern Europe' in Stuart Clark (ed.), *Languages of Witchcraft: Narrative, ideology and meaning in early modern culture* (Basingstoke, 2001).

Roger French and Andrew Wear, *The Medical Revolution of the Seventeenth Century* (Cambridge, 1989).

Phyllis J. Guskin, 'The context of witchcraft: The case of Jane Wenham (1712)', *Eighteenth-Century Studies*, 15(1) (Autumn, 1981), 48–71.

Sasha Handley, *Visions of an Unseen World: Ghost beliefs and ghost stories in eighteenth-century England* (2007).

Nathan Johnstone, *The Devil and Demonism in Early Modern England* (Cambridge, 2006)

Brian Levack, 'The end of witch trials' in Darren Oldridge, *The Witchcraft Reader* (2002).

Michael McDonald and Terence Murphy, *Sleepless Souls: Suicide in early modern England* (Oxford, 1990).

Raymond Martin and John Barresi, *The Naturalisation of the Soul: Self and personal identity in the eighteenth century* (2000).

Jeremy Schmidt, *Melancholy and the Care of the Soul: Religion, moral philosophy and madness in early modern England* (Aldershot, 2007).

Hillel Schwartz, *Knaves, Fools, Madmen and that Subtle Effluvium: A study of the opposition to the French Prophets in England 1707–1710*, University of Florida Monographs, Social Sciences no. 62 (1979).

——*The French Prophets: The history of a millenarian group in eighteenth century England* (Berkeley, 1980).

James Sharpe, *Witchcraft in Early Modern England* (2001).

Jane Shaw, *Miracles in Enlightenment England* (New Haven, 2006).

Andrew Sneddon, *Witchcraft and Whigs: The life of Bishop Francis Hutchinson 1660–1739* (Manchester, 2008).

S. E. Sprott, *Suicide: The English debate from Donne to Hume* (La Salle, Illinois, 1961).

D. P. Walker, *The Decline of Hell: Seventeenth century discussions of eternal torment* (Chicago, 1964).

Carl Zimmer, *Soul Made Flesh: The discovery of the brain and how it changed the world* (2004).

CONCLUSION

Paul Hazard, *The European Mind, 1680–1715*, English translation (1963).

Jonathan Israel, *Radical Enlightenment: Philosophy and the making of modernity, 1650–1750* (Oxford, 2001).

——*Enlightenment Contested: Philosophy, modernity and the emancipation of man, 1670–1752* (Oxford, 2006).

Roy Porter, *Enlightenment: Britain and the creation of the modern world* (2000).

——Mikulàs Teich (eds.), *The Enlightenment in National Context* (Cambridge, 1981).

John Robertson, *The Case for the Enlightenment: Scotland and Naples, 1680–1760* (Cambridge, 2005).

INDEX

Adams, John 203, 207
Adams, Thomas 221
Addison, Joseph 141, 163, 204, 230–1
Aesop 176
Aikenhead, Thomas 103, 108
Animal spirits 207–13, 236
Anne, Queen of England ix, 149–50, 218, 228
Arbitrary government 47, 51–3, 66, 247, 251
Arbuthnot, John 5
Aristotle 109
Ashburne, James 139
Ashurst, Sir William 69, 255
Association oath 64
Astell, Mary 8, 117, 122–5, 260
Atheism 55–6, 98–9, 101, 104, 106, 108, 135, 145, 155, 158, 162, 166, 194, 204–7, 231–4, 247
see also Religion
Aubrey, John 103

Bacon, Francis 138
Baker, John 229
Baldwin, Richard 244
Bank of England 64, 92
Baptist 56, 66, 75, 100, 110, 200, 247
Barber, John 140
Barefoot, Joseph 75
Barne, Miles 255
Battell, Ralph senior, minister of All Saints ix, 52, 61, 66
Battell, Ralph junior 61–3, 107, 209 254–5, 257
Baxter, Richard 210
Bayle, Pierre 243–4
Beaumont, John 233
Beckingham, Charles 97
Bekker, Balthazar 244
Bigamy 3, 99, 110, 125–140

Bigotry 106, 166, 189, 214, 215
see also Partisans and Fanaticism
Birmingham 192
Bisset, William 189, 214
Blount, Charles 146, 156, 202–3, 205
Boevey, James 103–7, 202, 204–5, 235
Bowd, Mr 31
Boyle, Robert 211
Braddon, Laurence 201
Bragge, Francis senior 215, 233
Bragge, Francis junior ix, 215–16, 220–33, 237–8
Bridgeman, Orlando 72
Browne, Sir Thomas 17, 232
Buckingham, George, duke of 100
Buckingham, Sir Owen 218
Bugg, Francis 79
Bull, John 5
Bunyan, John 199
Burke, Edmund 190
Burnet, Gilbert 133, 161, 172, 183–4
Burton, Robert 198–9
Burville, James 238
Butler, John 134–5

Caesar, Charles ix, 66, 95, 139–40, 215
Calvin, John (and Calvinism), 76–82, 105, 107, 147, 194, 247, 255, 257
Camlin, William ix, 11–12
Castlemaine see Cleveland
Catholicism see Religion, popery
Cato 204
Chapman, John 221
Charles I, King of England xi, 8, 45, 50, 57, 120, 144, 149–50, 170
Charles II, King of England xi, 45, 47, 50, 73, 78, 107, 136, 248
Chauncy, Arthur 223

Chauncy, Sir Henry ix, 58–61, 65, 66, 67, 72–4, 77, 214, 222, 224

Cherbury, Lord Herbert of 104, 202, 258

Child, John 200

Chishull, Edmund 215, 227

Chudleigh, Mary 123

Church of England see Religion

Clarke, Mary 119

Clarke, Thomas 95

Clavering, Ann 142, 150–1, 157

Clement, Edward 17–18

Cleveland, Barbara, duchess of (also known by her other title, Lady Castlemaine), 136–7

Cliff, Jeremiah 176

Clifford, Martin 100–1

Coatsworth, Dr Caleb 11–12, 17

Coffee house, frontispiece, 21, 34

Confucius 104

Consumer goods 115

Cowper, Anthony Ashley Cowper, first earl of Shaftesbury 47, 62

Cowper, Anthony Ashley Cowper, third earl of Shaftesbury 156, 166, 211–12

Cowper, Judith (Booth, first wife of William), 32, 40, 116, 125–31, 198

Cowper, Mary (Clavering, second wife of William), 113, 130, 150, 218

Cowper, Pennington (wife of Spencer), 33, 35, 198

Cowper, Sarah (wife of Sir William) ix, 2, 3, 6, 8–9, 44, 90–1, 95–6, 99–102, 116–25, 130, 138, 139, 141, 150–1, 157, 158, 160–6, 169, 194, 216–17, 241

Cowper, Sarah (daughter of William) ix, 130–1, 221–2, 228, 239–40

Cowper, Spencer ix, 1–3, 6, 8; , 12, 14–18, 27, 24, 30–4, 39–44, 45, 48–9, 63, 68–9, 82, 85–6, 89–98, 99, 112–13, 129, 142–3, 148, 151–2, 155, 156, 158–9, 168, 193, 197–8, 217–18, 232, 237, 241

Cowper, William (brother of Spencer and Lord Chancellor) ix, 1–2, 14, 34, 36, 44, 48–9, 63, 65–7, 70, 89–90, 95–6, 99, 107–8, 113, 125–32, 138–9, 141, 142–3, 149, 151, 153, 156–7, 159–60, 166, 219, 228, 239–41

Cowper, William (anatomist) ix, 13, 19–22, 26–7

Cowper, Sir William ix, 2, 8, 44, 46–53, 59–61, 63, 65–7, 70, 90–1, 95, 99–101, 107, 112–13, 116–19, 131–2, 202, 241, 260

Cox, Charles 91

Creech, Thomas 203

Cromwell, Oliver 56, 71, 116, 172, 213, 259

Crook, John 80, 114, 259

Culling, Elizabeth 126–31, 138–9

Culling, Mary 131

Culling, William 131

Curll, Edmund ix, 229

Davenant, Charles 165

Deism see Religion

Defoe, Daniel 131, 156, 181, 186, 196, 227, 229, 231

Deleau, Anne 137

Dell, Leonard 10, 64, 96

Delusion 78, 81, 82–8, 102, 205, 209–14, 231, 234, 242

Demonism see Devil and Witchcraft

Despair 193–213, 236–7 see also Suicide

Devil 4, 55–6, 82–5, 94, 102, 107, 133–4, 147, 169–70, 176–8, 189, 193–7, 199–200, 205–7, 210–15, 218, 220, 223–7, 229, 232, 235, 238, 242, 244

Dimsdale, John senior ix, 11–12, 24, 50–4, 59, 61, 64–8, 80, 95–6, 124

Dimsdale, John junior ix, 10, 27, 96

Dimsdale, Robert ix, 12, 24, 64–5

Dimsdale, Thomas 24

Dimsdale, William x, 80–1

Dissent see Religion

Dolben, John 148

Donne, John 204, 207

Drage, William 233

Drake, Dr James 124

Drake, Judith 123–5
Draper, Thomas 48
Dryden, John 23, 62, 111, 203
Dunton, John 91–2, 97

Edwards, George 204–5
Edwards, Thomas 211
Emblems 167–86
Enlightenment 1, 25, 46, 63, 70, 77–8,
    80, 97, 100, 117, 120, 123, 126,
    133, 180, 184, 187, 189, 192,
    193, 202, 206, 236, 240–5
Enthusiasm *see* Fanaticism
Epicurus 204
Essex, Arthur, earl of 200–1
Evelyn, John 205
Exclusion bills *see* James II

Fanaticism 2, 4, 5, 9, 54, 55–6, 70,
    77, 82–8, 143–92, 174–6,
    186–90, 195, 209–13, 248 *see
    also* Religion and Partisans
Fanshawe, Thomas 72–3
Feake, Christopher 55
Fiction 3–6, 37–9, 65–6, 86, 131,
    132, 140, 152, 230, 242 *see
    also* Truth
Fielding, Robert 136–7, 227
Filmer, Sir Robert 120 *see also*
    Patriarchalism
Filmer, Thomas 67
Finance 92–4, 242, 251
Fox, George 71, 81, 82, 113–14
France 17, 47, 59, 63, 64, 70, 190–1,
    243–5, 250 *see also* Louis XIV
French Prophets 187, 212, 238
Freedom of speech 143, 181–6
Freman, Mary 139
Freman, Ralph 96, 139, 215

Gardiner, Godfrey 215, 222, 224
Godrey, Mrs: Godfrey 215, 223–4
Garth, Samuel x, 21–3, 26
Gender 82–8, 98–141, 150–1, 220–2
    see also Marriage
George, King of England 48, 96
Gildon, Charles 202–4
Gilston, Matthew 221
Glanvill, Joseph 233, 236
Glorious Revolution *see* Revolution

Godolphin, William 139–40, 148
Goulston, Richard x, 95
Green, Theophilus 115–16
Green Ribbon Club 202
Gurrey, Mr, 16

Hale, Matthew 232
Hall, Mary 233
Hamilton, David 218–19, 261
Harcourt, Sir Simon 149, 159
Harley, Robert xi, 160, 163, 231
Harrington, James 183–4
Hatsell, Sir Henry, Judge 17, 68, 89
Hathaway, Richard 217–19, 223
Haworth, William x, 68–82, 105,
    200, 256
Heemskerck, Egbert van 87–8
Herbert, Lord, *see* Cherbury
Hertford xiii, 13, 15, 25, 37, 44,
    45–97, 112–17, 124, 126,
    131–2, 139, 158, 193, 197–8,
    215, 220, 226, 241–2, 245
Hertfordshire 215–40
Hewett, Sir Thomas 72
Hickeringill, Edmund 156
Higgins, Dr Francis 152–3
High Church *see* partisans
Hoadly, Benjamin x, 148, 152–3,
    158, 170, 172, 182, 183–4,
    189, 212–14
Hobbes, Thomas 62, 183–4, 202
Holland 87, 243–4
Holt, Sir John, Lord Chief Justice x,
    12, 90, 94, 217, 219
Hooke, Robert 21
Hutchinson, Francis 212–13, 222,
    237–9
Hypocrisy, frontispiece, 4, 6–7, 42,
    55–6, 62, 73–4, 82–8, 111–12,
    116, 121–3, 126–32, 138–40,
    142–8, 152, 155, 160–8, 177,
    187–90, 193, 204, 214

Images *see* Print
Immorality *see* Morality

Jamaica 74, 260
James II, King of England x, xi,
    47–8, 50, 52, 57, 59, 63, 64, 76,
    133, 144, 151, 200–2, 248, 250

James III, the Pretender 151–2, 161, 170, 172, 214
Jones, Benjamin 61, 64
Jones, Mr, Barrister 68

Keith, George 210–11
Kennett, White 214
Ketch, Jack 181
Keynton, Israel 66
King, Peter 151

Lacy, John 212
Lane, Sir Thomas x, 69, 218–19
Laroon, Marcellus 86–8
Laud, Archbishop William 170
Lawrence, William 133
Lechmere, Anthony 151
Leibniz, Gottfried 106
Leman, Sir William 66
Leslie, Charles 106–7, 133–4, 203, 269
L'Estrange, Sir Roger 176
Locke, John 120, 124, 151–2, 183–4, 201, 216, 244
Loftus, Dudley 132
London 2, 15, 19, 21, 22–4, 26, 28, 31, 33, 35, 40, 47, 67, 69, 86, 87, 93, 100, 108, 115, 127, 132, 134, 136, 142, 144, 152, 155, 179, 187, 188, 198, 205, 206, 218, 236
Louis XIV, King of France xi, 47, 244, 247
Low Church see Partisans
Low, Jane 31
Lucretius 203–4
Luther, Martin 76
Luttrell, Narcissus 152

Machiavelli, Nicholas 104
Madan, Martin 126, 132–3
Mandeville, Bernard de 112
Makin, Bathsua 124
Manley, Delarivier x, 3, 6, 8, 39–43, 126–32, 137–41, 143, 148, 165, 167, 186, 202, 241
Manley, John 137, 149
Marlborough, duke of 111, 139
Marriage 3, 8, 30–4, 40–4, 85–7, 98–100, 109–41 see also Bigamy

Marshall, Thomas x, 31–6
Martin, Mr 219
Masham, Abigail 149
Masham, Damaris 123–4
Marson, John x, 12, 16, 17, 31, 33, 35–6, 253, 254
Mary, Queen of England 1
Mazarin, Duchess of 122–3,
Medicine see Science
Melancholy see Despair and Suicide
Milton, John 123, 183–4, 194
Moderation 143–4, 146, 152, 155, 164, 169–70, 170, 187, 188, 190, 242
Mohamet 104, 146, 155
Monmouth, James, duke of 48
Montesquieu, Baron Charles de 128, 180
Morality 30, 37–8, 44, 55–6, 82–8, 98–141, 194, 205, 242 see also Bigamy, Polygamy
Morduck, Sarah 217–18, 223
Morley, Dr 20
Morphew, John 140, 187

Neville, Henry 133
Newton, Isaac 6, 21
Novel, rise of see Manley, Delarivier and Fiction
Nye, Stephen 216

Oldmixon, John 139–40
Orange, prince of see William III
Oxford University decree (1683) 183, 191–2

Parliament 49–50
  Acts
    Blasphemy 134
    Conventicle 72
    Corporation 49, 57, 248
    Licensing 64
    Occasional Conformity 144, 216, 249
    Toleration xi, 2, 5, 49, 59, 63, 79, 98, 99, 100, 102, 106, 143, 142–4, 146, 148, 151, 152, 155, 169–70, 188, 242–3, 251
    Triennial xi, 63
    Uniformity 49

Elections 49, 51–3, 59, 61, 63, 64–6, 68–9, 89, 95–6, 111, 131–2, 158, 185
Partisans 1–3, 7, 9, 11, 44, 45–69, 108–9, 139–41, 142–92, 196–7, 200–1, 213–19, 228–37, 240, 242–5, 248
  High Church 54–69, 72–3, 124, 141–92, 168–72, 176–7, 187–9, 194, 196, 200, 208, 213–17, 219, 229, 231–7, 240–1, 245, 248 see also Tory
  Low Church 145, 147, 148, 171–2, 176–8, 189, 214, 241, 249 see also Whig
  Tory 3, 47–8, 50, 52, 54–69, 95–7, 109, 111, 120, 157, 170, 176–7, 201, 230, 251 see also High Church
  Whig 3, 23, 39, 46–53, 59–60, 63–4, 67, 95–7, 110–12, 120–1, 125, 144–5, 157, 160, 166, 169, 176, 190–2, 200–2, 218–19, 229, 237–8, 239, 244–5, 251 see also Low Church and Revolution Principles
Patriarchalism 8, 88, 120–1, 125, 141, 242 see also Gender
Patrick, Simon 101–2
Paydon, John 135
Penn, William 69, 71
Pepys, Samuel 198
Pershall, Charlotte 139–40
Peterborough, earl of 141
Petitions 50, 59, 65–7, 71, 76, 91, 95, 158, 185
Pinkney, Dorcas 206–7
Plots
  Popish (1678) xi, 169, 172, 249, 251
  Rye House (1683) xi, 52
Plummer, Colonel 228
Politeness 124–5, 163–4, 186–7, 242
Political Language 55–7, 66, 68, 95, 99, 111, 116, 121–3, 141, 145, 147, 152–3, 158, 163, 167–72, 213–14, 216 see also Republicanism and Revolution Principles

Political Parties see Partisans
Pool, William 199
Poor 23, 51, 61, 88, 96, 195, 220–1, 236, 239
Popery see Religion
Polygamy see Bigamy and Marriage
Powell, Sir John x, 90, 227–8, 238
Pretender, the, see James III
Priestcraft 100–9, 133, 143, 145, 156, 162, 211, 214, 217, 233–5 see also Religion
Priestley, Joseph 192
Print 5, 37–8, 60, 62, 64, 65–7, 71, 77, 78, 80–1, 89, 90–4, 96, 102, 104, 122–3, 131–42, 155–6, 163–86, 212, 229–37, 238–9, 241–2, 249
  Images 82–8, 117–18, 119–110, 149–50, 152–4, 159, 165, 166–86, 253
Public 5, 7, 20, 21, 24, 25–30, 38, 91, 92, 96, 111, 122, 140, 152, 165, 167, 185–6, 229–30, 242 see also Print

Quakers see Religion

Radford, Henry 48
Radicati, Alberto 206
Reason 101–6, 189–90, 195, 202, 207, 235–8, 242–5 see also Science
Religion xi–xii, 2, 4–5, 9, 14, 46, 54–97, 98–141, 142–92, 194–240
  Church of England 49, 51, 53–64, 76–9, 98–102, 104, 108, 116, 123–5, 142–92, 195–6, 204, 215, 220, 224, 227, 247 see also Partisans, High Church, Low Church
  Dissent 49, 51, 54–97, 98–100, 108, 142–92, 198–202, 204, 208, 210–19, 229, 248, 251 see also Parliament, Acts, Toleration
  Deism 98–9, 102–9, 156, 202–4, 207
  Independents 54–6, 78–82, 248
  Presbyterians 54–6, 249

Religion (*cont.*)
    Quakers xi, 2–5, 8–9, 11, 16, 24,
      31, 40–1, 48, 55–6, 65–7, 69,
      70–97, 99, 101, 107, 112–16,
      131–2, 146, 155, 167, 187,
      189, 193–5, 199–200, 209–11,
      213, 224, 241, 250, 254
    Popery xi, 47–8, 51, 60, 80–1,
      133–4, 162, 176, 178, 202,
      234–7, 249
    Toleration *see* Parliament, Acts,
      Toleration
Republicanism 54–7, 62, 146, 158,
    166, 170–1, 184, 213, 250 *see*
    also Revolution, puritan
Resistance, right of *see* Revolution
    principles
Revolution
    Glorious (1688) xi, 1, 3, 8, 23, 48,
      52, 57, 59, 60–1, 63, 87, 104,
      108, 110, 144–6, 155, 157,
      160, 172, 184, 190–2, 243–4,
      250
    Revolution principles 48–50, 52–3,
      57, 59, 62–3, 99, 108–9, 110,
      116–17, 121, 142–3, 145–8,
      151–2, 155–6, 158, 169,
      190–2, 244, 250
    Puritan (1640s and 50s), 1, 30, 45,
      54, 56–7, 60, 62–3, 71, 104,
      106, 108, 146, 170–2, 187,
      189, 213, 243, 250
Ripa, Cesare 168
Rochester, earl of 107
Rogers, William 16, 33, 253
Royal Society 6, 21, 23, 207, 209,
    211, 233, 237 *see also* Science
Russell, Sarah 16

Sacheverell, Henry x, 2, 3–4, 6, 97,
    141–92, 196, 212–14, 216,
    229, 240, 241
Sacheverell Riots 142, 152–5, 160–1
St John, Henry 166
Salem 195, 222
Satire 165, 172, 186
Science 3, 6, 10–14, 17–29, 89, 124,
    195–7, 201, 205, 206, 207–13,
    217–19, 232–36, 242–3
Scott, Reginald 236

Self 7, 30–1, 82, 108, 115, 127,
    165–6, 173–9, 203,
    242, 258
Servants 119, 122
Sherlock, Thomas 266
Shower, Sir Bartholomew 67
Sidney, Algernon 120, 183–4
Slavery, *see* Political Language
Sloane, (Sir) Hans x, 3, 23–4, 27,
    237–8
Smart, Jonathan 75
Smith, John 204, 206
Society for Promoting Christian
    Knowledge 108
Spinke, Elizabeth 136
Spinke, John 136
Spinoza, Benedict 202, 243
Sprint, John 123
Squire, Mr 239–40
Stanhope, General James 151
Stebbing, Henry 266
Steele, Richard 141, 163
Stephens, William 103, 156
Stereotypes 8–9, 70, 82–9, 99, 107,
    118–19, 167–9, 197–8, 213,
    220, 222, 228, 230
Stevens (or Stephens), Ellis 16, 33
Stoakes, Mary 135
Story, John 114
Stout, Henry x, 3, 16, 51, 65, 69, 70,
    72–5, 78–82, 92, 114, 131,
    200, 255, 257, 260
Stout, Henry (Sarah's nephew), 89–90
Stout, John, Sarah's half-brother 34,
    59, 64–6, 69, 95, 257
Stout, Mary x, 8, 10–12, 71, 74, 76,
    78–82, 89–94, 194, 200
Stout, Sarah x, 1, 2, 3, 4, 6, 10–12,
    15–18, 23, 25, 30–44, 45, 56,
    67, 69–98, 112–16, 193–5,
    197–8, 206, 239, 241
Strafford, Thomas, earl of 171
Stratton, Nelson 48
Street, Anne 265, 266
Strutt, Robert 215, 224–5
Suicide 193–207, 223, 232, 242
Sweeting, Henry x, 74–5, 95
Swift, Jeremiah 75
Swift, Jonathan 5, 125, 132, 139,
    186, 227–8

Taylor, Christopher 82
Thorn, Anne 222–8, 234, 236, 238–9
Thornhill, John 179
Tillotson, John 101–2, 194
Tilly, John 137–8
Toland, John 102–3, 156, 183–4, 258
Toleration *see* Parliament, Acts
Toller, Bostock x, 89–90
Tory, *see* Partisans
Treby, Sir George 90
Trenchard, John 211–12, 235
Trevor, Sir Thomas 67
Truth 4–7, 14, 18–22, 25, 37, 39,
     79–81, 89, 101, 104–6, 111,
     114–15, 136–7, 179–80, 212,
     228–37, 242–3
Turner, John 135
Tutchin, John 156
Tyrrell, James 120–1
Tyte, Robert 73

Vernon, Sir Thomas 179
Villars, Charlotte 137
Voltaire, François-Marie
     Arouet 70–1, 180, 244

Wadsworth, Mary 137
Walkern 215
Walpole, Robert 151, 158, 190,
     239, 245
Webster, John 236–7
Wedgewood, Josiah 192
Wenham, Jane x, 2, 4–6, 9, 193,
     213–17, 220–41
Whig party *see* Partisans, Whigs
Whitehead, George 71
William III, King of England
     and Prince of Orange x, 1,
     48, 53, 59, 63–4, 144, 146,
     244, 250
Williams, Sir John 136
Willis, Thomas 207–8
Witchcraft 4, 7, 81, 97, 102,
     136, 193–7, 200, 207,
     210–40, 242
Wollstonecraft, Mary 110, 123
Woolley, Hannah 124
Wren, Christopher 207–8
Wright, Sir Nathaniel 90

Zeal *see* Fanaticism